From The Race Conscious Revolution
Essays by John Londen

## About The Author

'John Londen' is a pseudonym. Who I really am is not important.

As a White Neo-Tribalist, I believe that humanity is tribal and that with the constructs of liberal modernism in decline, the only sustainable future is a recognition of, and return to, our racial roots as the basis of social organisation.

This collection of essays sets out my thinking on politics today, particularly in a British context, and aims to help advance the concept of a New Tribe, which I believe is the future of Post-Nationalist politics in the 21st. century.

The essays are taken from my blog and from articles of mine published elsewhere. For convenience, they are grouped here under thematic headings.

You can visit my blog at http://www.johnlonden.com

References in what follows to White Independent Nation or 'WIN' are to the organisation found at http://www.win-white.org

"What we need is a Race Conscious Revolution. This Revolution will not be a single incident. It will not be traceable to any particular group of people, nor to a particular time or place. It will not be founded on any specific ideology or set of texts. It will be a gradual, imperceptible shift in consciousness, maybe over decades, even centuries. Much like the agricultural revolution, or the industrial revolution, it will mark the movement of European civilisation away from Jewish supremacy towards true white sovereignty."

John Londen.
From the essay: 'Down with Britain!'

# Contents

## 4. What Should Be Done?

## 5. Miscellaneous Subjects

# 1. The 'Nationalist' Problem

## 1.1.

### Escaping the Lotus: democracy and the 'leader syndrome'[1]

There is a great deal to be said on the whole issue of UKIP and Europe, but for now, I'll sketch out some initial thoughts I would like to offer on UKIP's recent apparent success and what I see as the wider issues.

1.      People flock to leaders and want their 'Messiah'. This is partly out of timidity and laziness. It's easier – and safer – to rely on others and vote with the herd rather than risk oneself. It's also the 'human' thing to do under certain conditions. The human mind is an organic system in its own right and can be shaped and moulded by certain influences. In the distant past, our early human ancestors had hive-like minds that equipped them to work in groups, which were essential for survival. These survival instincts have not left us, even in this 'liberal' society in which the concept of the 'individual' can take on its full force and expression. Modern politicians, like ancient rulers, are essentially psychologists with a shrewd understanding of these mind traps. Our potential as human beings is boundless, but our minds can also be suffocated and bound like Lotus feet. At the moment, the electorate are trapped within their 'Lotus minds', which gives expression to politically-illiterate choices, like UKIP.

2.      As a practical concept, 'democracy' is largely bogus in the West. Quaddafi's Libya had more democracy than we do. That we automatically tend to think of our people as 'voters' or the 'electorate' reflects how so-called 'politics' alienates them, us, from our true material interests. Most of those who opted for UKIP have no economic stake in society – though many are deluded in the belief that they do – and will not be affected one way or the other by UK membership of the EU. Yet they convince themselves that "We need to leave the EU, innit"...."We dunt wont foreigners runnin' our cuntry, gov", etc. Politics is not politics. It is a kind of anti-politics that is, quite literally, detached from reality. A similar observation can be made for voters and supporters of most, if not all, the other parties. It's not just UKIP voters.

3.      The issue of the EU is largely a red herring and has little to do with Nationalism. It's a distraction from two overarching issues of our time: 1. identity and culture, and their root, race; and 2. the end of capitalism and its replacement with democracy. The one major point that many Nationalists and pseudo-Nationalists miss, mainly because most other people miss it, is something learnt from the writings of the Jewish philosopher and historian, Oswald Spengler, which is that once people start referring to a 'Civilisation' as such, capitalised, then that civilisation is in terminal decline. While 'mainstream' society is preoccupied with membership of the EU and other marginal issues, the hierarchical system itself is crumbling.

4.      Dealing with the first issue: Whether the EU is an elite club for capitalists or a Euro-Bolshevik plot or something in-between, the reality is that non-whites will

---

[1] First published on 12 June 2014 at http://www.johnlonden.com

continue to want to travel to and enter the UK, legally or illegally, regardless of whether we are members of the EU. They did so before we joined the then-EEC, and they will continue to do so long after we leave the EU. UKIP itself is not committed to secession from the EU. Instead, it talks about 'withdrawal', which – I would suggest – could be interpreted in lots of different ways. For instance, 'withdrawal' could be interpreted to mean 'radical reform': the EU itself has sufficient institutional flexibility that it could encompass 'multi-speed' memberships. It already does, in effect, in that while EFTA and the regional Neighbourhoods are separate organisations, they act in concert with the EU and are – in reality – simply extensions of EU power. That is not to get teleological about Continental federalism, something that has – admittedly – gathered a sense of inevitability about it. This is not a question of 'liking' the EU, more a matter of acknowledging the reality that there is a possible middle-ground between narrow and obstinate Anglo-Saxon delusions of cyclopic autarky on the one hand and Napoleonic centralism on the other.

5. Turning to the second issue, the capitalist system itself is not sustainable. Eventually it will be abolished and replaced with a society based on co-operation and the control, use and distribution of resources for human need. Some people call this type of system 'socialism'. It can also be called 'co-operation' or 'democracy'. I think the best term for it is 'democracy' because it involves the realisation of human need in material reality – a literal democracy. Whereas today, in capitalism, human needs are cast aside or treated as spent and ignored, and with it we sacrifice such things as dignity, love, worth and value, in the democracy, dignity, love, worth and value will be central to decision-making. The first question is whether such a society can exist without meaningful culture. I think the answer to that has to be 'no'. People need the glue of identity. That being the case, we need to ask: Where does culture come from? Or, How does culture arise? The Nationalist position is that culture escheats to race. Even in a truly mixed-racial society, cultures would arise and with it, loyalties and identities – and thus races would evolve again.

6. These are the really interesting questions, and in my opinion, the mammoth and fundamental issues they raise cast UKIP and all the political babble of the elites – of whom UKIP are an intrinsic part – into total insignificance. If I were to broadcast these thoughts to a mainstream audience, they would think me mad and call for me to be sectioned – and in a sense they would be right, in that it is 'mad' to break out of the 'Lotus mind'. Nevertheless, I believe that all we now know and feel sure of will be swept aside, and one day, the things we know will seem like a joke to our descendants. I think this is where projects like White Independent Nation ('WIN') come into play, and also what I call the 'leader syndrome'. Going back to the way the human mind (as opposed to the brain) has evolved organically, all of us, without exception, are still burdened with this primitive cringe of looking for leaders to give us an answer to our problems. Organised religion is the ultimate expression of this, but religious believers, especially Christians, are easy to sneer at in this regard while overlooking the ways in which outbreaks of dim consciousness in our supposedly 'sophisticated' and 'rational' secular society can resemble a Moonie craze or the weird enactments of some other strange religious sect:

UKIP being a case in point, itself a kind of personality cult for the credulous and the clueless. Projects such as White Independent Nation are ahead of the curve, so to speak, in that – to my mind – they point the way to a democratic/communal style of Nationalism. Unless people can act for themselves and break out of their Lotus minds, nothing will change.

## 1.2

### Far-Right counter-culturalism: a dead-end[2]

It is now common to hear Nationalists say that we should give up on electoral politics as the current mixed-racialist society is what the public voted for and it's therefore what they deserve. This is an understandable sentiment, with an appealing logic, and there's a great deal of truth in it, but it's also true that the public have been consistently bullied and lied-to and a large section of the population have not voted for years. Of course, these are not excuses, and I do share the opinion of many other Nationalists on the subject: I think the public have brought all this on themselves and, given the opportunity, would not vote for their own liberation. This in part is why, in my opinion, the answer is for us to abandon electoral politics altogether and focus our resources on community building.

Now, I understand the arguments for UKIP and similar political alternatives, and if those parties can gain some influence that provides us with a protective umbrella, then that is all to the good, but what has not been mentioned is how our battle differs from the mixed-racialist one.

The social liberals and mixed-racialists were able to infiltrate the institutions in society and allow their ideology to slowly permeate through the system because of the invisibility of that ideology and its expediency and advantageousness for certain vested interests. The capitalist class wanted cheap immigrant labour. There was also pressure from other groups – feminists for example – for greater 'equality'. These factors allowed the metropolitan Left and their allies to work within the institutions they wanted to transform, both overtly and covertly.

As far as I can see, our beliefs do not carry the same attributes or advantages. What we stand for as Nationalists is something fundamentally different. We are not just a reactionary counter-culture, diverging from the values and attitudes of the mainstream. We are challenging the basic ideas on which society now works and calling for an altogether different society. You can't vote away black people. Yes, you can have a political party – i.e. UKIP – that hints about doing something along those lines, using other white ethnies such as Poles as a proxy target, but ultimately this 'Navajo codetalk' of the right-wing counter-culturalists is futile because the real objective – a white (European) society – is beyond the reach of the existing political system. What is needed now is a new system.

I do have this sense that white people are slowly waking up. It's in the air. It's almost tangible. The problem is that the nature of the game has now changed. At the moment, the whites who are now waking up are at the 'blaming and scapegoating stage' – it's the EU! It's a sinister cabal of Maoists! It's the Jews! The complexity, indeed complications, of the world are forgotten in favour of the blame game, which is just immature escapism. UKIP caters for this immaturity and political illiteracy perfectly. You'll notice how UKIP representatives – and other 'culturalists' – enjoy blaming others for problems that the public have voted for, or acquiesced in, themselves. It's not a solution. It's just a distraction from the real battle that needs to

---

[2] First published at http://www.johnlonden.com on 24 June 2014

be fought.

As many in Nationalism are rightly identifying, the blame is and always has been with the public themselves. This includes people like myself – I did not 'wake up' until later in life. I am as much to blame as anybody else. But blaming people, calling people childish names, doesn't get us anywhere.

The solution is boring and not for egotists: it involves changing public consciousness over many decades and building new white-conscious communities, and a new tribe.

## 1.3.

### 'Normalising' the far-Right: discussing the FN model[3]

A frequent topic of speculation among Nationalists is on how the British far-Right might emulate the success of ideologically-similar parties on the Continent. As I will explain briefly below, I believe that within the context of Nationalist aims and objectives, the records of these comparator parties have been vastly misunderstood. Their 'success' is largely illusory. A case in point is the Front Nationale of France. Now that Marine Le Pen has 'normalised' the FN, they are useful idiots, just like UKIP, but there is one important difference in political practices and culture on the Continent that allow 'far-Right' (not necessarily Nationalist) parties such as the FN to grow and build a more prominent profile, and thus appear to be more successful than their British counterparts.

Mainstream politicians on the Continent are more willing to work and co-operate with 'extremist' parties of both the Left and Right. This is down to a mix of Machiavellianism and practicality. There is felt to be a need to neutralise the threat the 'extremists' pose, and control them, because the electoral systems on the Continent tend to make it easier for fringe parties to participate and win seats than is the case in Britain. There's also more autonomy at the local level in these countries than in Britain, with the so-called 'extremists' regularly winning petty municipal positions from which they can build a support base, which then leads to regional success, and then national. Mainstream politicians find there is a need to control these burgeoning movements through various forms of co-operation and co-habitation, which absorb the 'extremists' into the Establishment, thus neutering any populist threat they might otherwise pose to elite interests.

These are among the reasons why parties such as Front Nationale – and indeed, other parties on both the far Left and far Right across Europe (not just in France, but in Germany, Italy and elsewhere) – seem to us to have a higher profile and be more successful. In reality, they remain fringe movements with only token influence and no real prospect of making a serious impact on social policy in their respective countries. Hence, I regard the 'Front Nationale model' as an illusory success. It's illusory not just on our (Nationalist) terms, but also on its own terms: looked at objectively, these parties achieve little.

It's a model for what can and will happen with UKIP and any other Judaised 'nationalist' party in the UK as our political system is pluralised. Of course, there are some within Nationalism who will be hoping for exactly that, which speaks for itself. UKIP will gain some nice influence, with one or two eye-catching initiatives (ban the burka?); they'll receive praise from the 'I Told You So' brigade when they manage to ginger an EU referendum; and, a few of the Aunt Sallies and Golf Club Gordons in the provinces will enjoy plastic positions in various meaningless elective bodies – but nothing will change.

Until Nationalists really start thinking about this and understanding that the UKIP/Front Nationale model is patriotism not Nationalism, and thus wrong, we'll just

---

[3] First published at http://www.johnlonden.com on 24 June 2014

keep running round in circles like a bunch of excited dogs.

## 1.4.

### UKIP and the Enoch Powell Cult[4]

UKIP is, in my view, a continuation of Powellite Conservatism, and its most visible aspect, the Farage Cult, is a pluperfect example of the 'leader syndrome' in operation.

The salient points are these:-

- the debate/discussion on immigration is fraudulent and managed;

- initiatives from parties (including UKIP) that encourage the impression they are interested in 'democracy' are only further extensions of this fraud;

- referenda and other forms of direct democracy change nothing because the questions and issues are decided in advance;

- UKIP's leaders and backers have no interest in controlling immigration in any meaningful way, as that would be against the interests of the people they really represent, but they have no scruple about giving the opposite impression;

- UKIP's support for global free trade and its supposed opposition to the EU are code language that it is in fact anti-white and pro-capitalist;

- political buzzwords and phrases have multiple meanings: 'democracy' means different things in different hands at different times. The same applies to 'controlling immigration' and 'freezing immigration', which could mean more immigration or less immigration;

- the historical myths around Enoch Powell are of significance to politics today because they influence Nationalists in clinging to democratic solutions that do not work [Powell held to the thesis that democracy would solve the problem of 'multi-culturalism'];

- in reality, democracy as it is presently constituted is the problem, not the solution;

- the 'Powell cult' has given birth to various 'democratic' (i.e. anti-white) parties, including UKIP, which is essentially the activist Eurosceptic wing of the Tory Party and a legacy of Powellite Conservatism;

- the longer Nationalists cling to leaders, the longer we will have to wait for a real solution – 'Farage' is a drug like heroin, and some people need a daily dose;

---

[4] First published on 29th. June 2014 at http://www.johnlonden.com

- finally, the support for UKIP and other Powellite solutions betrays a double naivety about democratic-style politics: first, that when you vote for something, you get it (which is hardly ever true in reality); and second, that choices are framed in the way that you want them to be, which is a backwards way of looking at history when in fact history is played out forwards. The 'Powell generation' knew what was coming, but they would never have presented the choice to the British public on racial terms, and they would never have allowed that choice;

- the 'dumb' white British public can see that they have been thoroughly conned, yet they carry on their dialogue within the same existing political solutions: Tory (UKIP) or Labour? Powell (Farage) or Cameron? Etc., etc.

## 1.5.

### Uncritical nationalism versus critical Nationalism[5]

One thing that separates me from most Nationalists is that I do not believe in leaders. That is not to say I reject the concept of leadership, which is necessary (or at least, useful) for any political movement (and any other practical human endeavour for that matter); but leadership is not contingent on the existence of leaders per se, and I firmly reject the notion that an effective political movement must always have a leader. In that sense – and other senses – I am a democrat as much as a fascist. Can two opposites exist in harmony? I believe so. My views are an idiosyncratic blend of the democratic and fascist, and the Nationalist and socialist. I will explain more during the course of this blog's existence, and as time goes on, you will – I hope – come to recognise a structural and ideological consistency: a system of belief that I will provisionally call Autonomous National Socialism. But more on that some other time.

Today, I would like to talk about a distinction I make between what I call 'critical Nationalism' and 'uncritical nationalism'. The terminology is borrowed from Karl Popper, who distinguished 'critical rationalism' from 'uncritical rationalism'. I believe that Popper's critique of justificatory methods in human knowledge can be extended into political theory and ideas, and is of particular relevance to 'the leader syndrome' (see my previous post: Escaping the Lotus: democracy and the 'leader syndrome').

A factor that distinguishes scientific knowledge from political knowledge is the reliance in science on knowledge (and the underpinning methodological doctrines of empiricism and falsificationism), while in political endeavour there is a reliance on truth (and its underpinning doctrine of authority). It is important for us to understand how the democratic concept cuts across this distinction. Science is fascist in nature, rather than democratic. (See my earlier discussion of Giddens' double hermeneutic in Nationalism and the Hermeneutical Dilemma: some brief thoughts). To a scientist, what matters is not certainty or absolute truth, but the search for truth, and with that, the provision of evidence in the form of experiments and observations, that might provide an explanation or account of the truth. This involves building, validating and destroying tentative conclusions – theses – with the aim that, at any one time, the body of scientific knowledge is closer to the truth. Scientific knowledge is always provisional, and any sense of authority is in its methodology: science is derived from the testability and falsifiability of any one of its tentative conclusions, which always stand ready to be undermined, minimised or destroyed as empirical findings dictate.

Political knowledge is, by contrast, democratic in nature and focused on the presentation of the truth with an attribute of certainty, regardless of whether what is presented is in fact true in the observational sense or valid in the rational or scientific sense. Regardless of the truth of a theory, statement or position, what matters is its social acceptability within the receiving group, or the likeability of the messenger, or some combination of the two.

I might observe that racial inequality is natural and inevitable and the very existence

---

[5] First published on 5th. July 2014 at http://www.johnlonden.com

of races is a demonstration of this res ipsa loquitur. In fact, that's the scientific position. I am not certain it is true, but I know that current scientific evidence supports it. It's a provisional truth, that is open to challenge and falsification. It also happens to be a common sense observation, but that is not what matters. Its authority is drawn from its [provisional] 'truthfulness', as it should be. Numerous studies show average differences between races in different areas of human endeavour, as does basic day-to-day observation. It may be an impolitic statement and deeply unpopular. It may be seen as vile and disgraceful, etc., by 'respectable people'. It may also be vigorously, perhaps violently, denied by some (if not most) scientists who, for varying motives, wish to interpret their science through politics – nonetheless, it is the truth to the limited extent that current science can provide valid conclusions. In that sense, science is 'fascist' by method, not due to its content (the racial example given here is incidental – we could be discussing any subject that science touches on), but because all scientific work must subsume to the overriding demands of its rigorous method. In a casual sense, we can say that findings that comply with its method and are repeated consistently are the 'truth', and for reasons of expediency, this practical short-cut is largely accepted. For example, things such as evolutionary theory and Big Bang theory are presented largely as fact in schools and in the media. Nothing can change the truth, except a modification or alteration of the theses that interpret it.

The converse of the scientific method is found in political knowledge, which deals with the reality of racial inequality quite differently. Political knowledge is 'democratic' in two senses. First, provisional knowledge, validated by scientific method and everyday observation, is denied in favour of 'the Truth', which is a fiction that is more socially acceptable and likeable. The 'fiction' might contain a strong element of actual truth-telling – and rarely, may simply be the truth. Indeed, as any professional politician will confirm, a really effective lie needs to contain a strong element of truth in order to convince people. Nonetheless, some lies can work because they are 'Big Lies'. Putting aside philosophical niceties, we 'know' that 2 + 2 equals 4, but if it were more socially acceptable that 2 and 2 should make 5 – especially if this deduction worked in the interests of a powerful group in society – then it is not inconceivable that this conclusion would be promoted by serious people and anyone who denied it would be ridiculed and verbally savaged, if not imprisoned. If you think this far-fetched, then consider how 'equality' is conceptualised in society. Equality among humans is empirical nonsense, just as 'equality' among wolves or sheep is nonsense. But the aim is not to make sense. The aim is acceptance and likeability.

The second feature of political knowledge is a deliberate politicisation of language, in that the subject term develops a double meaning. Much as we discussed the double meaning of 'democracy' in a previous post (democracy versus Democracy: or why the patient can't be restored), a canonical understanding of 'equality' is promoted that bears no relationship to material reality or lived experience, but reflects perceptions that society wishes to encourage – a kind of wish-thinking – and which also reflects certain perceptions the elite wish to encourage among society. We all wish for equality, democracy and other nice things because that's what we have been encouraged to wish for and it also seems civilised. The consequences of such views are not widely discussed.

All of us are susceptible to the fallacies of justificatory (political) knowledge – Popper's uncritical rationalism – which prioritises 'truth and 'certainty' over actual knowledge and observation. Often the fallacy can work in service of good (or at least, good intentions). An example is found in the global warming debate, and in particular the debate over whether, and to what extent, global trends in warming, if they exist, are caused by human activity. I must confess that I am not sufficiently informed about the science to offer a meaningful view on whether global warming is happening or what contributes to it, but based on what knowledge I have, I would tend to favour the anthropogenic thesis ('AGW'). This is for entirely precautionary reasons. The late Christopher Hitchens put it best: we can't run the experiment twice. We have only one chance to change our behaviour so as to mitigate our impact on the planet. As I see it, this is the best justification for the precautionary principle, and even if it turns out that the AGW thesis has been exaggerated or is wholly mistaken, it is best to exercise caution and reduce any damaging impact on the environment generally. This is one reason the so-called 'climate sceptics' annoy me a little in that, irrespective of the truthfulness of their position (something yet to be determined decisively, one way or the other), their scepticism does not take account of the need for us to end our supremacy over the Earth. We have no right to use the Earth like a dustbin. My position is what you might call 'cautious scepticism' or 'weak scepticism', but in adopting this view, it must be admitted that I am incorporating a disregard for the truth (in the sense of objective knowledge about the world) and prioritising my political view (a more subjective and unrealistic attitude to knowledge and truth). A belief that we should be more in touch with, and respectful of, our surrounding environment may represent 'good', but when this view takes on the uncritical pretensions of 'truth' as an unassailable reality and disregards actual knowledge and the inherent unattainability of absolute truth, then my position becomes dishonest (albeit, in my case, well-meaning).

I have encountered this same well-meaning disregard for truth among mixed-racialists, who think they are promoting good – the unity of the human race – which, in turn, explains their violent and aggressive reaction to those who are either sceptical and would prefer that different human sub-races retain their distinctive identities, or who point out that current science does not accord with the politics of the mixed-racialists. Some of these mixed-racialists have perhaps not considered fully the consequences of their views, which are now being played out in our society. We might call these well-meaning mixed racialists the 'idealists'. Others promote mixed-racialism for ideological reasons, believing that the deconstruction of the West, or the White Race, is necessary to achieve some political objective: a version of socialism, Islamic rule, or whatever. Both groups pursue the authoritarian approach that typifies political knowledge – i.e. lots of 'democracy' in which truth is overridden in favour of people's feelings. The White Nationalist slogan in response could almost be: "There are races. Just deal with it." The liberals/mixed-racialists/false flag conservatives would reply: "Yes we know that, but we'd rather pretend there isn't and call you Nazis." If there are races, then there is inequality. If there are sexes, then there is inequality. Difference means inequality, because that is Nature. Science has yet to present knowledge that might contradict this, but we live in hope that the mixed-racialists might be vindicated by some actual knowledge or verifiable observation.

The term 'equality' was used originally by the Enlightenment thinkers (for example, in the American Declaration of Independence) in a wholly different social and historical context to contemporary society. Theirs were white (or white-led) societies in which governments played only a minimal and distant part in people's lives, and in which women had dominion over the private and family sphere of life, which was much more important than it is today. Inequality was accepted as a fact of life, because that is what it was and still is. It didn't follow, and it still doesn't follow, that men are 'better' than women or vice versa, or that whites are 'better' than blacks or vice versa, etc. Rather, it meant there was a recognition of difference and society built itself around those differences, sometimes in frustrating and unjust ways, but mostly for the good of everyone. That does not mean that I think society should remain static. I am a socialist, not a conservative, but I believe that change should be progressive: i.e. it should be built on what is good about society, and so far as possible, facts about human beings should prevail. The denial of inequality and difference has led to a regression and devolution of the West: escalating violent crime, growing economic inequality (which, in my view, is the unjust type of inequality), and a loss of morals. These problems are the result of a bankrupt social system, capitalism, but they are also a demonstration of how the canonical equality that capitalism relies on does not work in practice – at least, not without considerable propaganda and governmental oppression.

The only way out of this problem for the equality activists is to reject science (which is where all the unwelcome 'truths' emanate from) and return to political knowledge, where 'equality' can be refashioned into an abstraction. Thus, although science (and everyday common sense) says there is inequality, no-one sees this because everything – including science itself – is interpreted through political knowledge. Ignorance Is Strength; Inequality Is Equality; and Authoritarianism Is Democracy. Of course, people do see inequality still – they must. The problem is in how they interpret the reality they see. They are persuaded either to ignore what they see and continue living in their own contented bubble as if it is not happening (and in the hope that some of the consequences won't affect them), or to treat it as either a failure of a particular government or political party, or the work of evil racists, or perhaps, the deliberate work of psychopathic rich men (normally Jews and their scapegoated surrogates, rich whites, are identified as the culprits). This is far preferable than the harsh alternative: which is confront reality and see society's breakdown for what it is: the failure of a failed and broken social system and paradigm of thought: i.e. Jewish (mixed racialist) capitalism – or capitalism for short, for that is what capitalism is.

It's in this context that I have long-believed that radical liberalism and mixed-racialism (and their attendant movements, such as militant feminism) are generally not revolutionary movements at all, but in fact are counter-revolutionary movements, for they belong to an uncritical tradition in which democracy becomes something that is vaguely nice – and thus an uncritical concept that, of course, 'everybody' believes in. Meanwhile, fascism (and any other revolutionary idea, including classical Marxism) becomes something that is vile and nasty and that, of course, 'everybody' disapproves of. Incidentally, this is why I am amused when I see Nationalists and right-wing types get into a frenzy about Cultural Marxism and 'liberals', terms that most of them only half-understand. What such people are doing is betraying a profound ignorance about the history of working class struggle and the place of

Nationalism in it, and they are also revealing that Nationalism as they conceive it is not a revolutionary idea, but just a propaganda front for shills and lackies of whoever happens to be in power, including Jews. So Nationalism has regretfully fallen into the uncritical tradition. Exhibit 'A' is the continuing success of the UK's very own Moonie cult: UKIP, a media party who seem to represent a mixture of golf club bores, right-wingers with clichéd views, and random disaffected people. Other exhibits in support for the uncritical tradition include: the Powellisation of the BNP (and to an extent, the National Front as well); the emerging popularity of 'thoughtful' social conservatives who are vaguely associated with civic nationalism, such as Peter Hitchens and Melanie Phillips, who are fact radical liberals of the uncritical tradition, though they like to pretend otherwise.

The truly revolutionary position is the Racial Nationalist one, for it asserts that a Nation cannot exist without racial homogeneity. A vague sense of ethnicity and patriotism – flag-waving, sports allegiance, culture and ritual and so on – which the civic nationalists focus on, is not enough. Without a racial under-girding, Nation means nothing. Singapore is a nation-state, but it can never be a Nation, and if the British Nation is 'singaporeanised' – i.e. turned into a mixed-racial population – then the artificial structure of the nation-state becomes irrelevant to Nationalists, as it no longer serves any racial purpose and is in fact traitorous. We have now arrived at that point: truly now, the Race is the Nation and the Nation is the Race. This signals a new opportunity, for a new White Nationalist/Sovereigntist Movement, but it also signals the sad end for British Nationalism as anything viable. In order to save the Race, we will have to ditch the nation-state. So it is a defeat, and it is as well to confront that fact.

There is one group of people, who deserve the blame and approbation for this: US – that is to say, you and me. The way to victory, I believes, starts with radical self-criticism. Blaming others, worshipping leaders, joining parties, putting an illiterate 'X' in a ballot every four years….all these non-activities are the hallmarks of the uncritical nationalists, and they are all proxies, projections even, in lieu of doing something useful. They are ways of deflecting the blame from where it really should be: ME AND YOU.

None of that is to say that I oppose voting or joining political parties. I am not advocating an 'all or nothing' approach. I realise that pluralism, even compromise, can be essential in politics if anything is to be achieved, but what I do oppose is people who do this uncritically (even non-strategically in some cases), out of a kind of Leninist loyalty or worship of a Great Leader or a made-up organisation such as a political party, or out of an understandable but misplaced loyalty to a nation-state (in this case the UK) that is in fact traitorous to whites. Admittedly, such people do have qualities: they show considerable gumption, and are in many ways a cut-above the 'dumb' whites who stay silent and stunned on their way to the abattoir. Nevertheless their pseudo-positivist mindsets (i.e. practising politics at face value) and their misplaced belief in the amulets of the uncritical tradition – 'democracy', voting, flag-waving, 'fair play' and so on – are just part of a circular and futile process that gives the existing fraudulent system an undeserved legitimacy, when in fact it should have been swept away long-ago.

Of course, I am not an innocent in this. In the 'YOU AND ME', I include myself. I was a 'dumb' white too. I was stupefied. In fact, my case was one of the worst. I joined the Labour Party as a young teenager and had ambitions to become a politician. I grew out of it quite early on, partly because my early active involvement in the mainstream, social democratic variety of left-wing politics immunised me against it. What you might see as a 'mistake' and something I should be ashamed of, was in fact a crucial part of my political development and maturity. Without that 'left-wing' phase, I would still be a plastic leader-worshipper, a Moonie cultist like some of you. So I'm glad I made that mistake. At some point I began to realise that it's all a con, and more importantly, I worked out my own explanation of why.

Along the way, I went down some interesting avenues. During my time in University as a law student, I joined a nearby coffee shop-style philosophy discussion group, consisting mainly of academics and what right-wing people might dismiss as 'liberal types'. Having been through a comprehensive school and survived the experience, albeit with considerable emotional and psychological damage, I had learned how to regurgitate the system's junk knowledge faithfully as one of its straight A students – a kind of Western version of the Soviet Young Pioneer. I did not know much philosophy (albeit, I was highly auto-didactic and well-read), so most of the discussion was beyond me, and I listened more than I spoke. This was an important experience for me because I first became aware of how deeply the left-wing current of thought had permeated into academic institutions, and it also made me recognise some of the contradictions and limitations in the left/liberal position.

However, I now realise that the people I conversed with back then were not really 'left-wing' as such, and certainly not 'socialist'. In fact they were 'metropolitan' and held a mindset that I would now call pseudo-positivist: they accepted the canonical understanding of politics and the conventional use of political language, and in that sense, today, those people would be closer politically to the average member of UKIP or the BNP than they are to me. The average UKIP and BNP member is liberal and part of the uncritical tradition, but doesn't realise it.

In my 20s, I joined a small Marxist group in the north of England, which was mainly about theoretical discussion. I had first read Das Kapital in my teens. Now I re-read it more thoroughly, along with the other works of Marx and Engels, in an effort to understand it all properly. Like most sincere Marxists, these people were gentle and kind, if a little too earnest and intellectually intolerant. They understood socialism very well but because they were convinced of their own truths (and to be fair, most of what they said was, and remains the truth), they would not listen to alternative perspectives. It was that unattractive intellectual attribute – commonly found among people who are in fact right and know they are right – that put me off them and forced me to re-assess and re-evaluate my views in the light of my growing experience. They would be appalled by my views now, but I am grateful to them. They opened my eyes to the truth and wisdom of Marxism and socialism – and also its limitations – and thus prevented me from sliding into the reactionary dead-end that most people find themselves in as they get older and more cynical about society. That has not happened to me because, thanks to the Marxists – who are largely correct in their analysis of capitalism – I have retained my optimism and I remain a 'young' person politically. I refuse to give in and I refuse to stop learning. I am a Nationalist now, but I belong to the critical tradition.

## 1.6.

### LibLabConUK: the uncritical nationalism of UKIP[6]

About fifteen years ago, a mantra began to emerge on the far-Right that the three main parties in Britain were part of a single political class whose members have essentially the same attitudes and ideas, and much the same policies. BNP members told us that it was time to unseat the 'LibLabCon', the elite alliance that was ruining Britain with its liberal, decadent politics. They were right, but what is interesting is how many of these same people are now giving their support to UKIP, a heavily watered-down version of the BNP that is closer to the three main parties than anything these people may have supported on the far-Right.

The 'LibLabConUK' version of the elite is much the same as the preceding version. It is wedded to the democratic liberal dogma, uses its buzz terminology and supports the electoral machine that keeps voters stupefied. Its continued existence is a tribute to the effectiveness of the liberal Leviathon in that it can accommodate huge public discontent over the direction of the country, and muffle any real opposition to mixed-racialism by co-opting a controlled, neutered version of the opposing view.

UKIP began in the early 1990s as a moderate 'non-racial' constitutionalist party, but evolved during the New Labour years to become the Eurosceptic wing of the Tory Party, little more than Purple Tories, with all the accompanying characteristics: a thinly-veiled reflexive racism that is slightly ashamed of itself; a vague, unfocused and rather simplistic business agenda based on clichéd ideas about cutting cost and regulations; dismissiveness about the problems of working class people, who are seen as cattle [the typical liberal mindset]; token opposition to immigration using white Europeans as a scapegoat, and a populist, ill-thought position on the EU based on an appeal to a fictionalised ethno-identity.

The facts about the EU and immigration are:

(i). we had mass non-white immigration long before we joined the then-EEC;

(ii). other countries that are not in the EU continue to suffer the same racial problems that we do;

(iii). there is absolutely no reason why leaving the EU will make the slightest difference to this; and

(iv). (crucially) even if the EU (or something like it) didn't exist, we would still face the same problems of regulation and migration, due to our obligations under UN treaties, the forces and influences of global capitalism and corporate lobbying by multi-nationals.

The key to a reasoned discussion on this subject is acceptance of these points. It may be that leaving the EU is, in fact, the best option – I have no strong view on the subject either way, since I do not see it as relevant to the racial issues, but it may be

---

[6] First published on 1th. July 2014 at http://www.johnlonden.com

that it is the right way forward from an economic or trade point-of-view. If so, then all well and good, but it should at least be acknowledged that UK secession is entirely a legality and would serve little more than a symbolic purpose. In or out of the EU, non-white immigration will continue unabated. Most people on the Right can't acknowledge this and prefer to put their fingers in their ears and shout: "I'm not listening". They prefer the comfort of received wisdom rather than the discomfort of independent thought. These right-wingers represent nationalism's real dirty secret – an embarrassing 'uncritical tradition' that colludes in the false liberal shibboleth of democracy, under the illusion of material gain and self-advancement.

Even if UKIP are sincere in their pledge to withdrawal Britain from the EU (following a referendum), the process of legal secession would take years to fulfil, if not decades, and there is a question mark over whether we can even withdrawal de facto from these arrangements, given the economic and geopolitical realities of the single market. In short, the UKIP position is simplistic and deceitful. It does not address the racial and social issues, which are the real problem. In fact, UKIP's neo-thatcherite free trade agenda might worsen our racial situation, not to mention further impoverish us.

UKIP's language is implicitly anti-white. When UKIP use the term 'free trade' (or similar), it's code for non-white immigration and non-white intrusion in British society. Other political language they use, such as 'controlling immigration', 'ending uncontrolled immigration', 'freezing immigration', 'withdrawal from the EU', etc., all entail ambiguity. 'Freezing immigration' might mean increasing or decreasing immigration, or something else altogether. UKIP talk about introducing a points system, which implies that they think non-white immigration to the UK is fine, as long as the applicant has a skill or a relevant and useful university degree. This is the liberal mentality in action.

What is often not appreciated by many well-meaning UKIP supporters (i.e. Farage Cultists) is how opposition to the EU can be consequentially anti-white. The agenda is clear in the public discussions, but most don't see it because opposition to the EU has – rightly or wrongly – become a reactionary mantra. That's not to say the EU is a good thing, necessarily – I'm not saying that – but the whole issue has been simplified hugely and some of the anti-white propaganda in the media is now blatant. Whereas you can't oppose non-white immigration openly, white immigrants (especially Eastern Europeans) who take advantage of 'freedom of movement' within the EU bloc are considered fair game for media vilification, including by UKIP spokespeople.

The more intelligent among UKIP's defenders make two points about this problem:-

1.    First, they argue that ethno-nationalism should be prioritised. A wider white identity cannot have any cohesiveness, and so it is legitimate on racial terms for UKIP to campaign against all mass immigration on the same terms, lumping all migrants together.

2.    Second, some UKIP supporters think opposition to Eastern European migrants is coded opposition to non-white immigration designed to bring the public to a general anti-immigration position, and that should UKIP gain power

and influence, they will then attend to the real problem, i.e. non-white immigration.

I am unconvinced by these defences, principally because the people who back and lead UKIP are business-oriented. There is nothing wrong with that in and of itself, of course, but it does strongly hint at where their priorities lie. In the end, they will choose whatever brings the country 'prosperity' or 'growth' or a 'trade deficit', or whatever. Racial integrity and solidarity in society will come a poor second, if they are considered at all. That is in their nature and it is what makes UKIP an enemy just as dangerous as the Labour Party or the Conservative Party.

Unfortunately, the message: "You've Been Had!" is not popular and the messenger is never thanked, so we must go through this 'rinse and repeat' farce again, as happened during the latter days of the BNP at its peak, and also with Thatcher's Conservative Party during the 1980s, with some Racial Nationalists engaging in disingenuous verbal gymnastics to tactically support a leader and a party that they know will not bring us any closer to a white society. UKIP's electoral "success" is only making the learning process more prolonged and painful. The harsh truth is that UKIP are, above all else, a liberal party and part of the same elite that we should be opposing, not propping up, even for tactical reasons.

**1.7.**

## The Scandal of UKIP and its MEPs[7]

Many Nationalists rightly disowned the BNP after revelations of mismanagement, misconduct and irregular financial practices within Griffin's Party. Oddly, many of these same people give UKIP a free pass, even though in describing itself as 'anti-EU' it must have breached every provision of the Trade Descriptions Act. Its cadre of MEPs are also not shy about drawing a salary from an institution they affect to despise, if not oppose, while maxing out their audit-free parliamentary expense accounts. Since 1999, when UKIP MEPs first entered the European Parliament, this purportedly 'anti-EU' party has bilked the taxpayer for hundreds of millions of pounds and believes in nothing except taking more.

UKIP supporters try to excuse this on the grounds of expediency. Quite shamelessly, and while keeping straight faces, they tell us that the largesse is justified (or, perhaps, justifiable) because if UKIP MEPs weren't there, then pro-EU MEPs would be. This excuse-making brings to mind UKIP's policy towards those in society from whom excuses are never accepted, the unemployed and those dependent on the 'generous' benefits handed out by the state. In regard to these unfortunate people, UKIP and its supporters are not as understanding or forgiving as the EU's benefit system is for their MEPs.

According to activists on the web[8], in its 2010 welfare policy, From Welfare to Workfare, UKIP described the unemployed as "a parasitic underclass of scroungers".

From the same source:

*"UKIP's welfare policies include forced unpaid work for all Housing and Council Tax Benefit claimants, Incapacity Benefit (now ESA) slashed to Job Seeker's Allowance rates and childcare support for working parents demolished."*

This seems to be based on the following paragraph in the shorter 2010 Policy Statement:

*"Require those on benefits – starting with Housing and Council Tax Benefit recipients in private rented homes – to take part in council-run local community projects called 'Workfare' schemes. The schemes will be in addition to council jobs."*

It took me a while to find the full policy document on the web, but eventually I located it here: https://stilllaughingattheukip.files.wordpress.com/2014/07/ukipwelfare.pdf I will not dissect it in this article. For one thing, it is unclear whether it is current. Rather, I will concentrate on its overall message and what that says about UKIP and the kind of country the party wants Britain to become. The passage which refers to 'the unemployed' as a 'parasitic underclass of scroungers' is below, in its full context:

---

[7] First published on 19th. July 2014 at http://www.johnlonden.com

[8] http://johnnyvoid.wordpress.com/2013/03/05/ukips-disappearing-welfare-policy-claimants-are-a-parasitic-underclass-of-scroungers-says-party/

*"It is intolerable that a large number of people choose to abuse the benefits system. Many people now see the benefits system, with its elaborate system of entitlements and payments as an alternative to work. This gives rise to a parasitic underclass of "scroungers", which represents both an unreasonable tax burden on the working population and is a factor in many social pathologies such as crime, anti-social behaviour and educational under achievement."*

That is from the 'Introduction', which continues with the following:

*"As well as those who cynically and shamelessly abuse the benefits system, there are a great number of decent, hard working people who wish to come off benefits, but are discouraged from doing so by the current benefits structure. They are too poor to enjoy a meaningful standard of living due to benefits payments, yet they fear taking up training courses as this will see their benefits cut or stopped altogether. Many of these people remain on benefits because they feel it provides a better "deal" than a minimum wage job. It is unacceptable that a sizeable percentage of people on benefits who could move out of benefits dependency and into work are discouraged from doing so by the structure of the current system."*

Here we see the classic premise of Tory welfare policy, dividing the poor into 'deserving' and 'undeserving'. The distinction seems cogent and does reflect experience – most of us have known at least one person who appears to live off the benefits system but could work – but that is not where our thoughts on the subject should end. A life on benefits is not an appealing alternative to work, even if some people get used to it or see it as easier than work. It is unpleasant and exclusion from employment or economic activity, whether willing or not, amounts to exclusion from mainstream society. The root of the problem lies not in a willingness among some people to 'scrounge', but in the lack of economic opportunity for all sections of the population – especially for the young and the unskilled. This in turn reflects decades of financial capitalism and under-investment in the skilled economy, the type of capitalism that UKIP likes (and are happy to admit as much), along with mass immigration of cheap labour willing to undercut and devalue indigenous labour – again, the type of thing that UKIP types like (though it won't admit to this part). In many white working class areas, there are no stable employment opportunities available, only casualised 'temp' work in warehouses and factories. Many people, both young and old, find the service jobs available in shops and other service industries frivolous and unfulfilling, not to mention that they are notoriously low paid. There is also no real vocational education system to speak of in the UK, as there is in, say, Germany, with the result that millions of young people are leaving full-time education without any form of skilled training or apprenticeship. Against this background, whatever the merits of UKIP's specific welfare policies (and some of their policies might be perfectly valid), to characterise people on benefits as "scroungers" who "abuse" the benefits system is obscenely disingenuous. It amounts to scapegoating the poor for the country's economic and social problems, which are caused by decades of deliberate policies – ironically (or perhaps not ironically) the very type of 'free market' policies that UKIP support – that have been harmful to the indigenous majority.

It's worth reflecting that in the eyes of the average UKIP supporter, all the various social and economic factors I mention above are merely 'excuses' for the poor, even if they are acknowledged at all. People should pull themselves up by their bootstraps, in much the same way that, presumably, 'deserving' UKIP MEPs have done. Of course, it is true that those who find themselves unemployed or in other similarly desperate circumstances should not rest on excuses and should not assume they can rely on state support unconditionally. It is fair to ask that as individuals we each take responsibility for our situation and contribute back to the society that pays for us. No doubt many of UKIP's policies reflect this reasonable position, and UKIP are, of course, right that people need to take responsibility for themselves. But that is just stating the obvious, and is in any case a bit simple in that it does not account for the context in which we are being asked to accept responsibility and take action. The problem with UKIP is that its attitude to the indigenous British population is much like that of the rest of the elite. UKIP is part of the Establishment. (See my previous essay, 'LibLabConUK: the uncritical nationalism of UKIP'). UKIP is a thatcherite pro-free trade party, meaning it sees the indigenous population not as a racial community, but as cattle to be used and exploited. This is why UKIP supporters justify everything in materialist terms: immigration is assessed according to its financial cost, welfare recipients are seen as 'scroungers' and a drain on the public purse, and so on. The reason UKIP, as Purple Tories, disparage the welfare system is that they know, in reality, that it is paid for by capitalists like them. The purpose of welfare is social control and the whole system is really a legacy of modernist industrialisation. It was understood from the beginning that capitalism is cyclical and that there will be periods when large numbers of industrial workers would be unemployed. It is necessary to provide sustenance to these people, frankly to avoid the possibility of social unrest, even revolution, which would be the inevitable and just outcome if people knew and understood the realities of capitalism. Without the benefits system to keep a lid on things, we would see an army of angry, disenfranchised people on the streets. It is also advantageous to capitalists to maintain an excluded group of unemployed as an incentive – a standing threat – to those in work. However, capitalists know that they have to pay for all this. (The fact that social insurance payments are deducted from wages and salaries gives the false impression that it is workers who pay for it and that we have 'entitlements', but in fact it is employers who fund the benefits system). It is therefore important for capitalists to maintain the impression that the money available for welfare is scarce and that those who 'abuse' it are 'robbing the taxpayer' (in fact, they are robbing capitalists). There is also a need for a constant threat that the 'benefits' will be withdrawn or that other repressive measures will be enacted. All this keeps the populace in line and also keeps ordinary people turning up for their pointless jobs and plastic 'career opportunities'.

UKIP might like to see itself as a 'business party', but that is just a euphemism for its true identity: it is a capitalist party, or part of the Capitalist Party (i.e. the LibLabConUK). UKIP's role is to advance the interests of capitalists – or Jews, to you and me. Capitalism is, after all, a Jewish racial strategy. (See 'The Smiling Jew and other clever wiles'). While UKIP might take us out of the EU – though even that is debatable – it would not stand in the way of so-called 'free market' forces, and in fact lauds the 'free market', which it puts before the interests of the indigenous British people. UKIP policies reflect this. Lower labour costs in reality mean more immigration, especially of the non-white variety, as this helps to divide the workforce. Non-white immigrants are also more pliable, and thus more employer-friendly. Less regulation in reality means fewer rights for workers. 'Free trade' is code for further abrogations of parliamentary sovereignty, in the interests of multi-nationals. UKIP hide their true intentions behind buzz words and scapegoats – be it white workers from Eastern Europe, 'benefit scroungers' from home or EU bureaucrats – and they latch on to whatever populist cause is currently trending. In reality, their policies, if implemented, would be a re-run of 1980s thatcherism and deeply harmful to the social fabric of the country and cohesivenss in society. UKIP is the Tory Party in drag: an extreme, colourful manifestation of its pent-up frustrations, bigotries and prejudices unleashed, incongruously, in a European talking shop. The free trade position brings out the classic Tory fissure between a commitment to neo-liberalism and an innate social conservatism, but it is clear to see that for UKIP, the 'free market' argument will always win out and any lingering social conservatism is for show. Their policy of 'no more uncontrolled immigration' is in fact a commitment to immigration. The only difference from the rest of the Establishment is the adoption of a more palatable wording. A typical LibLabConUK tactic.

Now, turning back to UKIP's own 'parasitic scroungers', its MEPs, it is tempting to ask which of them are 'deserving' and 'undeserving' according to UKIP's own policy criteria. The following is sourced (and paraphrased) from a 2013 analysis[9] by Rebecca Taylor, a Liberal Democrat MEP and member of the European Movement. I don't like the Liberal Democrats or the European Movement any more than I like Nigel Farage, but the fact is that Taylor's critique of Farage and UKIP is reasoned, valid and, for the most part, well-sourced.

Here are the relevant points:-

1.  Data derived from the Votewatch website in 2013 shows that UKIP MEPs miss more key votes than any other group in the European Parliament, with UKIP leader Nigel Farage having the fifth worst attendance record out of all 752 MEPs.

2.  In 2012, two UKIP MEPs were asked to repay £37,000.00 in allowances that they have improperly diverted to the Party. That scandal was significant in that the two MEPs claimed that this was an organised arrangement within UKIP. There has also been a criminal prosecution of a UKIP MEP for expenses fraud.

3.  During an interview with Andrew Neill, Mr. Farage was challenged on why he and his deputy, Paul Nuttall, do not publish their expense accounts.

    *"...he was asked why he and his deputy Mr Nuttall had not published their expenses for 2 years despite promising to do so. Mr Farage was unable to produce a convincing response, saying instead that he was "very busy" and that he had "lost some receipts".*

    To be fair, UKIP do have a webpage consisting of what is known as 'Transparency Reports', though it is not clear how long that has been up and the reports are in any case not comprehensive. Full details of MEPs'

---

[9] http://euromove.blogactiv.eu/2013/07/26/time-to-expose-ukip-meps-for-what-they-really-are-%E2%80%93-lazy-unprincipled/

entitlements and eligibility for salary, allowances and expenses is found on the relevant page of the European Parliament website[10], but nowhere is there a published account of how each MEP spends this money. MEPs are only entitled to a salary of 96,246.36 euros (around £76,182.01 at today's exchange rate), which seems fairly modest given the position – that is, for a hard-working MEP. You will note however there are a range of allowances and expense entitlements that bring an MEP's potential return up to quite a large amount. MEPs and their defenders would no doubt argue that the system of allowances is designed to off-set and cover legitimate expenses, and no doubt this is true, but the system itself is not fully-audited, the expenditure for each MEP is not published anywhere, and there has to be a lingering suspicion that the money is used to allow MEPs to live comfortably on the salary that they perhaps ought to be paid but cannot be paid for political reasons. A salary of, say, £200k would be more befitting to the post but would also ram home to ordinary people the cost of this additional layer of bureaucracy and government, and would perhaps also betray the real motives of UKIP MEPs, and other MEPs for that matter.

An explanation of how the system works in practice is given on the website of SNP MEP for Scotland, Alyn Smith[11]. As well as various office- and travel-related allowances, for which some degree of accounting or reporting has to be made to Brussels, MEPs are also entitled to a Daily subsistence allowance of 304 euros per day (£240.63 per day at today's rate). This allowance, I would suggest, is one of the key elements that increases an MEP's return, as there is no accountability as to how the subsistence allowance money is spent and it would not be difficult for an MEP to book accommodation and local travel in advance to minimise costs. What people also don't take account of are the inevitable perks and 'freebies' that MEPs will enjoy as they swan around Europe to Brussels, between Brussels and Strasbourg, or on some 'fact finding mission' or other.

4.  Back to the article, Taylor also claims that Farage:

    *"...has failed to attend 48% of Plenary votes, has never drafted a report and he is joint bottom when it comes to Parliamentary questions asked."*

    Interesting to note, but not mentioned by Taylor, is that the Daily subsistence allowance I refer to above is halved where an MEP fails to attend and take part in at least 50% of the plenary voting sessions. Clearly Farage knows this and has cynically attended for the requisite number of sessions so that he could claim his daily allowance.

5.  In November 2012, Belgian MEP Guy Verhofstadt accused Farage of being the EU's "biggest waste of money" after pointing out that he has never attended the Fisheries Committee (European Parliament) of which he is (or was) a member.

---

[10] http://www.europarl.europa.eu/aboutparliament/en/0081ddfaa4/MEPs.html
[11] http://www.alynsmith.eu/mep_allowances

6. On the subject of the Fisheries Committee, Mr. Farage is MEP for South-east England and so you would expect that he would take a keen interest in the subject and try to minimise any damaging impact of the Common Fisheries Policy on his constituents. However, Farage:

"...has never bothered to take part in Fisheries Committee meetings and when mammoth cross-party efforts by centre-right, Socialist, Liberal and Green MEPs ensured an historic reform of the CFP, which will end overfishing and safeguard the future of the fishing industry in Europe, Mr Farage was nowhere to be found. He did not even bother to show up to the fisheries committee final vote (which was very close) and he disappeared halfway through the plenary vote. In fact, according to Committee minutes, he attended just one of 42 Fisheries Committee meetings between February 2010 and January 2013, when he resigned from all Committees. Which is consistent with UKIP's record; UKIP MEPs have attended just 30% of Committee meetings."

7. On UKIP's attitude to the parliamentary committees, Taylor continues:-

"The real graft in Brussels is done in committee, so by skipping committee meetings UKIP miss the chance to exert any influence and help shape laws that affect their constituents. They claim that there is no point as they would be outvoted every time, which is patently ridiculous when key votes can (and often do) go one way or another with only a vote to spare."

8. Paul Nuttall, UKIP's deputy leader, is (or was) a member of the Environment, Public Health and Food Safety Committee of the European Parliament. He has a similar record to Farage, having only attended meetings of the Committee twice in three years, and he has not drafted a single report or opinion as an MEP. According to Votewatch, in 2013 Nuttall was 736th. out of 753 MEPs when it comes to plenary (i.e. full Parliament) sessions attended. Nuttall's poor record resulted in an unfavourable public incident around committee discussion of the EU Tobacco Directive. According to Taylor:

"[Nuttall's poor attendance record] is again "out of principle"; he thinks his time would be better used elsewhere. Or he does until he realises he might get some bad publicity as happened recently. The Environment, Public Health and Food Safety Committee recently debated and voted on the EU tobacco directive, which included the regulation of e-cigarettes. Like-minded MEPs from several parties worked to table sensible amendments on e-cigarettes and it all came to head in the Committee vote. Knowing that the key amendment on e-cigarettes required all the votes it could get and that Mr Nuttall never attends committee, e-cigarettes users (some of whom were Mr Nuttall's constituents) were encouraged to contact his office. Some were ignored, some received the same generic e-mail response they had received several months previously, and at least one was told Mr Nuttall would not attend the tobacco directive vote. They were dismayed and began complaining about him on Twitter. Then all of a sudden Mr Nuttall changed his mind and showed up at the Committee meeting (his 3rd visit in 3 years!), although he didn't bother to vote on many amendments."

UKIP could answer these criticisms in various ways. For instance, UKIP could argue that as an anti-EU party, any deeper participation among its MEPs would be superfluous. Other 'excuses' I have seen or heard are that the European Parliament is not in any case very powerful or impactful and so there is little point in participating in its decision-making; and that the views of UKIP MEPs will not be taken seriously or listened to by other MEPs; and that due to their antipathy to the whole EU project, UKIP MEPs will rarely agree one way or the other with the decisions taken and so there is little point in turning-up. I find these 'excuses' no more convincing than the 'work shy' excuses offered by UKIP's 'parasitical class of scroungers'. Work shy UKIP MEPs who do not wish to participate fully in the European Parliament should not stand for election in the first place, or if they feel they should stand for election on principle, then they should abstain and not take their seats in the Parliament. The fact is that the excuses offered by or on behalf of UKIP MEPs would not be accepted from benefit claimants, who UKIP expects to 'take responsibility' for themselves.

At best – and this is to be charitable – UKIP seems to be guilty of confusion, of not finding a definite role for itself as either an anti-EU party that abstains from participation in the European Parliament or as an anti-EU party that somehow seeks to reform the institutions from within and ameliorate the EU's worst excesses. UKIP wants to sit somewhere on the fence, in the middle of these two opposites. It's a classic case of wanting to have your cake and eat it. UKIP seems to be just a vehicle for a bunch of people to travel round the Continent living it off the taxpayer. Some people would call this fraud, and if the sheer scale of the expenditure involved – which now must be in the hundreds of millions – is anything to go by, not to mention the unaudited accounts and various scandals, the British taxpayer, who is being taken for a ride, should be up in arms. This is from the very people who claim to want to do something about the EU. However, it is also the case that what UKIP are doing is perfectly legal and the authorities can do nothing. It's a scam involving hundreds of millions in hot money, but it's 'legit'. That's the genius of it. Rather like a mafia boss who has, finally, decided to 'go legitimate', after years as a "stockbroker", Mr. Farage has finally landed on a scam that works and is legal at the same time. Laughing himself silly, and probably pinching himself in disbelief at his own good fortune, Mr. Farage – we'll call him 'Slick' – parades around as the UK's would-be Saviour from 'EU tyranny' or whatever the slogan is. However, to make the scam work, Slick and his co-conspirators…ahem, sorry, fellow MEPs…need to look busy. This explains why Slick enjoys making a spectacle of himself in the plenary sessions (that's the 'just over half' he bothers to turn up to – you know Slick!). It's part of the scam, his way of showing his face for the camera.

However, just because it is legal, that does not make it OK. In the first place, it is only 'legal' because the criminal law relating to fraud does not interact with electoral law in the sense that a group of politicians who stand on a false premise – i.e. UKIP – are not prosecutable in the same way that a regular businessperson might be. Legal or not, UKIP are still taking taxpayers' money under false pretences, pretending they are against the EU when they are bilking it, and in the full knowledge that they cannot practically enact their aim of withdrawal from the EU anyway. That it may be 'legal' within the narrow limits of the law does not excuse it. That being said, the matter is for you, the voter. What I don't like is this habit of blaming politicians for simply doing what comes naturally. Politicians were not brought up on some South Sea island. They are not a separate moral species. They came from our ranks and we vote for them. They are a reflection of the moral standards prevalent among the public-at-large and are just doing what most people would do in their position, which is the least amount of work for the most amount of money, using carefully-planned stunts to give the impression that they work assiduously on our behalf.

A real anti-EU party would abstain from the European Parliament altogether, and in so far as it might choose to contest European elections at all, its representatives would decline to take their seats if elected. Their absence would send a powerful message that a significant number of British voters do not recognise the legitimacy of European institutions and reject the European Union. Of course, such a strategy would have its difficulties, but the stance would be clear and uncompromising, and irresistible for many among the electorate who want to see some integrity and principle from their politicians, rather than more of the same. UKIP, and previously the BNP, do not display this clarity and integrity. They do recognise the legitimacy of the EU, implicitly. That is why they go. That is why they take the salaries, allowances and expenses, and all the perks, without complaint, rubbing it in our faces. Their 'anti-EU' position is false, a front, and in any event, not realistically achievable. Their leaders know this, but in the manner of commissars from a Soviet-style Politburo, they are only too happy to maintain the fictions that keep them in office and maintain their comfortable sinecures. The sad useful idiots who prop up these parties often do not realise this, or refuse to think about it. In the end, we come back to the same question that faces all of us. We need to stop blaming others for our racial plight and look in the mirror. It is up to you. That is what this has been about all along. You can either accept a fictitious 'reality' in which your life is run by demagogic leaders and their lies. Or you can start voting for yourself.

## 1.8.

## The Far-Right: conning us since 1945[12]

For seventy years, Nationalism in this country and the rest of Europe and North America has been dominated by the political Right, especially the far-Right. These people have created a rather shallow political movement, borrowing the superficial aspects of a fictional national identity invented by satirists at the beginning of the 18th. century. Their cause appeals to the unthinking, undeveloped mentality of the bigoted provincial who dislikes Johnny Foreigner: a kind of right-wing version of Dave Spart. These people do not represent me. They never have. Their simplistic messages have never appealed to my deep sense of feeling for these islands, for its geography, its unique people and culture, but above all, my allegiance to the White Race. I am a socialist, not a Zionist. My symbol is John Ball, not John Bull. The far-Right reflects no more my 'nationalist' tendency than a Catholic nun. That said, I think John Bull has had a bit of an unfair press. The original creation was the classic honest country yeoman: provincial, unpretentious and common-sensical, if a little blinkered. It was only later, around the time of the First World War, that the image of John Bull morphed into an authority figure and was used, for instance, on Army recruitment posters to enlist white men into the mass slaughter of that senseless war – a contrast with 'Tommy Atkins', who replaced John Bull as the representative of the ordinary Englishman. This transition in John Bull's propagandistic function from common man to a personification of authority reflected fundamental changes in British society and the working class experience: the movement from a society that was rural and agricultural in character to urban and industrial, and the resultant need for social control in society; the transition in the social relations of production from autonomy and landed peasantry to commerce and mass production; the change from strong families and communities to the strong state. The root of the far-Right's reactionary, authoritarian propaganda – indeed, the root of the modern state-fascism of the 20th. century – is the liberalism of the mass industrial society.

As such, the far-Right is just the latest in a long line of ideological vehicles for mass social control, working in the interests of capitalists. Its strategy seems to be to rely on an out-dated notion of Nationalism that was for all intents and purposes abolished by the Second World War. (See my essay: 'The Lessons of Leith'). The British have always had a more subdued attitude to patriotism than that found in other European countries. The British far-Right's pro-Zionist symbolism – the use of the Union Flag and John Bull imagery – does not connect with ordinary people and to a large extent plays into the hands of anti-whites and non-whites, who wish to co-opt the 'British' civic identity as their own. The various party political brands of the far-Right, including the National Front and the BNP, together with its 'normalised' outlets such as UKIP, are about managing dissent among the system's middle-managers and self-employed. The typical demographic of their supporters is not 'poor', but middle-class and the affluent working class, i.e. the petit bourgeosie. These tend to make up the majority of right-wing supporters and voters. The delusions that such people carry through their lives (what I call 'respectable deceits' in my essay, 'The Smiling Jew and other clever wiles') are similar to those among Labour and Conservative supporters and are based on the belief that they have a stake in the system. Voting

[12] First published on 25th. July 2014 at http://www.johnlonden.com

itself, and a lot of mainstream political activity, has now largely become the preserve of a modern parody of the Platonic citizenry, a sizeable minority who make up the system's client base and are the easiest to control because they believe either that the system already works in their favour or can be made to do so. As such, party politics – including the far-Right – has become just a way of diverting the frustrations of the 'affluent poor' into activity that is relatively harmless to the system. Thus any real opposition is suffocated without the need for violence. (See my essay, 'Democracy Keeps Us Dumb').

When I encounter these 'affluent poor' who accept the system implicitly, either by supporting it or seeking to reform it, one of my questions to them is why they choose to be so munificent towards their rich masters: the Jews and the capitalists? Why do they vote against their own racial and economic interests? Why would someone who has nothing expend so much time and energy in propping-up capitalism and Jewish supremacy, using received propaganda? Of course, these 'affluent poor' are in denial about their disenfranchisement. They don't accept that they have nothing. They still live under the delusion that they have a stake in the system. They own their own home and run their own business or hold down a well-paid job, or have some kind of plastic status, or whatever. These props fuel the delusion of citizenship, as does the promise of proxy say and influence through the attainment of political power and influence by 'their' party, UKIP. These are delusions, supported by lies that come from the mouths not of the elites, but of the 'affluent poor' themselves. They repeat and reinforce the positivistic mantras that the media feed them: democracy, human rights, legality, dictatorship, liberty, etc. ad nauseum. The question we should be asking these people is simple: Has lying worked? It's a simple enough question, maybe a little too simple, but sometimes the truth is straightforward. The reality is that lying hasn't worked. What these people want us to believe is that we should carry on lying nonetheless and vote for UKIP or the BNP or the BDP or LibertyGB or the National Front, or whatever. I have some time for the idea of tactically voting for these outfits on local issues, but the awkward truth is that electoral politics hasn't worked, largely because since the 1950s/60s, Nationalism has been controlled by the far-Right. They have not found a narrative that relates their cause to the needs and interests of ordinary people. All they have to offer is Zionist symbolism. Why should I vote for that? Why should I bow down to Jews? Keep your pin badges and your Pomp and Circumstance. I would rather go down fighting, thank you. The BNP, the National Front, Britain First, LibertyGB and UKIP are all the same: just the kosher Right under different names. They are all officially pro-Zionist or ultra-Zionist. They are all plugging the same line, using slightly different language and emphases. Enough is enough! We have to start voting for ourselves.

**FORWARD THE WHITE RESISTANCE!**

## 2.   The Jewish Problem

## 2.1.

### The Smiling Jew and other clever wiles[13]

Anthropologists think that smiling is based on an evolutionary impulse of some kind that has its origins deep in human history. Opinion differs as to what 'smiling' meant, or what its purpose was, at different times. One theory put forward is that due to our reduced canines, at some point smiling became a way of showing others that we are not a threat. Smiling might also have been a simple gesture of submission. Those who needed to join a group would have learnt to smile to show their submission and successfully integrate, while those who sought to express their dominance over others would refuse to smile.

Certainly in our society, one common strategy for ingratiation into a group or culture – be it the workplace or some social environment – is simply to smile. Smile, smile, smile. It is seen as a gesture of friendship, but from an evolutionary perspective, it can also be seen as a form of submission or compromise, needed for those who are genuinely submissive, but also by those who see submission or integration as merely a strategy for true dominance. The opposite behaviour, refusing to smile, can work equally powerfully, but is also risky because it is more visibly dominant and transparent in its intent. People who do not smile are typically seen as 'anti-social' or 'unfriendly'. They are a threat to the cohesiveness of the group because they do not follow group behaviour. Of course, in certain situations, visible unfriendliness and other signals of dominance are a requisite of professionalism.

In his seminal motivational book, *How To Win Friends And Influence People*, Dale Carnegie had a great deal to say about smiling. Here are some relevant excerpts from the book:-

*"You don't feel like smiling? Then what? Two things. First, force yourself to smile. If you are alone, force yourself to whistle or hum a tune or sing. Act as if you were already happy, and that will tend to make you happy."*

*"Here is the way the psychologist and philosopher William James put it: "Action seems to follow feeling, but really action and feeling go together; and by regulating the action, which is under the more direct control of the will, we can indirectly regulate the feeling, which is not."*

*"Your smile is a messenger of your good will. Your smile brightens the lives of all who see it. To someone who has seen a dozen people frown, scowl or turn their faces away, your smile is like the sun breaking through the clouds."*

*"Actions speak louder than words, and a smile says, "I like you, You make me happy. I am glad to see you." That is why dogs make such a hit. They are so glad to see us that they almost jump out of their skins. So, naturally, we are glad to see them."*

---

[13] First published on 12th. July 2014 at http://www.johnlonden.com

*"I am talking about a real smile, a heart-warming smile, a smile that comes from within, the kind of smile that will bring a good price in the marketplace."*

Carnegie was capitalism's answer to Lenin. The impact of his homespun philosophy is, I would argue, much more significant than anything written by a Friedman or Hayek. He didn't write this book for the good of humanity and he wasn't sponsored by the League of Nations. He was writing a book for business people. You might almost say that it was a propaganda piece for the Capitalist Party (i.e. the political elite). He began his famous motivational courses during a hiatus in the Great Depression of the 1930s, at a time when the future seemed more optimistic than later events justified, and when people were desperate for advice on how 'to get ahead'. Of course, as anyone who has travelled through reality knows, 'getting ahead' normally means more or less doing as you are told and colluding in the abuse and exploitation of others. Carnegie's innovation was to suggest that we should be nice while doing it, and actually really genuinely believe in it. Thus we would be less likely to complain about it and take up arms against the Capitalist Party, the people that Carnegie was really writing for.

The advice dispensed by Carnegie still appeals to the type of person the Americans call 'middle class' and we British variously call the 'striving classes', 'hard-workers', the 'affluent working class', 'White Van Man', or whatever – people who want to 'get ahead'. Traditionally such people were, and still mostly are, white. They are normally poor – 'affluent poor', you might say – but they share certain delusions, including an implicit belief in the system, or at least they are not as cynical about it as, say, a drop-out might be. Their consumerism and almost fanatical belief in home ownership fuelled the post-War booms in the Anglo-Saxon economies. I think it would be safe to say that I was brought up in this environment. My parents were manual workers with few or no academic qualifications, and I remember being instilled with certain ideas, some of which were valid, while others I can see in hindsight represented 'respectable deceits'. I was pressured to pursue a 'career' and cautioned against dropping out or falling in with 'undesirables' or the wrong crowd. These warnings, which were well-intended and contained much wisdom, nevertheless reflected a pining for respectability, and implicitly, a need among the post-War generation to put distance between themselves and their less materialist, less self-conscious parents. It also reflected, I think, a basic existential fear about the collapse of society and thus the collapse of the material prosperity that the 'affluent poor' enjoyed. This 'materialism' survives today and explains a great deal of what happens in mainstream politics.

Politics – whether the 'social' and 'workplace politics' of our everyday lives or the institutional forms – is the relational apotheosis of the Carnegie doctrine. The way we relate to each other in different aspects of our lives tends to reflect a deep need in society for compliant attitudes. A practical, seemingly trivial example of this would be the way in which any kind of vocal disturbance that disrupts the apparent equilibrium of daily life, whether a shouting match between a couple in the supermarket, or an impassioned political protest – will often prompt a response of visible shock on the part of onlookers. Increasingly, people value an equilibrium of calm and compliance to counter the anarchy and stress of their daily working lives. Extra-mural activities that are of no productive value, such as protest, dissent, anger, are being stigmatised as dysfunctional. The archetype of the 'angry white man' –

whether he is in a committee meeting or on a golf course – is offered as an unattractive example that we are urged not to emulate.

There is nothing new in this, to be fair – a need for compliance and group think is, to an extent, a reflection of innate human impulses – but what is new, at least for our time, is the way in which compliance and consensus are being fetishised. We must not 'rock the boat', cause 'trouble', give 'offence' nor do anything that might threaten 'investment' into our local areas. We must all become Smiling Jews. Society is being reduced to a series of transactions, in which human value is measured by a shekel. This naive hyper-materialism permeates debate even among Nationalists. UKIP has co-opted those whose real loyalty is to the 'respectable deceits' of the post-War generation. In the end, they will do what is expected of them in the workplace, in the community and in politics, in the hope that they might be able to change the environment a little, make it slightly more favourable to whites. This is done with the best of intentions, but it serves wickedness and evil, and in any case won't work. You know the drill by now – leave your troubles at the door and be 'professional', don't rock the boat. Smile!

The Smiling Jew that each of us sees in the mirror is just the more visible element of a deeper culture that has its hold on the West. Those Nationalists who believe they can invent a counter-culture to reverse it and re-create a white society, or something like it, are mistaken. What is needed is a new society. The strategy must be separatism. The reason goes back to the nature of our real enemy. Jews understand the difference between power and influence, and prefer the latter, using overt submissiveness and ingratiation as a strategy for racial domination. Whether the Jew is Levy, Leveson or Mandelson, they do not overtly take power themselves – at least not the top positions – but instead tend to act as hired hands, right-hand men, to the putative (white) leaders, using the influence this gives them to steer institutions and entire countries. This strategy is partly self-selected, due to their natural physical unattractiveness, with the result that Jews tend to be obsessed with money, finance and capital, and are skilled in areas that require back room, bureaucratic 'expertise' – law, finance, administration, media production. It's how the Jew parasite survives, and the virus needs a host.

Liberalism, the ideology that Jews promote, is an ideal vehicle for this survival strategy. It encourages whites to be 'open-minded', 'tolerant', 'nice' and so on – Smile! It discourages conservatism, scepticism, criticism, dissent. It is a concept, not a tangible enemy, and so cannot be fought easily. Meanwhile, the Jew hides skilfully among the host population. Liberalism helps him to do this, as a society that is 'open' and tolerant of different cultures is less likely to single out the Jew, but the Jew also uses miscegenation for this purpose, a kind of physical expression of liberal values, so that subsequent generations of Jews increasingly resemble the host group phenotypically, while retaining their true racial and cultural allegiance. The crocodile smile of the Jew is a reflection of both his submissiveness and his dominance. He submits to his host, the white society, knowing cleverly that this is the key to his true long-term domination. In contrast, the white man's smile is the signal of his final capitulation and submission to the Jew. The white man as The Smiling Jew – the white man Judaised, finally – is what the Jew is really thinking when he gives you that crocodile smile. Above all else, we, the workers, are to be 'friendly' and 'smiling' – a veritable Rainbow Nation of fluffy loveliness, all equal and tolerant.

Sometimes the Jew also makes use of the 'unsmile'. This is an indirect method of thought control using the manipulation of behaviour similar to the 'smile'. It is in fact an emotional corollary to the smile. We are asked not to smile for our passport photographs, nor make jokes at airport security. Official business is grim and serious and the authorities must not be laughed-at. There is also the emotional bullying inflicted on The Unsmiling Jew in that he must be seen to react to certain events in a po-faced way; he must condemn dissenting public figures harshly; he must agree with the treatment of certain forms of speech as a serious 'crime'; and he must use only a licensed form of speech, widely known as political correctness. What people often don't appreciate is how the term 'political correctness' is deeply misleading. The notion is that political correctness itself is just a modern form of politeness and self-censure, a kind of legalistic application of language, a formality and almost harmless. When viewed in that limited way, political correctness can indeed be seen as just an advanced form of etiquette for people who live side-by-side with others of a different culture. In reality, the doctrine is of much deeper significance and importance. A better term for it would be emotional correctness. The Unsmiling Jew is the essential counterpoint of The Smiling Jew. He is told what to think, feel and say, and when, and even why. And he is made to feel guilty for his 'incorrect' feelings. Above all else, it is not enough to comply, the individual must also be happy about it and if he is not happy – usually evinced by a smile, a penchant for meaningless chatter and gossip and an interest in mindless TV soaps and sport events – then he is viewed as neurotic and dysfunctional, a 'weirdo', an outcast. So smile! But be careful when you smile.

Meanwhile, you will notice that the Rainbow Nation's commissars, the celebrity white traitors and Jews, and their various hired idiots in the media, the police, politics, law, business, and academia, your boss at work – honorary Jews in short – are all permitted to be stern and unfriendly. They are, after all, the ruling class – or its collaborationist branch – and must express their dominance. This dominance entails the imposition of new values on white society, some of them entirely alien. We have already had to suffer the ignominy of homosexual equality, a sign of 'civilisation' the Jews tell us. Now, it seems, we must be 'tolerant' and 'smile' in the face of the sexualisation of our children. We are reassured that child abuse is never tolerated, but already we are seeing tiny glimpses of an emerging toleration. Some people really do think that paedophilia is just another sexual orientation, rather than a psychiatric condition. Typically, such people see problems such as homosexuality and paedophilia through a legalistic perspective. They advocate changes in the law so that this or that 'orientation' can be normalised by legislative fiat. This legal permissiveness has taken place against the backdrop of broader economic changes in society, especially the financialisation of capital and the focus on service industries, which have reduced the industrial power of working people and led to the diminished role of men in society, and with it the weakening of the family. The media and advertising industries have slowly crept into the sanctified realm of childhood innocence, like unwelcome stalkers in the night, intruding their profanity on ordinary people who tend to ape what they see in the imagery around them. Permissive attitudes have played a role in increasing the opportunities for men to indulge base desires unchecked. One undesirable result of this is an increasing role for the state in policing sexual conduct, with its courts acting as a kind of surrogate parent to an infantilised population. Executive dominance over the legislature has also left the courts without their traditional independence and without any respect for the presumption of innocence. The sexual perversion of the elite, stocked with homosexuals, and the infiltration by ethnic minorities, have resulted in a raft of anti-white legislative measures that have created a confused moral climate.

Against this background, a long-running scandal of institutionalised paedophilia and child abuse has re-surfaced over the last week. What we are being asked to believe is that these allegations cannot be properly investigated or prosecuted for a variety of reasons, including but not limited to missing documents and the memory loss of key witnesses and suspects. One suspect is Greville Ewan Janner, Baron Janner of Braunstone. It is an open secret that Lord Janner, a Jewish Labour Law Lord, is a suspected paedophile. He has been investigated several times by the police for various child abuse allegations, but charges have never been brought. When asked to explain this, a range of dubious excuses are brought forth by the police. The latest announcement is that he will probably not now face criminal charges due to his 'dementia'. The Houses of Degeneracy – formerly known as Parliament – will go to great lengths to protect itself, but on this occasion it seems that Janner will probably not be thrown to the wolves as a distraction. That he is a well-connected Jew and promulgator of Holocaust propaganda of course has absolutely nothing to do with it. No such scruples were exercised for white men accused of paedophilia – Hall and Harris, being examples – and rightly so in that they were guilty, but they too are elderly, like Janner. Only, they are not Jewish.

Janner himself is an interesting figure. A lawyer and author, he is a sort of modern version of Dale Carnegie for the more sophisticated. Titles of his books include On Meetings, On Chairing, On Presentation and How To Win Meetings. His Janner's Complete Speechmaker shows all the brutal self-analytical qualities of Carnegie. This is someone who understands not just speech-making, but human beings as well.

"The first and last sentences of a speech are crucial. The importance of a clear, resounding, and striking first sentence and a well-rounded peroration cannot be over-emphasised. You must catch the interest of your audience from the start and send them away satisfied at the end." [p.5].

"Personalise your message. Give your audience true incentive to listen. Whet their appetites for the substance to come." [p6].

Throughout the book, Janner warns against the perils of jargon and cliché, the over-use of the vertical pronoun, common verbal grammatical errors, how to deal with nerves, various social faux-pas and other ways that the amateur speech-maker might trip himself up. Janner also likes the sound of his own voice:

"Part of the price of the pleasure of hearing your own voice is the need to endure the speeches of others." [p131].

Unlike Carnegie, Janner was born into privilege and advantage, the son of Barnett Janner, a member of the House of Lords. It is interesting that he has nevertheless developed an almost neurotic obsession, expressed through his books, with the finest minutiae of social advancement and success. People of privileged backgrounds do not normally concern themselves with such things, except as a kind of commentary on the sub-culture among their own class. It's a subject that is normally the province of the more insecure and self-made. It is tempting to think of Janner's counterpart, Carnegie, the son of a poor Mid West farmer, as that kind of figure, someone who craved social acceptance through the pursuit of material success – a classic American 20th. century materialist, in other words – but Carnegie was more complex than that. He did end up changing the spelling of his name to ape the great steel magnate (it was originally spelled Carnegey), but in the beginning he had innocent dreams of becoming an adult education teacher and then an actor, failing at the latter. He actually fell into the more cynical area of motivational schtick, for which he would become famous, entirely by accident. Out-of-work and homeless during the Depression, he decided to combine his liking for teaching and his skill as a salesman. It is easy to see how a person in such desperate circumstances of poverty – in Carnegie's case, he was living at a YMCA in New York – might have been driven towards a point-of-view that, if anything embraced the values of the system fanatically and ingratiatingly, including a kind of obsessive-compulsive interest in the details of human behaviour and the value of compliance and 'getting on'. The alternative – bitter rejection of the system – would have got him nowhere.

Janner, on the other hand, has never had this type of poverty to drive him, yet much like Carnegie, he seems to concern himself with how people can get on in life and the details of success and social acceptance. Among his other titles are Janner on Communication and Janner's Complete Letterwriter. Coincidentally, I found the latter book years ago at a second-hand bookshop, at a time when I was involved in Labour politics myself and knew about Janner (though I'd never met him), and my first thought was: Why would a successful politician, barrister and QC want to write a scratty little book on letter-writing? Now that I am aware of some unpleasant rumours about Lord Janner, my question widens to: What does Janner's interest in writing 'how-to' books say about him? What's his psychology? Appropriately, it's a very Jewish question, so let's employ some Jewish methods and start with the father.

The key to Janner might be found in his relationship with his father, Barnett Janner. Although he has never suffered hardship, Janner will have had to cope with the pressure of being the son of a highly-successful, self-made man, who was a lawyer and Member of Parliament, then a member of the House of Lords, and held the position of President of the Board of British Jews. All of these attainments ensured a high profile for his father, and thus the family, within the Jewish community. Barnett Janner was not necessarily the scion of privilege, though detailed information about his background is hard to find. He was born in Lithuania and his family emigrated to Britain when he was nine months old, where his father became a furniture dealer in Cardiff. Barnett, having achieved on his own merits, would have harboured similar expectations of his children. The pressure would have been considerable and might have been detrimental psychologically to his son, either pushing him into a life he did not want, or maybe turning him into an unpleasant, callous, single-minded individual. Janner went on to equal his father's achievements, becoming a barrister, an author, a Member of Parliament, President of the Board of Deputies of British Jews, and then a peer. He became a Member of Parliament by taking over his father's Leicester seat on his retirement in 1970. Both were Labour politicians, and having succeeded his father, they were clearly close politically, both advocating Zionist causes. Zionism is Jewish geopolitical nationalism. Zionists believe in the creation and sustaining of a Jewish homeland in Palestine.

Zionism is important to all Jews, but some oppose it, a larger number affect to oppose it, still more pretend to, a smaller number support it, and almost-all Jews in some way believe in it (whether they support it or not). As a side-note, it is the case that some deeply-religious Jews are sincerely anti-Zionist and virulently oppose the State of Israel. This is because they believe the existence of a Jewish nation-state threatens Jewish existence itself. They prefer the strategy of maintaining Judaism as a tribe, rather than rely on a geopolitical entity that can be attacked. However, that view is rather principled and esoteric and definitely in the minority. In fact, most anti-Zionist Jews tend to be liberal-left types and insincere. For the Jewish Left, opposing Israel is a kind of teenage reaction or rebel style trip – an example of this tendency is Noam Chomsky, who intellectualises liberal Jewish anti-Zionism, whereas in fact if you study his writings and statements closely, you'll realise he upholds Israel. This fake opposition is very important. Another subtle tendency of 'pro-Zionism' disguised as something else is found among conservative Jewish writers like Peter Hitchens, an atheist who pretends to be a Christian and stern moralist and who paradoxically admits he is Zionist. You might have noticed that he makes easy concessions to the Palestinian side in order to appear 'balanced' – a common tactic.

In order to ensure Israel remains in existence, it is necessary for Jews to bring influence to bear on Western governments, which can only happen if Jews are made to appear sympathetic to the West so that the interests of Jews (specifically, Zionist Jews) and the West are made to appear to dovetail. They do this in various ways. Fake opposition is deployed, as outlined above, to ensure that the parameters of contrary views and feelings are kept within certain limits. Fake anti-Zionists like Chomsky often make heavy and dramatic use of abstract legalistic language – reference is made to human rights, Nuremberg standards, etc. – as a form of linguistic submission and ingratiation towards what are supposed to be Western ideas. The method is in fact part of a strategy of dominance. Hitchens, the 'reasonable' Zionist uses similar liberal parameters to judge Israeli actions. Neither Chomsky nor Hitchens – nor other Jews who fall into their respective ideological camps – will mention the real reasons for Israel's existence and its actions, which is the racial preservation and advancement of the Jewish people.

It's important to note that there is nothing necessarily wrong or immoral in this activity, in and of itself. Jews have as much right to genetic preservation as any other group, and they also have the right to lie and trick us about it. They can't be blamed for this. My purpose is to point out the deceit and its impact on European (white) civilisation. What we see is a narrative presented in piously humanistic, liberal, 'Western' terms – a positivistic, legalistic narrative devoid of actual meaning. If Chomsky, Hitchens & co. were actually intent on telling the truth, they would begin by admitting and accepting their own pro-Jewish racism, and they would point out what Israel is for and why its collapse can never be allowed to happen by any self-respecting Jew. People like the Janners played an important role in this deceitful pro-Israel narrative, by advancing 20th. century British Zionism, a movement within Britain's traditional institutions that persuaded our government to adopt policies favourable to Israel and to Jews in general. The essential features were – Holocaust education, equality laws, joining the EEC and mass immigration. A liberal climate in society is more favourable to Jewish survival. The Janners' loyalty was not to Britain, but to their race, the Jews. In its own way, this loyalty was admirable, but it was also detrimental to the interests of indigenous whites.

We now come to the possible relationship between the allegations of paedophilia against Greville Janner, his politics and his strange penchant for writing self-help books. Janner's need for acceptance and pressure to emulate his father gave fuel to his ambition, but Janner was also part of a distinct and different racial group with its own interests that were, and are, separate from whites. Janner, the racist and Jewish supremacist, inculcated in Jewish culture, steeped in the rabid Zionism of his father, a bitter contemporary of the Holocaust, sees white people as cattle that he can legitimately control, trick and deceive – and possibly also sexually abuse, though that allegation remains unproven. Power is pursued for its own sake, of course, but also out of loyalty to family, tribe and race. In that respect, the Jews of today understand the survivalist importance of race and culture better than the whites of today. Janner's patronising attitude and his obsession with social etiquette and superiority to the cattle whites is encapsulated in his books, which are the projection of a complex. With his didactic barbs about the minutiae of success, he taunts whites using the pettily repressive mores and norms of their own culture.

Unfortunately, most whites do not recognise the deeper motives in the behaviour of powerful and influential figures. Institutionalised paedophilia, even if proven, will just be seen as the disgusting actions of individuals, not the degeneracy of an entire political system. That's because presentation is more important than the truth, something that Janner knows a thing or two about. We whites are mostly social rather than intellectual as a race. This has its advantages, but its downsides include the fact that we are easily manipulated by clever Jews. Buzz words are more effective in diverting the focus of the average white than a detailed, truth-seeking scrutiny of the facts, even to the extent that the truth – the Jewish face that is staring back at us from the television screen – will be ignored in favour of the usual mantra: "democracy", "human rights", "equality", "justice", "fairness", the language of the cynical, lying Jew. The role of the white man is to smile back – or else.

The ultimate liberal shibboleth of our time is the Holocaust, that Greville Janner helped to invent and promote – first as a wartime Army investigator, then as a politician. In The Complete Speechmaker, Janner writes:

"About the only time that deliberate exaggeration helps the presentation of a serious case is when that case is thin. 'If something is too silly to say, you can always sing it,' says the operatic librettist. 'If logic and argument are surplus' says the skilled speaker, 'then it is just possible that if you should loud enough, exaggerate sufficiently, thump with sufficient force, you may numb the minds of your audience.' [p16].

I cannot, for the life of me, think what 'Lord' Janner must be referring to.

The question arises: how many 'Janners' must be publicised and how much of this sickening degeneracy must white people put up with before they begin to question the system more fundamentally?  When is the White Man going to stop smiling and become angry again?

## 2.2.

### The Nervous Jew: deconstructing Peter Hitchens[14]

One of the more admirable aspects of the political writing of the Jew Noam Chomsky is the way he is prepared to de-construct the liberal hypocrisy of professional intellectuals. Chomsky has demonstrated time and again the limitations of positivist/liberal thinking and the emptiness of buzz phrases like 'democracy', 'liberty' and 'human rights' when deployed in defence of societies that are as undemocratic and unjust as those the West targets for its propaganda. That Chomsky is also a rank hypocrite who uses the same tactics himself is less noticed and less remarked on, but that having been noted, it remains the case that his writings are useful in that they prompt us to ask a very important question: What role do society's intellectuals play in maintaining repressive systems at home and abroad?

Peter Hitchens is a professional intellectual of some interest to me, for the following reasons:-

(1).   He is Jewish and strongly Zionist, but affects to be devoutly Christian. Admittedly, there is little difference between the two positions, and certainly no contradiction as far as I can see, since Christianity and Judaism are more or less the same moral belief system, albeit with some important but superficial differences. But the important point is that Hitchens' 'pretend Christianity' allows him to pursue the classic Jewish tactic of hiding among whites and affecting to adopt Western values.

(2).   Although he makes no serious attempt to hide his Zionism, Hitchens does like to distract from it a little by putting forward easy and obvious concessions to the Palestinian side. He does this to appear as the 'reasonable Zionist'. When Israel commits an obvious atrocity, it's likely Hitchens will have some condemnatory formulation prepared in response to it, while at the same time also pointing out (perhaps rightly, in fairness) that people should not adopt a simplistic view of things and arrantly castigate Israel.

(3).   The third reason is Hitchens' apparent conservatism. I say 'apparent' because like much else about him, in Hitchens' case what appears to be conservatism is in fact something else. That 'something else' is not quite alien to conservatism – I am suggesting Hitchens is a propagandist, not a liar – it is more of a hybrid that serves a hidden or difficult-to-see purpose. The purpose is racial. Hitchens (like Chomsky and other media Jews) is a pro-Jewish racist.

To explain this and how it relates to Hitchens' conservatism, we should consider the extent to which British conservatism and British Zionism dovetail. Both have an interest in preserving the system they have successfully infiltrated and in attacking any political or social force that might threaten it. In Hitchens' case, this has led to a rather pronounced brand of traditional social conservatism. I would argue that Peter Hitchens serves as the personification of British conservative-Zionist intellectual

---

[14] First published on 13th. July 2014 at http://www.johnlonden.com

confluence and is in fact the archetypal practitioner of the 'respectable deceit' referred to in my previous article (The Smiling Jew and other clever wiles). Such people tend to see anyone who questions the system fundamentally as a 'crank' or 'troublemaker'.

Indeed, one thing you will notice about Hitchens is the way that he hypocritically often makes use of mockery and personal insult against his opponents, while complaining loudly whenever the same is dished out to him. This is because Hitchens is actually engaged in a racial struggle, the type of struggle in which loyalty to one's Race must come before intellectual honesty and objectivity. For Hitchens, the personal actually is the political. He sees his political opponents as existential enemies who might threaten not just the illusions of material prosperity that support the 'respectable deceits' of his post-War generation, but also the survival of the Jewish race. Hitchens is, in short, still fighting the left-wing battles of his (alleged) Trotskyist youth, using much the same obnoxious methods, only deploying different language.

I strongly suspect Hitchens' Trotskyist period is largely a fiction and that his actual involvement in anything remotely rebellious was very small and resembled juvenile pranksterism more than Trotskyism. However, I have no evidence for this – it's just an intuitive suspicion on my part. It would make an interesting project for an investigative journalist to pursue, and if my suspicion is correct, it would also prove him a liar, and raise lots of interesting and serious questions about who he really is and what he is up to. However, it may not be of any great importance either way. In truth, even if we accept Hitchens on his own terms, his Trotskyism was not as significant as he pretends. Hitchens talks up these radical movements, conjuring up dark visions of enemies within, in much the same fashion that people on the far-Right like to, but the reality is more prosaic. Trotskyists are essentially left-wing radicals who follow the general politics of Leon Trotsky. I have some experience of my own in the matter. I was never a Trotskyist, but I was in the Labour Party and held quite left-wing views, and I knew Trotskyists and other sorts of state-communists (as I would call them, though admittedly use of the term 'state' risks being a little clumsy with regard to the ideology of Trotsky, but that's another matter). Their views are not significantly far removed from democratic socialists in the Labour Party, though they pretend to be, and people like Hitchens, who want to give the impression of an edgy radical past, pretend that they are. They aren't. Of course, Hitchens acknowledges this himself, rightly pointing out how the modern Labour Party has achieved many of the aims of the radical left of his youth. Where perhaps he errors in in assuming that this means the modern Labour Party and the contemporary Left and the radicals of his era are, more or less, one and the same movement. There is merit in the theory, but things are not quite that simple.

Cultural conservatives like Hitchens tend to emphasise what I call 'idealism' over 'materialism'. To Hitchens, being radical is about idealism and effecting cultural changes and has no bearing on the deeper racial (genetic) and economic interests in society. To put that in plain terms, using an example: to Hitchens, militant feminism is just the assertion of radical women against some kind of prevailing social orthodoxy. Most people are persuaded by this type of view, but it serves an ulterior purpose in that it means that most people don't stop to consider what vested interests (racial and economic) might really be driving feminism and push for its success. The latter is the materialist perspective. Of course, the idealist/materialist dichotomy is a simplification: Hitchens' presentation of his views can sometimes embrace social complexity, as is the case for all of us, but the point is that in postulating a continuation of radical liberalism from the Sixties to the Blair government, Hitchens does not take into account of the forces that drive social change, which are primarily racial and economic and outside the remit of national governments. In other words, Hitchens doesn't want us to consider that the way our society is organised into owners and non-owners – i.e. capitalism – and the existence of different racial groups might have bearing on social and cultural change. Instead, like other conservatives, Hitchens adopts the 'culture wars' narrative. Feminists are just men-haters. Left-wingers are just 'commies'. Blair is just a silly drip or a 'war-monger'. The advantage of a purely cultural narrative like this that it is evacuated of materialist analysis is that it allows the propagandist to blame everything on a concept – it might be 'liberals' or 'feminist man-haters' or whatever. Hitchens, and people like him, would rather we don't grasp that the reason the UK went to war in Iraq is because we have a capitalist government under the influence of Zionist Jews. Instead, Blair is a 'liar' or an 'interventionist liberal'. Of course, Blair may be these things as well – I'm not dismissing these views entirely – and by engaging in this type of second-hand critique, Hitchens does run the risk that the dog might stop looking at the finger and see what the finger is pointing at. However, my point is that there is more to it than what people like Hitchens like to pretend. Hitchens would like us to believe that everything happens in a vacuum and cannot be explained rationally and that we should instead be satisfied with blame, scape-goating and name-calling, and perhaps, the comfort of a superannuated rational actor in God. He doesn't want us to look for more rational explanations, as this might cause us to start asking some uncomfortable questions about the way society is run.

There is of course nothing wrong with the notion that the Left have managed to effect considerable cultural change in society over the last sixty years, but this hasn't happened because of a bunch of bolshie commies and man-hating feminists. Hitchens can afford to be candid about his own supposed radical past because he is certain we will accept this second-rate explanation, which is given credence by his 'confessional'. It is part of a front that he has constructed to distract from his true agenda, which is the racial interests of Jews. It helps to create in the mind of the naive observer an impression of knowledge and reasonableness, especially given that Hitchens likes to claim he has left this 'radical' past behind. The clue as to the truth of this claim is apparent whenever you see him speak or read his words on a page: his rhetorical and argumentative methods remain left-wing in that he can be prating, hectoring, simplistic and personal – and above all else, manipulative – in the way he puts across his points, often resembling an excited student at a university debating society. What we can see with Hitchens, as with anyone else, is a continuation, in which he has been pursuing the same cause all along: not as some mad, frenzied radical 'liberal', but as one of the Jews.

An article that appeared on Hitchens' blog today caught my attention and I will offer my analysis of part of it. One thing that immediately grabs attention about Hitchens – and the linked article offers a very good example of this – is his consummate skill as a propagandist, both as a speaker and writer. It is almost as if he has received some professional training in the art of rhetorical persuasion, such is the cogency of his prose. To deconstruct his prose, I adopt here the method of textual analysis, based on the premise that in small details we will often find important truths, about the author and society in general. As for the article itself, to borrow a rhetorical flourish often used by Noam Chomsky – the piece is 'a classic in the genre'. It's an example of how British conservatism and British Zionism converge. Surely one for the archives, it should be regarded as a 'useful study' (as Chomsky likes to put it) of a particularly disreputable intellectual ferment.

My comments are interleaved with the prose...

*"We're queuing meekly in security, clutching a one-way ticket to disaster...*

*"We have become a nation of suspects. The last wisps of British liberty are being stripped away and, as usual, this is happening with the keen support of millions.*

Hitchens begins by cleverly framing his arguments as 'We'. The idea is that you and I are now suspects and should fear a strong state. Hitchens would like us all to stand by him and his fellow Jews. It's a tactic of submission to the reader, a plea that we should share in the impending Shoah. The 'We' is actually the Jews, including Hitchens. The Jews are the suspects in the real crime – the ongoing genetic eradication of the White Race. Everyone knows this at an intuitive level – it's the elephant in the room – but no-one dares admit it, even to themselves. Hitchens, The Nervous Jew, wants to keep it that way.

The 'British liberty' referred to is in fact British Zionism, which is what the British state really stands for. Hitchens wants us to cling on to various teary-eyed myths, like jury trials, presumption of innocence, lay juries and, no doubt, impartial judges in horsehair wigs. Of course, these may be fine and civilised traditions in their own right, but they are also useful as heart-pulling levers for propagandists like Hitchens who have no real arguments. The 'stripping away' referred to is the stripping away of Jewish assets and the removal of Jews, which is what Hitchens really fears might happen if public discontent goes much further.

The reference to "the keen support of millions" suggests a fear of popular opinion. Hitchens would rather we do not have our say, but instead listen to Jews like him, and preferably keep jolly quiet and vote UKIP.

*"First we have a scandal, entirely without hard evidence so far, which supposedly affects the whole of Parliament.*

Not true. The Westminster paedophile scandal has evidence to support it. All that's needed is a simple web search to find references to corroborated stories of abuse by household names and high-profile figures. Hitchens here is, at best, disingenuous. As a London journalist, he must know what the allegations involve.

*"Scandals of this kind – vague, general and fed by rumour – are a feature of societies on the eve of regime change.*

In the first part of that sentence, Hitchens is – again – being disingenuous. First, Hitchens uses the term 'scandal', which I think is telling. 'Scandal' is a media term.

To people like Hitchens, this sort of thing is something rather disreputable and embarrassing involving a few dirty old men. That's the way he wants you and I to think about it too. The word 'scandal' is a verbal fail-safe, to ensure that we don't question any further or see the whole situation as anything more than an example of bad morals among elite types.

In fact, this is not a 'scandal' at all. This sort of behaviour is to be expected among perverts, which is what these people actually are. It's just another example of why these people have no legitimacy and no right to rule over us any longer. To talk of 'scandal' is to trivialise what in fact is the total moral collapse of a political system.

But let's humour Hitchens and go along with his own trickery. We can start by observing that Hitchens is wrong on his own terms. The 'scandal', as he calls it, involves specific allegations of specific acts of abuse by specific people who have exercised, or still, exercise power and influence. Hitchens knows this. It is not 'vague', 'general' or 'fed by rumour'. These are actual allegations that have been historically investigated by the police and considered by the CPS, in some cases only to have been dropped on highly-dubious pretexts. They are now being investigated again, by the police, and there is also to be a public inquiry. Why would there be a public inquiry if the allegations were without evidence (which Hitchens knows is not the case anyway)? Of course, a public inquiry can result entirely from political or parliamentary pressure, but even if we accept that's the case here, then where has that pressure come from? Thin air?

Hitchens' tactic is the old and tired one of trying to portray as hysterics those who are concerned about elite behaviour and whether it is institutionalised. It's not an argument.

The second part of the sentence does, however, contain an isolated truth – albeit you have to take the wording out of context. Hitchens is 'right' in that we are indeed in a society on the eve of 'regime change'. That's why Hitchens, The Nervous Jew, is imploring us to think twice. 'We' are all suspects, when in fact he knows very well it is the Jews and their useful idiots who are in the firing line, not just for isolated acts of paedophilia and sexual abuse, but for their attack on the White Race.

*"They discredit ancient institutions and make troublemakers look virtuous.*
*Hitchens likes 'ancient institutions' but doesn't like 'troublemakers'. Righto. I'm sure*
*we'll all sleep better at night knowing that.*

This is an example of the way that Hitchens uses buzz phraseology to govern interpretation of events. Any system based on deceit needs to do this, often for what is thought to be good or honourable ends. Good things are 'ancient'. Bad things involve 'troublemakers' and so on. Hitchens probably believes this sincerely and believes that people who challenge his precious system mean ill. And he would be right. Many people are waking up and do mean ill – towards him and his fellow Jews. That is what makes him, rightly, nervous.

*"The charge of child sex abuse is so horrible that anyone who is accused of it is*
*automatically presumed guilty and shunned by all, so it is more or less unstoppable*
*once it has been launched.*

Not true and disingenuous anyway. If someone is suspected of committing child abuse and there is the basis of a case, then that is of proper interest to society and the authorities. What is popularly thought about child abuse is separate from what did or did not actually occur and is not an excuse for cover ups, which is what Hitchens implicitly condones – just as Tebbit admits that the Thatcher administration (and no doubt other governments) covered-up abuse to protect 'the system', and thus condoned abuse. The point of this 'scandal', as Hitchens calls it, is that there is strong evidence that cover ups have occurred. Whereas figures such as Rolf Harris and Stuart Hall, both white, have been prosecuted and convicted, despite their senescence, and rightly so, key political figures suspected of child abuse and paedophilia remain unmolested by the law. It is also significant, I think, that despite the large scale of his paedophilic activity, Jimmy Savile was never brought before a court to answer for his actions. Savile was well-connected politically, whereas those who have been prosecuted in the wake of the Yewtree frenzy seem to have no political connections nor any significant involvement in politics.

Our lives belong to us, not to an elite. Our country belongs to us, not to Jews and their media fictions. The significance of the Westminster paedophile scandal is that it is a rare shard of truth that vividly cuts through the media fictions and 'respectable deceits' of this system, and any hierarchical system. All that the elites have in response is the teary-eyed liberal buzz phrases of Hitchens and his fake conservatism, plus credit bubbles, celebrities, pop stars, and official bullying. One day, this system will collapse – for the betterment of all.

So I disagree with the prevailing pessimism among Nationalists and I consider that we are fortunate to live in these interesting times. Our mettle, intellect, character and ingenuity are being tested and as a Race we will emerge from this stronger – and wiser. At the moment, whites are failing the intellectual test. We have not yet identified our true enemy, and we wilfully refuse to, instead buying into the fear peddled by conservative Zionists like Hitchens, and others. Hitchens employs Orwellian allegory, threatening us with a dystopian future lest we peer beneath the surface of the Jews' invented reality. I think of Nineteen Eighty-Four, its vision now common currency among reactionaries, and I draw from it renewed strength, not fear. I remember that at least Winston Smith could identify his real enemy. We, the dumb whites, stunned and stupefied into calm compliance, haven't yet even managed that. In some respects, the fictional Winston was mentally freer than most whites today. We need to acknowledge that the true enemy is the Jews. Muslim fanatics, Asian paedophile gangs and gun-toting blacks are all serious problems, true, but they are merely the more visible and obvious manifestations of a broken society. They are not the cause. The collapse of Western society – the event that Hitchens, The Nervous Jew fears – would bring these issues into focus and would identify to whites their true enemy – Jews like Hitchens. Hitchens, being thoughtful, knows this and that is why he rails against the excesses of his fellow travellers. The Nervous Jew has much to fear.

# 3. The White Problem

## 3.1.

## Problems of Abrahamic Morality: religion as race[16]

One of the points I touched on in my previous essay (The Nervous Jew: deconstructing Peter Hitchens), is the way that the intellectual elites in the West have turned away from materialist explanations of society and have returned to a kind of primitivist idealism. In this climate, genetic and economic explanations for what happens in society are ignored in favour of superficial explanations that attribute human behaviour to second-rank ideologies and 'bolshie' behaviour: be it 'man-hating feminists', 'fanatical Muslims', 'angry white racist men', 'decadent liberals', or whatever.

There is strong peer pressure among Western intellectuals – almost an 'ideology of ideology' – not to allow society to be explained rationally, i.e. in racial/genetic and economic terms. A great deal of the mantra we hear on socio-cultural issues reflects this. Relevant to us would be: "Islam is not a race, it's a religion." "Judaism is not a race, it's a religion". "Britain has been ruined by trendy liberals". And so on. At the moment, Islam is the most popular target of this intellectual frenzy. We are expected to believe that radical Muslims are just a random bunch of religious fanatics with no particular motive other than a belief in a Sky God. Of course, many, if not most, radical Muslims will indeed be sincere in their faith and religiosity, but the real fanaticism is about race. These Muslims are pursuing a racial survival strategy. That most of them don't fully realise or understand it themselves is of crucial importance. In fact, the strategy depends on the unconsciousness (and fear) of most of those who pursue it, because to question religious purpose would be akin to questioning race, which is but a short step away from undermining the genetic advancement of the racial group. To question, or unintentionally challenge and undermine the very tenets of a racial and group survival strategy is genetic suicide. Hence the continuing usefulness of Sky God Worship for Muslims, despite its transparent absurdity. Religion, which is inherently faith-based and lends itself to fanaticism and irrationalism, fits the bill well as an ideological vessel for chauvinistic racial conquest.

Religions are political ideologies. That is their true purpose. They rely on faith and not questioning things. You will note however that 'doubting' the Sky God is fine, even necessary. It is important for the racial group to maintain its intellectual vitality and criticality, therefore a theological dialectic as well as sympathetic interaction with science and other rigorous disciplines is encouraged. However, a climate of fear and submission is also necessary so as to ensure that ordinary Muslims do not stray from the core racial survival strategy. Let us also observe that race is about genes. This is not openly acknowledged by intellectuals in the West (it is elsewhere, but that's another story), who prefer to encourage the misconception that race is just skin colour – the classic 'idealistic' perspective. The syllogism is: race is just skin colour, your colour of skin doesn't matter much, and so racists are just unreasoned fanatics and can be ignored or treated as criminals. One of the reasons this

---

[15] First published on 14th. July 2014 at http://www.johnlonden.com

narrative is crucial to the elites is that genes are not conscious actors. Once this is grasped, a great deal becomes clear. The most successful populations are those that consist of blind vessels: the unthinking herd is important for survival. Hence we get back to the political importance of religions. If Muslims were to begin rejecting their religious faith, in effect they would be abandoning their unconscious genetic destiny and supplanting it with an idealist destiny of 'race as skin colour', race as something that does not matter. Then the racial strategy would begin to fail. This is why, although it is not uncommon to come across Muslims who are quite secular and even atheistic, it remains a rare thing to encounter a Muslim who rejects his cultural identity altogether and has detached himself from Islam. Partly this is due to certain special features of Islam – among which are its legalism and its practical communalism. A key feature of Islamic legalism is the concept of apostasy: a Muslim who openly renounces his faith, in word or deed, might face severe consequences in his community or generally. We can also observe that Muslims place a high importance on community and value hierarchy, compliance and submission, which discourage informal dissent. What Muslims mean by 'peace' – a word they often use – is submission, through silence and the suffocation of dissent, both within and without.

The 'religion as race' idea can be applied almost-universally, and Judaism is no exception. In fact, the Jews are an exemplar of the model and I would have normally begun this essay with them. I didn't for three reasons. First because it is important to deconstruct the present, counter-productive obsession with 'radical Muslims'. A sizeable number of nationalists, and many more with views broadly sympathetic to us, seem to think that if only Islam can be reformed or the radical Muslims can be sent away, then a key part of the national problem will be solved. It won't. We need to understand that the problem is racial. All Muslims are radical, it's just that some are more honest about it than others. This is the case because Islam is a racial strategy. Second, the Jewish problem is complicated. At the moment, it is easy for influential Jews, and their white collaborators, to dismiss anyone who points to the Jewish racial strategy and pro-Jewish racism as a krank or nut. Most people will accept the slur implicitly and not question further. It's a little bit like when a dog looks at the finger rather than what its owner is pointing at. We are all 'dog-brained' in this sense. I began by staring at the finger (radical Muslims). This is what the media owners wanted me to bark at. In time, I began to realise that the finger was pointing somewhere – at the Jews. But it took me a long time.

The third factor is perhaps the most interesting and important. The racial relationship between Islam and Judaism is a topic that is currently not widely discussed but deserves serious attention. Islam, an anti-white, racial chauvinist creed, is the Jews' little pet. One thing that needs to be understood about Jews is that they thrive on conflict, provocation and antagonism. I mentioned in a previous essay (The Smiling Jew and other clever wiles) how whites are primarily social rather than intellectual. Jews are the opposite, in that they tend to emphasise the cerebral and intellectual over the social and thrive on conflict and hatred, both between each other and against outsiders. It's how they have survived tribally, and from a group evolutionary perspective it makes perfect sense. You survive by hating. However, Jews need reasoned justifications for this survivalist mentality, and so they co-opt the notional concepts of the host population. For example, in the West, this meant that Jews corrupted racial equality, which was a nameless materialist and natural concept that – to our modern understanding – meant simply the equality of people of similar capability, i.e. within the same racial group. The Jews turned this 'materialist equality' into an idealistic concept of inalienability and unattainability, based on religious mythology, in order to engineer conditions more favourable for their own survival, and thus implicitly less favourable for whites. Jews use Islamic fundamentalism similarly as a tool to pressure and divide whites and create Israelised societies in the West that are favourable to Jews. Christianity also serves a purpose for Jews, just as Islam does, as do the major Jewish secular responses to the Western Enlightenment: liberalism and industrial capitalism.

This brings us to one of the central problems of the West. Whites no longer have their own successful racial survival strategy. Instead, our lives are directed towards the interests of a minority – capitalists, who own society's resources. Instead of thinking as a racial bloc, whites think as selfish self-interested individuals and live and work in a competitive society, in which their relationship to production is as wage slave and in which they have no real economic stake. The capitalism system is anarchic and unplanned and its productive forces take no account of the needs of the community, resulting in needless waste and antagonism, which are the basis for most of the social problems – including many of those that are simplistically attributed to racial differences. The capitalist class is influenced and dominated by Jews. Capitalism – both its so-called 'free market' model and its statist model of 'communism' – is a Jewish slave system. Its subsidiary ideologies, such as Christianity and secular liberalism, help the elites govern populations by providing moral ballast for the inherent contradictions in the capitalist system and by furnishing ethical rationalisations for the blatant unfairness and injustice we see in our own societies and elsewhere.

Christianity is an extension of Judaism into the West – the legal, moral and economic system of Jews imposed on whites. As the scientific method and reason became the more acceptable basis for explaining the physical and social world, Christianity and other organised religions went into gradual decline in the West and so the Jews required a different justificatory ideology for capitalism: liberalism. The liberal notion of equality is a moral gospel used to justify inequality. If people believe that the elites are interested in making society more equal, then they will not be interested in pursuing genuine equality, a social condition that does not have a name since it would simply be the natural state of affairs among people of similar capabilities: i.e. among a racial community. Since the Jews cannot allow racial communities to exist among whites, it is necessary to deconstruct the natural and obvious concept of equality as an essential social component of race, and as a materialist reality that is not opposed to racial integrity but in fact an integral part of it – racial socialism, in other words – and replace it with a fictitious ideal of equality that is not achievable and serves its purpose in fragmenting white racial consciousness.

There is one additional problem I should mention. Some Nationalists and conservatives make the mistake of thinking that it was the decline of Christianity in the West that prompted the decline of white racial unity and consciousness, and that we need only restore institutionalised faith to bring back a sense of national and racial cohesiveness. This error is of course understandable and forgivable. I myself have always been atheist, but I do like old churches and I admire the softness and tolerance of Christianity, especially the Church of England – which, after all, is my culture. And which of us doesn't hark back to earlier times, actual and imagined? The problem lies in the fact that we have a culture that is not fit for purpose. To explain, let us approach the problem comparatively. The Chinese Revolutionaries did not waste time worrying about the preservation of false gods and obscure mumbo jumbo in the interests of 'cultural preservation'. It may be attractive to do so, but the Chinese – like the Bolsheviks – were entirely ruthless and unsentimental in their recognition of the national interest, which is what their movements are really about. The Bolsheviks and the Maoists industrialised their economies and re-engineered their peoples culturally. Whether what they did was 'right' or 'wrong' is a separate issue. The point is that there was no room for teary-eyed liberal sentiment, for remembrance of halcyon bygone days and mythical cultures except to the extent that such would help assist national objectives. To preserve their race, they first destroyed or re-engineered the culture that had not been serving the race. That is the point about culture that conservative types often do not grasp. Culture serves the race. It is an expression of the genetic interests of the dominant group and escheats to blood. Replace the blood, and you replace the interest served. To the dim reactionary Tory, someone like Chairman Mao might be a dirty commie and really rather caddish. In reality, Mao was simply someone who pursued the economic and racial interests of a particular group, in the same way that regular people do. He was just particularly successful at it. Conversely, the dim left-winger rails against Thatcher, as if she was some kind of demon personified rather than simply an ordinary person who did what ordinary people do: which is pursue the interests of one's own group, in this case the Jews and capitalists whom she chose to make common cause with. As for the Labour Party, its social democracy is simply a strategy for managing capitalism, i.e. the interests of Jews and their white collaborators.

What conservatives see as the decline of religion – and other idealist forms of social and political thought – was, in my view, actually a civilised and necessary advancement for the West. The problem is not that religious nonsense was replaced, but in what replaced it. To argue that whites should seek their salvation in a return to some kind of primitivist Middle Eastern mumbo-jumbo just because the secular ideologies that supplanted it have been found just as wanting is a poor analysis. If anything, what whites need is their own 'Maoism'. We need a conscious racial ideology free of poisonous Abrahamic morality, free of Jewish influence.

## 3.2.

### The Morality Problem: liberalism as a white construct[16]

Many years ago, when I was still on the Left politically and naive about racial issues, I was an avid watcher of Michael Moore, including his political TV series, TV Nation, and his various books and pseudo-documentary films. I watched and read everything of his: my own (embarrassing) empirical example, if you like, of the leader syndrome. One particular Michael Moore book stands out in my memory: Stupid White Men, which – if I recall correctly – I bought and read almost as soon as it was published in the UK. It was a truly terrible book, and I even threw it in the dustbin – the only time I have ever done that with a book. I normally have much more respect for books, even the ones I dislike intensely (and there have been a few like that), because I assume a great effort is expended in the business of writing and publishing, and I do think it is ignorant to treat a book, any book, with disregard.

Thinking back now, it occurs to me that I might have been harsh on Moore and that he understands something about white people that is important, but not obvious. What I am referring to is the white tendency to assume the burden of others, sometimes directly, sometimes indirectly, and sometimes by proxy, and often in political language that does not make the paternalism obvious. When I was on the Left, one thing that puzzled me for a long time was what appeared to me to be the sheer mean-spiritedness of right-wing/conservative types (I used to lump them all together, and to an extent still do today, albeit for more rational reasons now than before). Quite simply, I could not understand how one group of people could be so mean. This was especially the case when I looked at American politics. If British Tories can be cruel, their rugged U.S. Republican counterparts across the Atlantic can seem positively uncivilised to cosseted British eyes. What I think I hadn't grasped was the relationship of conservative moral outrage and condemnation to its apparent opposite, and that in fact one is just the flip side of the other. Conservative condemnation is liberal compassion expressed in its own political language, sympathetic to the values of provincial whites It is just another manifestation of the white tendency to assume the burdens of others, just as traditional welfare liberalism represents the same tendency in the language of 'liberal'/leftist whites. Moral condemnation of welfare and poverty is prominent in the mainstream politics of all Western societies, and even in those societies in which whites do not want to live around blacks – for example, historically South Africa, which was an apartheid society that had blacks as the labouring class, even though its whites wanted to live separately. Whites seem to adopt in their behaviour, thought and attitudes a paternalism towards non-whites – blacks especially – that often does not even extend to their fellow whites.

This is liberalism – or as I would put it, 'fake white liberal paternalism'. It comes in 'liberal' and 'conservative' flavours, depending on what you prefer, but it is basically the same thing. It is trait of moral concern found across the mainstream political spectrum, including among some of the most right-wing and conservative people, who fulminate about welfare and government dependency, expressing their view of society as a moral economy in which non-whites (and poor whites) must adhere to

---

[16] First published on 24th. July 2014 at http://www.johnlonden.com

white values. Where I think we can sometimes misunderstand the (admittedly simplistic) Left-Right divide in Western politics is in assuming that left-wing political thought is underpinned by a radically different moral economy to that of the Right. The political Right, especially white conservatives, rail against what they see as left-wing clientist policies that promote welfare dependency. The criticism is largely based on reality, but what is not openly admitted is the necessity of left-wing clientism for a multi-racial society as a whole to function and not explode into civil conflagration. The moral economy is the same, because the interests are the same, and the Left-Right dichotomy is, in truth, simply a stage for different actors to play out a fictitious melodrama. The public, both white and black, only see the puppet shadows on the wall and do not surmise who has been holding the puppets and playing them all along. The Orwellian propaganda of fake white liberal paternalism is practised most starkly in the United States.

News and current affairs in the US are largely framed and influenced by racial issues. A sharp racial divide exists, eliding people of different races by issue and party, largely due to the fact that white Americans have had to live alongside blacks much longer than white Europeans. Healthcare is really a race issue. Prisons are really about race. The Republican Party is essentially a white party (though 'white' seems to have an expansive meaning in this context, embracing also non-white groups that aren't black). Complaints from Republicans about welfare and healthcare intervention, affirmative action politics, and so on, are really coded attacks on black culture and reflect a resentment among white Americans about the extent to which they have to subsidise the black community (or so they think). Conversely, the Democratic Party is the party of so-called white 'liberals', Jews and other non-whites. Most Democrats seem to support the elite culture of paternalism openly, whereas Republicans like to pretend they don't, or at least pretend they don't like it. In fact, they do support it, and they do like it, for reasons I will explain momentarily.

The repeated theme of right-wing populists is moralist – the white tendency to assume the burdens of others, this time through the tax system. The debate is centred around the extent to which support should be given or at all. Likewise left-wing populists adopt a moral tone that is just as transparently about getting whites to support blacks through the tax system. The Right (and some on the Left: what American elite types call 'progressives') hold that the welfare subsidy cannot continue. The argument is that while it keeps a lid on American society – keeping a growing and restless non-white minority in check – it is not financially or economically sustainable. Actually, that is the very reason it must continue, because its real purposes are served well, which are ideological. One misconception is that American politics is non-ideological when in fact it is deeply ideological. The ideology is that of capitalism. The purpose of welfare is that it is a rent that the rich pay to the poor in return for control of society. This is only possible because real power is with the poor, the working classes. This is why even the most right-wing Republicans support an extensive welfare system in the United States. The system serves a purpose for the elite. Or it just wouldn't exist. It keeps the people with real power in check, i.e. the masses. The propaganda attempts to convince us of the opposite, that it is the rich who are powerful and that the people receive welfare as some kind of paternalistic concession. This is hogwash, but the propaganda works – people really do think this. The propaganda takes various forms, but the underpinning rationale for all of it are the aims of the moral economy. Some white conservatives genuinely believe that they are on a mission to rescue the poor from government dependency. Others are more concerned with the financial algebra of what they see as government dependency. Many white liberals see welfare paternalism as a moral duty, others try to rationalise it as a necessary step-up from poverty and destitution. What all these different threads of ideological justification share is an underlying faith in maintaining white liberal paternalism. Each side of the debate will argue heatedly and make all sorts of accusations against the other while hiding their common interest, which is to maintain elite control by handing out scraps to ordinary people, depriving the masses, black and white, of their birth right: a true stake in society. Capitalism, like any hierarchical social system, relies on pacification, lies, ignorance and collusion with the elite among those who can be bought-off.

The fakery and propaganda distracts the masses from the real issues and puts off until another time any resolution of the deep-seated problems faced by America, and other Western societies. This makes sense because to confront the problems would require a social revolution – in other words, democracy (or 'socialism' or whatever you want to call it). Thus, it is necessary and expedient to fudge the issues and to use the political system as a moderator between the competing interests. This has some unintended effects which, in the long-run, are causing fissures in the system and may eventually bring it to collapse. First, to avoid discussion about the deepening economic inequality in society and the inherent unfairness of capitalism, certain scapegoats are set up for blame. These include rich whites (the Jews do this) or blacks (the whites do this) or poor whites (the blacks do this). The actual problem, economic inequality, is a subject that Jews and rich whites don't want raised – even though, arguably, it actually threatens their interests as much as everybody else's. If present trends continue, the future of capitalism itself could be on the line due to the widening and deepening wealth and income gap between the elite and ordinary people. Poor whites are bought-off through the propaganda of some White Nationalists, who (not unreasonably, it must be said) seek to blame blacks for detroitisation of black-majority areas and (rightly) point to high black involvement in violent crime, the high black prison population, and other problems. It is argued, a little simplistically but not inaccurately, that these issues are due to 'inherent' racial differences. There is some merit in those observations, but the causes are more complex than simply race and, if we are honest, include the socio-economic and cultural legacy of slavery as an institution in North America. Nevertheless, the narrative is very effective in diluting and diverting opposition to the system and serves a secondary purpose in that it allows Americans to defer the awkward but necessary resolution they must one day come to on the race question as a de facto segregated society and certain other uncomfortable cultural questions in that society, caused by the 1965 revolution in immigration law and America's deep history as, in effect, a biracial state. It is fashionable among intellectuals in Europe, who are influenced by scientific Marxism, to dismiss cultural questions and sneer at the preoccupation among American conservatives with such matters (while ignoring the desecration of their own culture), but culture is important because it is about how people live their lives.

That American white liberal paternalism is fake and will one day collapse is simultaneously known and denied in an Orwellian fashion, and a similar observation can be made about other Western countries. As in America, in Britain there is a significant underclass whose needs and interests are, in practice, ignored. It is this international underclass that will one day be the ferment for a revolution. Whether the revolution is spasmodic, or one event, or in fact an evolutionary social movement that is technical in character (much like an industrial or technological revolution), is open to speculation. I suspect the latter. In fact, I think the 'anti-hierarchical revolution' is already happening, all around us, imperceptible to most people, but real nonetheless. But I – we – cannot know for sure. Only history will tell. For now, a vital question that arises for race conscious whites is whether this new revolutionary consciousness is, or will, be based on, or allow for, racial and cultural differences. My central contention is that we must focus our work on making sure it will. We must disregard the fake, paternalistic structures of our present society, including its electoral politics and its media fictions that keep the uneasy alliances and contradictions of capitalism in check, and we must instead build a parallel white republic-in-waiting: a community of white conscious individuals ready to think and act collectively in a future non-hierarchical world. If nothing else, we must do this so as to ensure the survival of the White Race.

The major intellectual obstacle faced by White Nationalists in this task is the problem identified by Michael Moore in Stupid White Men: the white predilection for assuming the burdens of other races – what might be called 'liberal morality' – as opposed to 'racial morality' (the latter being what I would regard as real morality). Whether intentionally or not, it is clear to me that Moore identifies the liberal moral tendency among white conservatives, whom he criticises for their meanness. Of course, Moore did not understand that what he was describing was in fact liberalism by another name, just articulated differently from what is called left-liberalism. He did not recognise that the fulminations of social and moral conservatism are based on the very same basic belief system that inspires the moral outrage of liberal whites, only using different political language, with the rhetoric of one side catalysing the other. This liberalism seems to be characteristically white, and possibly originated in the Anglo-Saxon part of the European world as a secular counterpoint to Christianity, borrowing its basic precepts. It entails an implicit belief in capitalism as a moral economy and involves a strong attachment to spiritual self-immolation and Protestant asceticism. It is a characteristic that has made white societies racially and culturally vulnerable and that has been used advantageously by Jews to infiltrate and direct the policies of Western governments in an anti-white direction: including the introduction of mass immigration, among other things. White conservatives like to argue instead that the decline of the West, even the West's post-modern collapse, began with an identifiable series of events – the so-called 'Sixties': some kind of radical social, academic and cultural movement in Europe and the United States. The conventional view seems to be that the Sixties were a departure, a rejection of the surrounding society by some sort of youth culture made up of baby-boomers. I see it slightly differently. To my mind, the Sixties, in so far as it existed as a coherent phenomenon at all, was a continuation of the liberal canonical tradition. It wasn't so much a rebellion against parenthood and authority as an affirmation of it, only in a more infantile sense than in the past. Surface rebellion was combined with deep authoritarianism, the compliance being achieved through the wider dispensation of cheap recreational drugs and permissive sexual relations, which were used to pacify and control what could have otherwise been a dangerous source of unrest against the capitalist system among disaffected baby-boomers. Meanwhile, legislative measures were enacted to undermine the indigenous white majorities in Western countries – especially through mass non-white immigration. The mistake that cultural conservatives make is in wrongly identifying the Sixties as a some kind of revolutionary movement. If anything, the Sixties was a counter-revolutionary movement and its problems, including mass immigration, widespread recreational drug use, mindless rock music and so on are also counter-revolutionary nature: they assist the Leviathon rather than weaken it. The Sixties certainly encouraged the potential for radical social change in the West, but only in directions favourable to Jews and elite whites.

People seem to look back on the Sixties nostalgically, as a gala parade of colour, brightness and innocent libertinism, when in fact for most ordinary people it was a dark decade, marked by economic crises and policies that attacked and fragmented the white working class, and flooded the country with cheap foreign labour. It was a decade that also signalled the beginning of the end of the influence of traditional manufacturing and trade unions. This reality is masked by vapid talk of a liberal cultural revolution involving naive politicians, militant feminists, sex, drugs and rock music. What was culturally significant about these more superficial aspects of the Sixties was what they represented about the shift in 'meaning'. The previous institutional definitions of what is 'right' and 'wrong' had been established based on a pre-War type of moral economy in which each ordinary person was expected to be upstanding, self-reliant and respectful of the institutions, formal and informal, that regulated societal conduct: the family, the Church, the community and so on. These institutions were far more influential and important in people's everyday lives than the state – love and warmth in the family, solidarity in the workplace, kinship and racial identity in the wider national space. In the Sixties, the moral economy shifted towards a brutal form of equalitarianism, necessary for a type of capitalism that was becoming increasingly financialised and based on high technology and bureaucratic expertise. This happened against a background of meaningless rock music that encouraged promiscuity and other reckless, ultra-individualistic attitudes. These types of attitudes are implicitly anti-family and designed to break social cohesion and encourage each of us to think about the primacy of our individual desires. In this new moral climate, the social bonds that were regulated through the various old institutions began to breakdown as loyalty shifted from society to the individual, so that the family, workplace and nation became a less stable and permanent feature of people's lives. In an absence of 'meaning' at this informal social level, there is tyranny – the need for a strong state. At the same time, this type of liberal, less-bonded society is more welcoming (or less unwelcoming) to aliens and outsiders – like Jews and other non-white immigrants – and it becomes easier for business people and multi-nationals to control and exploit the population. All this was concealed beneath positivistic buzz words and terminology. The Sixties was about 'freedom', 'peace', 'democracy', things that were in fact lessened and weakened.

One of the great symbolic movements of The Sixties was the agitation against America's war in Vietnam. The purpose of the Vietnam War was to quell the spread of a geopolitical movement that the United States called 'communism', but in fact was just a type of state-capitalism that happened to be antagonistic to the United States and its sphere of influence. One group of Jews, the Bolsheviks, had seized control in Czarist Russia and established a new imperial and aristocratic system, based superficially on Marxist-Lenninist ideology and governed by a bureaucratic elite. This was just another form of capitalism. Another group of Jews, the liberal capitalists, had taken control of the United States and established a centralised system of financial control with notional market forces. This was also a form of capitalism. Both systems served the interests of Jews and rich whites, but used ideology and propaganda to encourage the fiction of popular consent, legality and justification. The two state-capitalist systems faced each other in a bi-polar Cold War that was in fact just a part of the ideological and propagandist fiction used to trick and con people into accepting the moral legitimacy of whichever system they lived under. The Vietnam War was a proxy war fought between these two superpowers. The confrontation between the pro-war and anti-war movements were a microcosm of the deceitful play-off between the two power 'systems'. Rather than question the system itself, the elites sought to lead public debate into the limited avenues of either a pro-war or anti-war position. Neither position challenged the system itself. In fact, each position in its own way served to legitimise the system by giving the appearance that political dissent could be effective within capitalist societies and that capitalist governments could be responsive to popular movements. That is why the anti-war movement of the Vietnam era was itself counter-revolutionary and conformist, and the ideological outcrops of The Sixties, such as militant feminism, are also counter-revolutionary and conformist. They encourage conformity to the liberalism of the elite: the essential features of which are control of the masses through fantasy politics and false choices; fake opposition parties and movements; the control and manipulation of political language; and fake welfare paternalism, as a means of 'buying-off' potential sources of unrest, such as the unemployed.

Crucial to this propaganda system is the positivistic interpretation of political language. Instead of examining and understanding what certain words meaning and assessing the system against rational criteria that relate to the substantive meaning, political language is treated as simply a pragmatic, man-made phenomenon without any social. moral or economic basis. This allows liberal intellectuals to use words such as 'democracy' without any need to understand the basis of the term or its meaning or evaluate its usage and application to the actual political system or the actions of powerful people. The word 'democracy' itself has at least two valid meanings. It can be seen as a double concept. There is the meaning that it carries in the West, and then there is its actual true meaning. The meaning that democracy carries in the West – its canonical meaning, if you like – is what is common currency in the media and institutions. It is a mechanism to keep us 'dumb' because, in brief, it is a way of maintaining a hierarchy based on economic power, a truth that is hidden behind positivist buzz phraseology about 'democracy' and 'equality' and false notions of legality, such as 'human rights'. The questions are decided in advance and everything is stage-managed. Whites are encouraged in their 'liberal morality' to assume the burdens of elite Jews and their white collaborators. That is Western 'liberal democracy'. Actual democracy – its non-canonical meaning – bears no relation to this and is in most respects its opposite. This is the basis on which those whites who support UKIP are fundamentally opposed to people like me. I am willing to see the system for what it really is and face it head-on. They aren't. They want to carry on living in a dream world and support politicians who wear the right rosette. This 'democracy' encourages a fanciful idea that you can somehow get what **you** want by putting an 'X' – the mark of an illiterate – in a box every few years. UKIP supporters seem to think that political leaders mean what they say and say what they think and that if we vote for something, then it will happen in the way presented. So, in this dream world, if UKIP say they want to 'freeze immigration', this of course means that rates of immigration will decrease or that support for UKIP will put pressure on politicians of other parties to support a decrease in the rate of immigration, or both. It doesn't occur to these types of people that 'freeze immigration' might mean that the rate of immigration increases. When UKIP say they want to leave the EU, the liberal mind swallows this because it is thought that the promise means literally that. It doesn't occur to many people that in fact what this might mean is much the same relationship with the EU, in or out.

In my view, the purpose of political parties is to uphold the existing economic system, control public opinion and suppress dissent. Their role is to represent the interests of the powerful, i.e. people who own significant capital. They are not there to uphold the interests of the weak, i.e. us. That is the way the world works. It's what liberalism really is and really means. This reality is never admitted into discussion, because no-one entertains the idea that 'democracy' is a double-concept. The reason no-one other than a few Marxists want to admit this is because that: (i). would involve some independent thought; and, (ii). would involve an admission that most of us (including you and I) have been fooled. No-one wants to admit they have been fooled, so we keep going with this merry-go-round...fake elections and leader cults...demonising Poles and 'Eurocrats'...voting for Purple Tories and Blue Tories...It's like a bad soap opera: which is precisely how it is intended. It's meant to distract you AND alienate you from your true interests. It's not real politics. It's just fantasy.

What is the way out of this intellectual morass? What we need (among other things) is a racial morality, not a liberal morality. We need to let go of the unfortunate, masochistic group tendency identified by Michael Moore and start thinking in terms of race. The next time you feel like fulminating about blacks or the cost of welfare or some similar subject, remember that this is what the system wants you to do. We are often told that we are weak and 'they' are powerful. But the terms 'strong' and 'weak' are malleable. The only reason we are 'weak' is because we have been indoctrinated with that mentality. In reality, we are strong and the 'powerful' are in fact terrified of us. What is required is for people to reject these leader cults and the moral poison of fake liberalism and wake up to their own strength.

## 3.3.

## Race Consciousness and the Ebola Scare[17]

Some people believe in democracy. Other people believe in unicorns. What the two beliefs have in common is irreason: an inability or unwillingness to accept reality. Reality itself is the product of both reason and observation, with each having a dependency on the other, so that our reasoned understanding of things influences our observations and how we interpret them, while our observations influence how we reason about the world. The most powerful of the forces underpinning reality is simple, everyday observation. Often the path to reality – that is to say, a realistic understanding of our situation – begins by simply looking. If we would just take off the myopic goggles provided to us by the media, our friends and workplace colleagues and all the other apparatuses of indoctrination, and simply look, with our own eyes, we would begin to recognise a new, more truthful reality. The irreasoned masses bypass this simple process of observation partly because of peer pressure and the motive power of group thinking – which has deep evolutionary origins and which we all succumb to from time-to-time – and also because they are engaging in wish-thought – the supplicant of reason – which, again, we all succumb to at important points in our everyday lives. We all wish that things could be a certain way, and sometimes, in consequence, we block out simple observation and the reasoned conclusions that irresistibly flow from them and instead see things as we would wish them to be. We then apply our actions accordingly, in defiance of reality. The reality is that capitalism is a social system designed to exploit the majority of working people, but most people will still turn up for work in the morning. Sometimes, the fantastical nature of the irreasoned belief is too much, even for the type of highly-indoctrinated mind that is a feature of modern society; often, it becomes squarely apparent to the confused mind that the irreasoned belief is so inimical to one's own existential or material interests that the contradiction has to be confronted, if only privately and quietly, in one's own mental world.

One common result of this disjunction is what is known as cognitive dissonance: a term that is now memetically cited with increasing frequency in pseudo-intellectual discussion. Cognitive dissonance is, in fact, just another word for maturity. It is the mental strain experienced by an individual who has come to realise that the interests promoted in society are contrary to his own, and perhaps, contrary to the interests of society itself. Society has put in place powerful forces to combat maturity, including TV soaps, mindless pop music, football teams, permissiveness in drug-taking and social relations. All these are designed to distract attention and smooth-over the stresses and neuroses that arise in the mature mind. Of course, these distractions do not work with the more intelligent, educated or effective person. For that type of maturity, a more sophisticated intellectual fantasy world needs to be constructed and sustained. This may take the form of very basic political ideas, such as the notion that democracy is the best system, that ordinary people have a stake in society and that hard work makes you successful. These ideas are supported by fictions, such as voting, home ownership, plastic careers and important-sounding job titles. Political language and conceptualisation plays an important part in constructing and maintaining the fantasy world. People are trained to think that political language

---

[17] First published on 30th. July 2014 at http://www.johnlonden.com

and concepts have no social, moral, economic or racial basis, as such, but simply represent the outcome of practical experience. This is what I term a 'pseudo-positivist' outlook. An example would be the treatment of 'democracy'. Democracy is seen not for what it truly is – a system of social control and the expression of group interests – but rather, as the most practically beneficial way of running and organising society. In that kind of intellectual environment, lacking as it does any contextual insight, it is easy to posit that 'democracy' is the 'right' or 'moral' way whereas anything anti-democratic is the 'wrong' or 'immoral' way. Most of the time, such assertions are lies, or at least hypocritical, but the lack of any understanding of what democracy is contextually or whose interests it serves results in a situation where any meaningful discussion is outside the parameters of accepted debate and those who question the system tend to be stigmatised and ignored. The liberal mind is the perfection of linguistic pseudo-positivism: it supports state, even military, intervention in the lives of individuals, families, groups, even whole nations, on the pretext of 'democracy' or some other political phrase or concept polluted with positivism. What helps the liberal virus is that most people are mentally exoteric: they base their perceptions and judgements on the information they receive and they plan their lives according to the experience of themselves and others. This is a perfectly intelligent way to think, to an extent, but it is also ideal basis for social control. The content of received knowledge and information is dominated conceptually by the interests of the elite. Without this control, the fantasy world would start to break down under the irresistible influence of reason and observation. We can see that our society is not democratic – that conclusion is the result of plain reason and observation – but most refuse to pursue this line of thinking further, still less articulate it. Instead, the positivist mindset is dominant and the ordinary person – the modern liberal – parrots uncritically the mantra of democracy, human rights, equality and so on.

One of the cruder tricks deployed by the media to control us is through the dissemination of scare stories. Normally, this kind of yellow journalism focuses on providing a hysterical interpretation of events that plays to the base instincts of people, so as to attract attention to the right narratives and distract attention from incidences and narratives that might point the way to harsher truths about society. The usual topics are crime and health scares. It is important to understand what while dishonest hack journalism is commercially-motivated and intended to sustain readership, its editorial preoccupations also reflect whatever is the political climate of the time. In a white race conscious society, crime stories would be expected to not only feature blacks in significant number, but also emphasise the racial and ethnic identities of the perpetrators. In our mixed-racial society, it is necessary to undermine confidence among the still-dominant socio-economic group, whites – especially white Britons – and so violent crime by whites against non-whites tends to be sensationalised. Non-British whites are also used as a scapegoat for the problems of mass immigration, especially if the white group has little or no power or influence, as is the case with Poles, Romanians and Bulgarians, who represents an easy target. Muslims and Asians generally are becoming more influential, and so attacks on that group are restricted to 'radicals' and 'fundamentalists', who can still be targeted for sensationalist coverage, whereas 'ordinary' Asians and Muslims cannot (generally) be targeted in the same way that ordinary whites, especially non-British whites, can be. Jews are not the subject of this type of sensationalism at all, except in the narrow sense that they can be portrayed as perpetual 'victims' of the 'race crimes' of everybody else, especially whites but also Muslims. When it comes to this kind of sensationalist coverage about 'race', positivist linguistics is deployed classically to encourage a fantasy perception of what is going on, so that instead of seeing things in terms of a conflict between different racial groups with competing racial and economic interests – which is the normal, reasoned way of seeing things – ordinary people are encouraged to divide the protagonists into 'haters', 'racists', 'bigots', Nazis' and 'victims'. Supposedly, if we are to believe the newspapers, Muslims are for the most part peace-loving and only a few of them are fanatical. A more rational journalist might pose to himself, and the public, the question of what, in fact, all Muslims want from their religion. He may come to the conclusion that in fact all Muslims are radical, but only some are honest about it, and the 'radicalism' itself is simply an expression of a racial interest that Islam has evolved to promote in host societies. If we believe the newspapers, we are asked to accept that whites who are race conscious and articulate this are just a bunch of wannabe Nazi dictators who want to kill Jews. What in fact they may be is something duller and more prosaic – just people who have pride in their identity, like normal people do, and who simply want to maintain the European, Western characteristics of Britain and Europe – which is surely to be expected, and is in any case a laudable goal. We are asked to believe by those same sensationalist journalists that Jews are the victims of everybody else. No-one asks the rational question: what have Jews done to carry this unfortunate stigma?

Those who highlight Jewish influence in society are labelled kranks, misfits, losers and crazies, as if it is irrational to question who benefits from the way society works or to suggest that what happens in society might have a social, economic, financial and racial basis. When in fact Jewish crimes are, rightly and justly, highlighted by the media, as is the case with the ongoing coverage of Israel's brutality in Gaza, this is always represented through the concave lens of pseudo-positivism: we are told that the Israelis (not the Jews) are committing atrocities or genocide or breaching human rights. It is not explained that these crimes are an expression not so much of Israeli nationalism, but Jewish Racial Nationalism and the need for Jews to maintain their own racial state. The original Zionists were of the Jewish Left and desired settlement in Palestine. Over time, this tendency – which became characterised as 'Traditionalist Zionism' – faced a rival, in the form of Revisionist (conservative) Zionism. The Revisionists demanded nothing less than a Jewish state. They won out and the Traditionists gradually melted away as the State of Israel became a geopolitical reality, but they did not go away completely. The cleave is reflected in Israeli domestic politics to this day. The Likud party of Netanyahu is the modern version of the Revisionist tendency, while the weaker tendency in Israel, towards conciliation, is represented by much of the Israeli Labor Party, which has its origins in Traditionalism. The division is largely meaningless as both sides believe in maintaining the tribal integrity of Jews, which is the real issue. The permanent, relentless state of alert that exists in Israel assists in maintaining the Jews' sense of tribal identity and in repelling outsiders, but this is not reflected in the coverage of the Western media, where the matter is decontextualised, allowing apologists for the Jews to defend pro-Jewish racism on terms that are amenable to them, using the false narrative of legality: specifically, Israeli civil and military defence against Hamas. No matter how brutal or inhumane Israel's offensive operations become, so long as Israel's own race-free narrative is accepted, then the truth can be easily hidden and concealed, or at worst, manipulated, controlled or minimised.

If people were to take off their liberal goggles and actually look, what they would see in Gaza is Jewish people defending their own racial interests. To an extent, this is admirable, but this revelation would also be highly-dangerous for Jews if popularised, for it would expose to an otherwise oblivious public a rare but accurate diagnosis of their motivations and it would not be long before people would start to apply the same motivation to the actions of Jews in Britain and other Western societies. There is no reason why we should not do so, and there would be nothing worse for the Jews than if we were to do so. Suddenly, Racial Nationalists and those who are sympathetic to us would have a riposte: "You are only saying that/calling for that because you are a Jew!" It really is a simple matter of 'Who benefits?'. Thus, the alarmism and scare stories over Gaza serve an important defensive purpose for Jews. They prevent ordinary white people from seeing the massive elephant in the room: the 'European Gaza' that the Jews in the West have constructed and still maintain. It is in the Jews' interests that we should feel that we are besieged by Muslims, their age-old enemy in Palestine, and now ours  thanks to the Jews. The 'Israelisation' of our society ferments the threats and divisions that Jews thrive on and that keep them together as a tribal group, while sowing division and mistrust among whites.

To highlight that Jews and Jewish values have a critical influence in society for the benefit of Jews is certainly a conspiracy theory. What it is not is a form of conspiracism. The former type of explanatory phenomenon – 'conspiracy theory' – is rational and, even if shown to not be valid, is still based on reason, logic and observation. The latter type of explanatory phenomenon – 'conspiracism' – is irrational, irreasoned and tends not to be based on observation. The difference can, perhaps, be illuminated by an example. Consider the contrast between someone complaining about rule by lizard-hybrid beings (an example of conspiracism), with someone suggesting that Jews might have too much influence in society (an example of conspiracy theory). Conspiracism, then, is a belief in conspiracy for its own sake, irrespective of the empirical merits of the theory or explanation; whereas conspiracy theory is simply what all of us, from governments downward, have engaged in most of the time: the official U.S. government explanation for the 9/11 attacks is a conspiracy theory in that it is believed a conspiracy of Al Qaeda operatives planned it and did it. Conspiracy theory – whether it is about Jews or Al Qaeda or something else – is based on a rational understanding of the world, a commitment to reason combined with a belief in the validity of empiricism and observation, and an acknowledgement that conspiratorial power and influence can be exercised subtly and unconsciously in the advancement of underlying interests in the society, both on a large- and small-scale. The notion that Jews run society is not the same as blaming Jews for society. Blaming others is an immature and unintellectual impulse. We are concerned here with cause and effect, not hating or blaming – but hating and blaming are an important tool of distraction. Most people block out questions about society, or accept the licensed explanations offered to them by powerful interests. Typically these official explanations, even when they have a valid or rational basis, can take the form of hating or blaming politicians and other prominent figures or groups – e.g. Tony Blair is called a liar and vilified – or they can involve blaming some vague, intangible concept – for instance, militant feminists or 'liberals' or Marxists are said to be to blame for social and moral degeneration in Western society. Or it can just be blaming groups in an unanalytical way: for example, blaming Jewish capitalists or bankers or blaming blacks for gun crime, or whatever. This 'blaming' gets us nowhere unless it is replaced, or at least accompanied by, a dispassionate analysis of (a). what is not satisfactory about society; (b). which groups or individuals benefit from the way society is run; and, (c). whether there can be any causation established between the problem, its effects and those who appear to make decisions. That's an intellectual exercise that requires time, thought and patience. Our society is structured in a way that is inimical to this kind of analytical activity. Instead, we are expected to act as receivers and repeaters of information, which itself has undergone the rigours of editorial concision; and when our opinion is asked for at all, we are expected to reduce a complex world into the narrow, pedestrian mould of 'acceptable' opinion, often resulting in the regurgitation of soundbites that conveniently dispatch the issues of the day on terms that are expedient to the interests of the powerful. Social media assists this process of intellectual suffocation. Twitter, for instance, which has become a popular social media site, is based on the practice of micro-blogging, a comment format that lends itself to repetition of whatever opinions and attitudes are trending rather than original thought and insight. Twitter also encourages a mob mentality, so that people who express opinions that are contrary to, or outside, the dominant fantasy world of irreason can be verbally attacked and threatened at will, with little recourse.

What is interesting is the way that every now and then we see a tear in the manufactured reality of this fantasy world. The existential racial threats presented by the realities of mass non-white immigration and liberal mixed-racialism cannot be hidden or denied with any real conviction. They have the potential to cause cognitive dissonance among even the most 'educated' and liberal whites. What these whites are starting to realise, albeit slowly and sub-consciously, is that we have our own Gaza here in Europe. This is gradually becoming apparent even among white people who would otherwise never consider themselves to be 'racist' and indeed would be quick to sneer condescendingly at others who express opinions even vaguely xenophobic, regarding such as unsophisticated buffoonery.

Consider these contributions from readers of the liberal newspaper, the Independent, posted in the comments section of an Ebola story[18]:-

*Coming to a multicultural hospital in Britain soon....................*

*You open your borders to all and sundry and this is the end result.*

*All this talk about quarantine, sealing borders etc !! The UK cannot even prevent TB carriers from SE Asia entering the country. Some of the highest incidences are in East Lancashire which have larger Asian Heritage populations*

---

[18] http://www.independent.co.uk/life-style/health-and-families/health-news/is-ebola-coming-to-britain-uk-health-officials-issue-warning-to-doctors-as-outbreak-fears-grow-9634779.html

*What if someone decides to weaponise this virus ? Say a group decides to acquire a bottle of Ebola laden bodily fluids from some poor African family. This would indeed be a potent weapon if smuggled to the west.*

*So why are we still allowing people from these third-world hell holes into the country? We should be establishing a quarantine zone around the affected regions on land, sea and in the air.*

*It will spread through the London ghetto's like wild fire.*

*And Birmingham, Manchester, Bradford, Leeds, etc. etc.*

*Yes, but what are the downsides?*

*The symptoms of Ebola are almost indistinguishable from those associated with the aftermath of eating Nando's chicken:*
*Fever*
*Headache*
*Joint and muscle aches*
*Weakness*
*Diahhorea*
*Vomiting*
*Stomach pain*
*Lack of appetite*

*Or any kebab.*

*Except Ebola victims have a better chance of survival.*

*Bushmeat, HIV/AIDS, benefit tourism, scam marriages, religion, fraud and scams, FGM, witchcraft and now Ebola; is there no end to it? There probably will be now!*

*Its called "enrichment and diversity".*

*It's not called the Dark Continent for nothing.*

*And no doubt if we start turning people back at Heathrow the left will be ranting about "racism".*

*Spot on. Better a dead non-racist than a live racist is their motto.*

*Invite the third in, you have third world problems.*
*Shame the cretins running the country can't see that!*

I would suggest that only a few years ago these types of comments would have been next to-unthinkable at the foot of an article in a national liberal newspaper, and would only have been tolerated rarely in that environment, maybe from the odd reader or two.  My suspicion is that for some of these people, it will have been the first time in their lives that they have found the courage to comment in this way publicly, albeit under an online pseudonym.  A newspaper like the Independent, with its social liberal reputation, is simply not commonly associated with comments like this, and the few that do make what are (on the Establishment's own terms) 'racist' comments would usually expect to see their comments removed by the moderators, and would be lucky not to be banned from the site.  The Ebola scare is of course just the latest example of media scare-mongering.  Unless it were to mutate into airborne form, the virus presents a minimal threat to the more advanced healthcare systems of the West, but it would be a mistake to dismiss any media scare story without looking at the underlying causes and what it suggests about the direction of public opinion.  Whatever Ebola may be in the medical and public health sense, Ebola as a political phenomenon is a conduit of the fears of a more enlightened public who are starting to experience cognitive dissonance – i.e. maturity.  People are starting to recognise that 'diversity' brings costs with it.  We are always being told that we need immigrants in our society.  No-one stops to consider that the immigrants might need us, and might even need us more than we need them.  That kind of rational examination isn't popular among the elite, but as reason and observation continues to erode the fantasy world constructed for the masses, the media are running out of options.  Scare stories like Ebola are cyclical – we had a similar round of Ebola scares a few years ago – and these stories are often planted in the media for an ulterior purpose, in that they can distract the attention of the viewer from larger scandals.  The Westminster paedophile 'scandal' is cyclical and comes up every few years, reflecting the pressures brought to bear on the media to conceal a larger problem.  (See my essay: 'Pervertocratic Pervocracy: the political science of child abuse').  The latest Establishment paedophile stories focused on narrow issues around documentary evidence and unpopular individuals.  This so-called 'scandal' probably succeeded in diverting attention from the real issue, which is that child abuse seems to be, or has been, committed on a large-scale among the Establishment and has been systematically covered-up.

Sometimes the media use disjointed stories to distract attention.  On the face of it, there would seem to be no connection between Ebola and Jewish attrition in Gaza, but if we think a little deeper, we can see connections between the two stories.  The Ebola scare is really a manifestation of the innate, instinctual, impulsive drive among social animals to repel 'the Other', the alien, the invader.  Ebola itself is a metaphoric surrogate for the real target: non-white foreigners who we know would destroy our society.  It is these same instincts that drive the Jewish Racial Nationalists who fire their rockets into civilian Gaza.  Like it or not, it is the instinct to repel outsiders that is the motive force behind a great deal of social action.  Without it, there would be no effective community; we would all just be a collection of individuals and consumers pursuing selfish lives, and civilisation itself would be fundamentally different – that is, if we had a civilisation at all. It is likely that each of the commenters who posted something beneath the Independent article referenced above see themselves as quite 'normal', 'ordinary' people who are not 'racist' in any way. It is likely that they will go on with their daily lives and not think much about Ebola again. They affect to be frightened, but deep down they know that the media have constructed a scare story to help them sustain the fantasy that keeps our manufactured reality going, keeps us showing up for work, keeps us voting, keeps us doing all the 'normal' things that 'normal' people do. Some of these same people might also have commented on the other scare story – Gaza – but will certainly not think about the 'European Gaza' that is being constructed by the Jews before their very eyes. That blip of maturity and racial consciousness that they exhibited when commenting on Ebola is a sign of hope for us. It means the patient is still alive and can be revived, but it is going to take a concerted effort, and in the meantime our own metaphorical Gaza is being constructed, brick by brick – a prison of our own making. One day the metaphor will take literal form and we will have to fight, not a distant outbreak of Ebola, but the suicidal irreason on our own doorsteps.

3.4.

## White Liberal Supremacism: a dangerous tendency[19]

It's instructive sometimes to look at issues from the point-of-view of an opposing group. It's also an interesting intellectual exercise in its own right. A few years ago, I spent some time – about six months – going to church and mixing socially with religious people, because I wanted to find out why people have faith and think about the world in that way. As an atheist, I needed to immerse myself in their world and think like them in order to understand them. I did not actually come to believe in God as a result of this, but I did come to a better understanding of Christianity, religion and faith. I imagine a similar exercise along racial lines would be useful. I have already been a white liberal, so I need not go back to that. I've had that experience in spades. If it were feasible and practical for me, I would be tempted to spend some time immersing myself in the black, Asian, Jewish or Islamic worlds to better understand that point-of-view. 'Know Your Enemies' is an important basis for embarking on any type of warfare, but especially the legalistic, cultural, demographic and intellectual warfare that we face in Europe.

What does white liberalism mean to a non-white person? I'm particularly interested here in the perceptions of blacks, for reasons I will explain in a moment. By 'white liberalism', I refer to a belief in mixed-racialism, positive action for non-whites and other compassionate policies, even if these are at the expense of the racial interests of whites, if those interests are acknowledged at all. This so-called liberalism is really a kind of fake paternalism (see my essay, 'The Morality Problem: liberalism as a white construct'), in which the white person is asserting his individual selfish self-interest and disregarding the interests of his racial group, behaviour that consumer capitalism is built on and encourages. White liberalism is an example of where the class basis of society interacts with the racial basis of society, and one triumphs over the other: in this case, economic interest trumps racial interest (if the racial community is recognised or considered at all by the social actor). I think blacks especially recognise this at a sub-conscious level and probably associate white liberalism with fakery and insincerity because they sense that it is the expression of some kind of economic or business interest rather than a general concern for the welfare of a group or society at large. This brings me to why blacks as a group are of particular interest to me when it comes to discussions about white liberalism. Blacks generally fulfil all the key socio-economic indicators of deprivation. As a group, they tend to be the poorest and have the lowest occupational status, the lowest measured IQs and the lowest educational attainment. As the 'downtrodden' group, they will readily diagnose the motivations of these apparently munificent whites who seem to be trying to help them and will perceive that the actions of white liberals are entirely self-interested and narcissistic – particularly when these are harmful to other whites of comparable socio-economic status to most blacks.

Of course, this 'white liberalism as racism' thesis is nothing new, but what I think is novel is an examination of the way in which 'liberal racism', if we can call it that, is based not on a recognition of some wider racial interest among whites, but rather on the narrower economic interests of affluent whites. The involvement of Jews is of

---

[19] First published on 31st. July 2014 at http://www.johnlonden.com

course highly-important in this. That the class system of capitalism serves the interests of a Jewish elite and the fact that most of the Jewish-backed propaganda amounts to white racial self-hatred is beyond question as far as I am concerned, but the purpose of this essay is to evaluate the mechanics of the white liberal phenomenon, and in particular why some whites act in this way, apparently against their own racial interest. While I certainly think that white liberalism is just a condescending form of racial supremacism against non-whites, I believe the motivations for it are primarily class-based rather than race-based and are not in most cases about having a psychological pathology such as self-hate. Instead, it reflects simple economic (class) interest. This would explain the more visible pathology noticed among middle-class anti-fascists and anti-racists – a tendency to exhibit 'hate' against 'racists' and 'fascists', which I would argue is a way of projecting their own innate white liberal racism. These middle-class 'sandal-wearers' and 'beardie-weirdies' – the types who fit Orwell's description of the 'lifestyle Left' in The Road To Wigan Pier – are themselves deeply racialist and conscious of it, but unlike Nationalists, they feel guilt or self-consciousness about it. What 'white guilt' really amounts to, when you boil it down, is a recognition that racialism must exist in any meaningful community (or you could not have community) and also a recognition that white liberalism is just a polite expression of naked class interest. This 'white guilt' is the post-modern version of medieval Catholic indulgencies. It's payment for the position of privilege that these whites and Jews enjoy and it reflects the fear that such people feel that their privileges might one day be challenged and confiscated by an insurgent working class. The motivation for their hatred of Nationalists is therefore not difficult to rationalise: it is fuelled by fear of class war and also by resentment that the truth is being spoken back to them. It's no coincidence that ordinary Nationalists tend on the whole to be characterised by the Left and also by the media as uncouth working class types and are openly denigrated for their supposed stupidity, illiteracy and lack of sophistication – a form of class hatred. Rather like viewing an ugly and unflattering aspect of one's visage in the mirror, to the Left, Nationalists are the mirror held up to them, revealing nakedly their hypocrisy and self-interest.

This brings us to how Nationalists might like to exploit this Achilles heel in the mixed-racial Left and its white liberal foot soldiers. We've had the Mantra, which is an excellent way of exploiting the geopolitical hypocrisy of anti-white liberalism. I would like to propose that when Nationalists are confronted by white liberals, they consider something more interrogative to use in addition to the Mantra. Something that takes advantage of the weak point that white liberals have, which is their naked class hatred of ordinary whites and their hidden 'racism' against non-whites. In response to accusations of 'hate', 'racism' and what not, we might like to use some of these lines (and others similar):

'Tell me, why do you condescend to blacks so much?'

'Why don't you make them take responsibility for their actions?'

'Why do you hate ordinary white people so much?'

'Why are you always trying to help non-whites? Do you think you're better than them?'

*'So you think we all came from Africa? Does that mean you think whites are more evolved than African blacks?'*

These are just for starters. I am sure we can all think up more. They will touch a nerve, because they go right to the underlying, unspoken motivations of most white liberals. It's important to understand that these hidden, darker motivations are not always consciously on the mind of the white liberal. Even the activist will normally have convinced themselves of their own idealism and righteousness, while wider economic interests tend to be acted on unconsciously and often with no direct or immediate tangible benefit for the advocate. The son or daughter of a secure, comfortable middle-class upbringing who attends university and is active against 'fascists' and 'racists' may believe that what they are doing is 'right' in the sense that they believe in the ideological justifications put forward for such political action, but the reality, I would suggest, is that what is operating in their actions is unconscious socio-economic interest: a need to keep both non-whites and poor whites down, and in particular a form of class supremacism against other whites. Undoubtedly, as already mentioned above, the more fanatical anti-racists are also exorcising a crude psychological projection: betraying guilt at their own necessary racialism and projecting it on to others as a form of denial. These people tend to be (though are not always) economically-privileged whites who can afford not to live with the consequences of their own views. It's also no coincidence that anti-racism generally has become a tool of authority – it's a way of talking down to people, dividing and controlling the workplace, sensationalising news and scaremongering and so on.

The current political obsession with the 'Out of Africa' theory of human evolution is an example of how white liberals like to condescend to blacks especially. I actually happen to accept the theory as it is based on the best available current science, though it can also be annoying to discuss this with dim-witted liberals who seem to think that just because human beings might have originated in Africa this must mean that all our ancestors were black. Some even try and suggest this means we are all black. Some Nationalists reject the Out of Africa theory, as they see it as politically-inconvenient. I don't share that view, and in any case I believe the matter has to be guided by current science, but that's a different discussion. What I have noticed is how the Out of Africa thesis is just another stick with which to beat blacks. If we have common genetic ancestry, then this would imply that race is a natural result of some kind of micro-evolutionary process of the human species in which whites could be said to be superior to blacks – a very condescending idea, if not repugnant, but perfectly reflecting the attitudes of white liberals, who are implicitly supremacist. Of course, white liberals would deny that these are their true feelings about blacks and would assert that the 'Out of Africa' theory merely suggests that we are 'all the same' in the genetic sense and that any racial differences that might exist are insignificant on the social and cultural level. They know this cannot be true. We are patently not all the same and the Out of Africa theory, if accepted, demonstrates this in that it suggests that different racial groups have evolved into being to suit differing environments. If we were all the 'same', then we would not need an Out of Africa theory, as such, to explain the differences that exist. The theory has been fashioned partly to explain human evolution retroactively and implies that some racial groups have developed more than others. That liberals miss this point is an example of how the summative interpretation of scientific theory can be twisted to suit ignorant political ends and a fanatical desire to level-down and deny a legitimate recognition of differences. In my view the source of this fanaticism is not directly self-hatred for the most part, as Nationalists seem to think (though this will apply in many cases). Rather, it is just the assertion of class interest. Privileged whites like to maintain the fiction of 'sameness' because it helps to conceal the true reality of their exploitation of people of all races. It's an ideological agenda, but more in furtherance of class than some kind of twisted racial cause.

Another example of 'white liberal supremacy' is the contemporary tendency among Western intellectuals to favour civilisational universality. Not only must we have 'sameness' on racial/genetic questions, they tell us, but we must also all be part of the same global culture as well. In extreme cases, this tendency has led us into military intervention and war, in the name of supposedly humanistic ideals. I have already discussed in previous essays what I call linguistic pseudo-positivism (For discussions on this, see for example: 'Race Consciousness and the Ebola Scare' and 'The Morality Problem: liberalism as a white construct'). It is the use of political language and concepts in such a way that they are evacuated of any social, economic, racial or moral meaning and context, and instead applied practically. So, for example, 'democracy' is not presented truthfully as a concept that serves the interests of a group. Rather it is presented positivistically, as either a 'good'/'bad' or 'right'/'wrong' notion, and on the basis that democracy is 'good', it is used as a pretext for demands that all other countries emulate the political economy of the West. Positivistic language is linked closely to political correctness and is used to restrict the mental parameters of ordinary people. So any discussion that contextualises events in the news – be it about the racial interests of Jews or Muslims or the economic interests of capitalists – is rendered almost impossible unless the individual is willing to adopt an entirely new political language, or rather, a new interpretation of the existing language that allows for hermeneutical complexity and context. To take an example: we will all be familiar with the videos that are now appearing on the web with increasing regularity, showing people in the Islamic world – usually women and children – being stoned to death, often after having been buried up to the neck. These disgusting practices can only be the hallmark of a sick culture, but there is also a need to put aside our (understandable) outrage, consider the matter more objectively, and ask what such practices really represent. What we have here is a culture clash. They have their way of doing things, which to us often seem barbaric (and to be fair, sometimes seem barbaric to the more educated among their own populations). We have our way of doing things, which to them sometimes seem decadent and destructive (and to be fair, they would be right about that a lot of the time). These cultural differences arise because of race. Culture is just an expression of the wish of the genetic group to perpetuate itself by adopting mores, norms, attitudes, institutions and rituals. Recognising this helps us to look at these videos with a degree of objectivity and understand that all these people are doing is perpetuating a culture. In a sense, the root of the problem isn't that we are 'better' than them and they need to catch-up with us, as liberal universalism would seem to imply. If anything, the problem is that we are not doing the same as them. We are clinging on to a culture that no longer serves our racial interest, that no longer sustains us. So yes, we can condemn these people – and I'll join in with the condemnation – but we should also remember that whether we are 'better' is a moot point. What isn't moot is that they are far more effective than us at preserving a survivalist morality and culture, and while they may be the 'moral ants' of civilisation in some respects, it's this so-called 'backwardness' that may well help them survive us and thrive long after the White Race has faded into history.

That all this IS about race and culture is not an obvious point. Most people don't seem to understand where culture comes from and that it is purposeful rather than accidental. A great many of the objections that Muslims, for instance, have about our society are quite valid. Likewise, and conversely, we might see some of their practices as cruel and barbaric. Again, what we are really looking at in the arguments between whites and Muslims is a culture clash. Once this is understood, it becomes possible to see things more clearly and recognise: first, the dangers of ignoring racial and cultural questions within our own society; second, the dangers of interfering in the cultures of other races. It is tempting to want to intervene and 'civilise' these people, but that would be a mistake. It is this liberal 'supremacist' tendency of assuming civilisational burdens that has got us into this mess in the first place in which we are now threatened with racial extinction. The irony of all this is that those of us who, in response to the racial problem, rationally call for separation, rather than supremacy, are unfairly labelled as the bad guys. The real villains are those whites who, whether due to self-hating or simple greed, maintain a system of supremacy over the rest of us, white and non-white, insist that we mix and so lose our identity and sense of community, and deny us racial and economic sovereignty, that which is our liberty. It is not, however, for us to demand things such as racial and economic sovereignty as birthrights. There is no right to a co-operative society in which resources are shared and owned democratically and in which an elite group can never again arise to dominate the people. That society has to be fought for. Similarly, there is no right for different races to exist, nor should there be, but there is a right for each distinctive race to fight for its existence in the same genetic struggle that belongs to all living things. That is the struggle we are engaged in now. It is, surely, a worthy struggle, whether we are all out of Africa or not.

## 3.5.

### David Duke and 'liberal' national-socialism[20]

One of the things that I think Nationalists have to start doing is being a bit more sceptical and questioning about some of these personalities who have led 'the movement' over the last seventy years. Nationalism belongs to white people, and we have the right to look critically on those who were meant to stand for our racial interests but who have failed for one reason or another. Some of them (this does not apply to all) have been happy to take the money or enjoyed high public profiles but have not delivered. Of course, failure is not a crime in and of itself, but it should prompt questions. It is not really good enough to continue with the same tactics and methods over and again, nor should we be surprised at repeated failure if the course being followed is a repetition of previous failed strategies. The reality facing us is that Racial Nationalism has been beaten back into a tiny corner of the internet and an even lesser space of civic life in Britain, with actual activity sporadic in nature and consisting of poorly-attended meetings and the odd public demonstration. We also face a legal, political and social environment that is not just hostile to white conscious people, but to all white people: to the extent that, some pseudo-nationalists in UKIP think that the right way to criticise mass immigration is to attack other white people coming in from Europe rather than point to the really damaging phenomenon of decades of non-white immigration. As matters stand, we have no strong leader or personality (assuming leaders is something you like) and we have no unifying strategy or direction, but I would suggest that this void has existed for quite some years now and we have just been living on borrowed time.

The underlying problem was always that Nationalists did not have a message that connected with ordinary people. That is for two reasons: the first internal, the other external. The internal reason was that, from the beginning of the post-War period, the far-Right became the dominant tendency within this movement and consequently there was no organisation, structure or base of ideas to link racial causes with the cause of labour and socialism: in other words, there was nothing to connect the idea of a racially homogeneous society with people's everyday lives. In fact, the message of the far-Right was not generally racial as such, but patriotic. Whatever we might think about the education system, people are more educated nowadays than ever. We can argue over the quality of that education, which is a separate issue, and it could also be observed that the 'education' largely consists of being schooled in various politically-correct epithets – all true – but I would suggest that the idea that people are dumbed-down by TV and other frivolous pursuits or that the education system itself is dumbed-down, while also containing some truth, is a little too simplistic and does not take into account the complexity of what has occurred. What we are dealing with is, on the one hand, a population that is more leisured, self-centred and affluent than in the past, largely based on credit and equity, and with the social independence that goes with it; but on the other hand, a people that are not as literate and are more willing to treat politics as a series of retail choices, with nice fuzzy messages being seen as more appealing than weighty discussion. These socio-cultural changes really began in the 1950s with the advent of the consumer society and continued into the 1960s with the decline of traditional industries and the

---

[20] First published on 5th. August 2014 at http://www.johnlonden.com

emergence of a more individualistic culture. During the 1980s, the government's attack on trade unions broke solidarity in the industrial workplace and created a sense of a country that valued entrepreneurial attitudes.

The last gasp of right-wing 'collectivism' was the National Front phenomenon of the late 1970s. After this faded, the National Front began to fall apart ideologically as it could not find a coherent intellectual response to thatcherism and the changes in society that had begun 30 years before and had produced a very different society that was in tension with the more social and statist beliefs of the far-Right's old guard. By the late 1990s, the image of the then-leading Nationalist party, the BNP, was starting to look dated, while in the United States, Nationalists had no significant profile at all outside of alternative media. A younger group within Nationalism (including within the BNP) looked to remedy this ossification by revising the presentation of Nationalism. Under the Griffin-Duke-Black troika, a period of liberalisation and moderation was instituted. At a meeting of the American Friends of the BNP in Texas in April 2000, Griffin said this (in the presence of David Duke and other leading American White Nationalists)[21]:

*"There is a difference between selling out your ideas and selling your ideas. The BNP isn't about selling out its ideas, which are your ideas too......But we are determined, now, to sell them, and that means basically to use the saleable words, as I say: freedom, security, identity, democracy....Nobody can criticise them. Nobody can come at you and attack you on those ideas. They are saleable.....Perhaps one day, once, by being rather more subtle, we've got ourselves in a position where we control the British broadcast media; then perhaps one day the British people might change their mind and say 'yes, every last one must go'....Perhaps they will one day, but if you want that out as your sole aim to start with: you're going to get absolutely nowhere, so instead of talking about racial purity, you talk about identity..."*

The speech from which these words were taken was found and broadcast by opponents of Nationalism who wanted to expose Griffin for his insincerity and cynicism and present the BNP as a 'Trojan horse' for a more extremist agenda. But the issues with 'far-Right liberalism' are larger than the BNP and its former leader. The new liberal tendency emerged across the far-Right and reflected long-term changes in society that its leadership believed they needed to adapt to. In Griffin's case, the Establishment (whether with his covert co-operation or not) set out on a determined course to attack and undermine him from the beginning, using a complicit and rather corrupt media. This was 'necessary' because, in simple terms, a liberalised far-Right would be more attractive to the white electorate who could, at last, express their latent racial consciousness through support for a more 'respectable' political party. Such a party might still pose a threat to mass immigration and multi-culturalism, if it were to gain important influence at a local and national level.

In fact, the BNP had fallen into a trap. Griffin was half-correct. It was important to 'denazify' Nationalism and detoxify its message so that the old psychological barriers that had been erected by the media and that prevented reasonable, sensible people from thinking in racial terms could be removed. The problem is that in rightly

---

[21] http://blog.thecst.org.uk/?p=750

avoiding one trap, Griffin fell into another. That is not to say Griffin was stupid. In hindsight, we can see that his use of the four buzz words – freedom, security, identity, democracy – was quite clever in its own way, and it did work in broadening the appeal for what would otherwise have been a marginal political movement. But by expressing racial nationalism in liberal language, he allowed anti-white opponents to argue the case for white genetic eradication on their own terms rather than on Nationalist terms. It was like stepping unprepared into enemy territory and trying to fight a war by borrowing the enemy's weapons. Instead of finding a political language of its own, the far-Right sought to fight using the language of the most virulent opponents of Nationalism. To explain why, and to illuminate the point, let us de-construct each of Griffin's four catchphrases in turn:-

**Freedom** This harks back to typical conservative Burkean nostrums of the English constitution and other quaint myths: the notion of the 'free-born Englishman' and what not. I call it 'myth', but in fairness it does have some basis in reality, in that English – and British – government has traditionally been quite reserved with an emphasis on self-government. The Griffin BNP sought to resurrect such notions in the belief that they would appeal to the romantic aspect of the British mind and various mythologies about a time when the government did not interfere in the freedoms of ordinary people. It's therefore a counterpoint to the type of political correctness and microscopic state intervention that characterises a multi-cultural society. So one can see the logic. The problem is that the BNP wasn't campaigning in some kind of neo-feudal society made up of freeborn agricultural peasants of native stock, but rather in a mass, urban post-industrial society that, while still overwhelmingly white, had largely accepted mixed-racial ideas and contained a large contingent of non-whites. Against this background, a party that argues for 'freedom' just ends up attacking one of the symptoms of a mixed-racial society, not the cause, and in the long-run, even if successful in gaining influence, such efforts can only assist in cementing the sickness by alleviating and ameliorating some of its harsher effects on white people. In truth, a genuine racial nationalist movement cannot appeal to saleable notions of 'freedom', which are freedom only to get into debt, to race-mix and to ignore the long-term consequences of one's actions. Race-conscious freedom is inherently socialist in nature and exactly opposite of the liberal sense of freedom. It means asking the individual to recognising that he is part of a larger racial community, on which his own welfare and the welfare of others depends. How this racial message can be made appealing is a different discussion, but the point is that by co-opting the canonical notion of freedom, the BNP contributed to making the British people less free. Losing your homeland is no kind of freedom at all, even if you do have a nice new car and live in a hip culture.

**Security** This reflects the far-Right traditionalist interest in the 'law and order' agenda and its advocacy of a 'crime control' approach to the problem of crime and anti-social behaviour. The slogan acts as code to whites who have legitimate and well-founded fears about the non-white impact on crime levels. However, it also plays into the hands of anti-whites who want to suppress Nationalism and who favour the use of repressive measures against Nationalists to do so. In effect, while liberals advocate sociological approaches to crime for the ordinary population (and perhaps rightly so), they are happy to deploy harsh crime control measures against Nationalists and others who are politically-inconvenient.

**Identity** The use of this term reflects the post-modern sense of insecurity and uncertainty that is endemic in an alienated society. The idea is to give people a feeling of belonging and community that is lacking by appealing to a unified sense of who we are. This is perfectly laudable, but it would be more substantive if predicated on race, which in the majority of cases is a pretty sure denominator. By talking about 'identity' rather than race, the BNP turned what is a simple fact into a moveable and flexible concept and gave an opening to its opponents to frame the debate in terms of what is meant by 'this' or 'that' identity – usually 'British' identity, as the name of the Party suggests an attachment to Britain and the demonym 'British' can be made to seem inherently fluid and civic in nature. Of course, we can always have an argument about what is meant by 'white' people, and there are also various media traps in race-based advocacy – such as DNA tests (see the case of Craig Cobb as an example) – that can be used to undermine us, but these largely come out of an obsession with identity, which appeals to narcissistic impulses, rather than a fixation on race, which is more rigid and scientific in its basis. It is much harder to undermine a message built on 'race', rigid and unchanging, than on 'identity', which is inherently flexible and as in Cobb's case, can even be demarcated by dubious science and percentages. What we need is less identity and more race. Alas, it seems that under Griffin, racial purity was segued into a civic, non-racial concept of identity. That is what the BNP now stands for – admittedly, under force of law – but the process for turning the BNP into a civic nationalist party was begun by Griffin long before the infamous 2009 legal case.

**Democracy** The reasons for the use of this word, and the problems with it, echo the points in Freedom above. A nice fuzzy word that helps lots of people feel good about themselves, but the problem is that it can be made to mean practically anything. One has to ask what kind of democracy exists in a society that no longer serves the interests of the white racial group (if it ever did) and in which whites are out-voted by other, more effective racial blocs.

What all these nice-sounding words have in common is that they are the building block of a political language that is shorn of context and meaning, and as such is manipulative. It is part of a phenomenon in modern liberal society that I call pseudo-positivism: i.e. the removal of social, economic, and racial meaning from language and its replacement with connotations and interactions that reflect whatever is practically-accepted or 'works best' in society. (See, my essays: 'Race Consciousness and the Ebola Scare', 'The Mechanics of Virtual Resistance', 'Uncritical nationalism versus critical Nationalism', 'Nationalism and the Hermeneutical Dilemma: some brief thoughts', 'democracy versus Democracy, or Why the patient can't be restored'). The most nefarious manifestation of the liberal, pseudo-positivist mindset is political correctness, something the BNP attacked vociferously while adopting its own style of linguistic correctness under Griffin. Thus Griffin's 'liberalisation' agenda, with its emphasis on language and presentation, had the effect of de-racinating the BNP.

Another new aspect of white nationalism that has come to prominence over the last ten years or so is the video movement. This is perhaps encapsulated best by the efforts of David Duke, who has almost become nationalism's answer to Michael Moore, only a little more substantial than his counterpart. What David Duke and Michael Moore share is that they are both liberal – each of a different type. Duke's video channel on YouTube is worth visiting just to get a sense of what we are dealing with. Duke has obviously changed his physical appearance and style to match his new-found Griffin-like liberalism. The white beard, which looks comforting; the professorial manner; the spouting of dreary 'Rights of Man' twaddle; the talk of racial rights. The idea is that Duke should appeal to the innate sense of fairness found in the 'reasonable man', the man on the street. It is a reflection of our times that he has to do it not by being racial, as such, but by being liberal, implicitly Zionist and linguistically correct. That I should make this accusation might at first seem odd and contradictory. Duke's main area of interest is Jews and Israel, and he explicitly attacks Zionism, so most people would not think of him as Zionist. I would beg to differ. Zionism is the interest served by Duke's attacks on it. Much like those sages of the British National Front, Mr. Duke can protest and affect to be an anti-Zionist all he likes, but in my eyes he is just another tool of the Jewish Racial State: implicitly ultra-Zionist. To explain why, I would propose here to examine from a racial perspective an issue currently in the news: Israel's attacks on Gaza.

The 'debate'/'discussion' on Gaza is, I would contend, a case in point of the implicit Zionist tendency among the far-Right. The argument seems to be that there is some kind of external, universal standard that people and nations must adhere to in moral conduct. I would challenge this, as I think it is in reality just a lazy assumption. Any such standards are merely a guide, at best. In reality, life is a fight for survival. Culture, when looked at objectively, and whether it is Islam or Judaism or the zero-conscious non-culture of ethnic Europeans, is just a tool, a vessel, a means for a racial group to advance its own genetic perpetuation with varying degrees of success. That we Europeans have lost our culture and sit like zombies in front of Third World-manufactured blocks of substrate does not give us the right to sit in judgement on other cultures who are still successful at perpetuating the genes of their peoples. Those who think, for instance, that radical Muslims are primitive and uncivilised because they stone people, may have cause to re-evaluate their concept of 'civilisation' if those same Muslims are more successful than us in spreading their genes. What's civilised or not does not depend on shallow, ignorant, self-centred, back-of-a-postcard notions of 'niceness' and 'conscience' that have been handed to us by media Jews, for their own ends. The harsh truth is that rest of the world – outside Europe and the Anglosphere – has no time for our 'civilisation' and childish decadence.

The Israelis will not stop their attrition on Gaza and the Palestinians, even if we ask them nicely. The reason they are invading Gaza is because they realise that they have to fight for their existence. They won't stop until they have annihilated the so-called 'Palestinians', through a combination of force and guile, just as they won't stop their intellectual and cultural assault on our societies, no matter how outraged people get. And quite rightly so. 'Rightly so' because they have as much right to fight for their existence as the so-called 'Palestinians' do, and just as much right as white people do. They have the right to trick, and lie to us, and deceive us. That is not to condone such behaviour. I am not myself a Zionist in any sense and I am not a friend of the Jews. It's simply to look at the situation objectively. Human rights mean nothing to a drowning man, and they mean nothing to a people fighting for its existence. That white people don't seem interested in fighting for their existence and would rather sit on their sofas attacking those who do is neither here nor there. The problem isn't that Jews are psychopaths. The problem is that we're not more like

Jews. We're not prepared to defend ourselves racially any more, unlike Jews, who – to their credit – are. Instead, we've become this giggling, drug- and drink-fuelled, TV-obsessed mass of narcissists and emotional basket-cases who weep and cry about dead kiddies in a war thousands of miles away that we will never be able to contextualise or understand. It's really just the mentality of children, which is what the White Race has become – just a bunch of fat, over-indulged moral teenagers whose politics is whatever uninformed, de-anchored, decontextualised juvenilia the global Jewish media can throw at us, while laughing at us behind our backs.

The more Duke and other far-Right figures, both in the UK and North America, blather and feign outrage at Gaza, the more Zionist they look. Duke tends to talk in terms of the right of racial groups to exist, and often refers to established legalities that supposedly support this, but the reality is that there is no right for any race, group or individual to exist. There is, however, a right for a people or race to fight for their existence. Our argument should be that if the Arabs (Palestinians) and the Jews (Israelis) have this right, then so should whites. This is an argument that needs to be made not to non-whites, whose racial interests are contrary to ours and whom we are 'fighting', but to our fellow whites. It is not that whites as a racial group have inherent or inalienable rights or that a world with white people would be better; rather, it is that there is a right for white people to fight for their existence in the common genetic struggle: including against the 'European Gaza' that the Jews have created in our homelands.

This is why I have never been able to take the 'new David Duke' and his nonsense seriously, so for a long time now I have simply assumed that he was some kind of state puppet and that he had taken the American equivalent of The M(15)cGuinness Option, if you like, though it did also occur to me that he might be engaging in a legitimate tactic to insinuate himself into the agenda of non-whites in order to undermine them. Actually, both explanations are equally plausible and need not be mutually exclusive. The videos showcase Duke as the thorough-going narcissist that he is – not always a bad quality, but a quality that would support some combination of state involvement/Jew shilling, political expediency and base money-making. However, recently I have begun to develop in my own mind an alternative, more sophisticated rationalisation for his actions, which I think needs to be considered alongside other, more obvious and baser explanations. Duke clearly shares the genuine fear among all of us that whites will become a demographic minority in their own countries, and this is what may have prompted what he sees as a need to 'liberalise' White Nationalism and turn it into a rights movement – and to an extent, that may also be what motivated the Griffin BNP, which, as discussed above, transformed itself from a racial narrative under Tyndall into more of a liberal, rights-based narrative under Griffin. 'Rights for whites' is an old slogan for the far-Right, but whereas in the past it might have represented an inarticulate and somewhat incongruous expression of white racial assertiveness, today increasingly under Duke's 'liberal' national-socialism it has become a plaintive plea for more multi-culturalism, not less. Of course, it is not difficult to appreciate the logic: if other non-white groups have the right to exist and expressively flourish, then so should whites, and so on. The difficulty with all this emphasis on 'rights' is that it is a Jewish strategy that is being borrowed and like most of their ways of doing things, it entails huge risks. What the Jews are counting on is that, like a good-natured pup, the dumb white keeps looking at the finger and not where it's pointing. One might ask: If Jews and other groups are not allowed a 'racial morality' and cannot attack Gaza to the extent their capability allows, then maybe white people shouldn't be allowed a similar right to fight for their existence and should instead bow down and accept whatever second-class status might be on offer in this new multi-cultural society – so long as they can exist. If the Jews of 3,000 years ago had been satisfied merely with existing, then they most probably would not be still here today. It was their willingness to fight, and indeed risk their existence, that propelled them. What Duke and his semitically-correct counterparts on the American Right ask us to do is conform to some fictitious liberal morality, which we know is fanciful, and be beholden to Jews, who can easily smooth over the contradictions in their own position. Wouldn't a better approach be simply to point out that if the Jews can fight for their existence in Palestine (a matter on which we should take a neutral position), then likewise we white people should be able to fight for our existence too? Buying into all this liberal pap may be the line of least resistance/popular, but ultimately it's self-defeating. The only answer is to adopt a properly racial position. That means neutrality on Palestine and to also point out, both to Jews and the putative anti-Zionists, that just as Jews have a right to fight for their existence, so do whites.

End Notes

I couldn't fit the below neatly into the essay, so I include it below.

First, continuing my 'Developed Mantra' theme, a good question to ask Jews would be:

*If you Jews can defend yourselves in Israel, then why do you think it is wrong for whites in Europe to do similar?*

Better still, an adapted form of that question should be put to whites – especially those who, with a bit of persuasion, might be sympathetic to us.

On the implicit 'Zionism' of the 'controlled opposition' in the West – i.e. far-Right and the far-Left – I have not mentioned much of the far-Left in this regard, but now will, very briefly: One reason the so-called 'anti-Zionist' Left serves the Jews very well is that it provides cover for the real Gaza, which is the Jewish attack on whites, and means that any criticism of Israel is made to look like a criticism of Jews and therefore 'anti-semitism'. Obviously, the far-Right's own 'anti-Zionism' can only aid this objective, which is why genuine Racial Nationalists should be neutral on Palestine and should instead ask Jews about their own influence in our society: the 'European Gaza', and should also ask whites to direct their attention to this large and ignored 'elephant in the room'.

My opinion is that Zionism and anti-Zionism are simply two sides of the same coin – much like most anti-capitalists are actually just supporters of capitalism in a different form. They may not be conscious of their own complicitly, but that is not necessarily an excuse.

In the case of the far-Right – including the BNP, the National Front, the BDP, etc., etc. – they have all worked to serve Zionist interests in one way or another. It may be that in most cases this service was unrendered unconsciously and 'by omission' –

I have no problem accepting that, but having genuine motives is not enough. The truth matters. The whole history of the British far-Right is something that needs a revisionist re-examination: including its Zionism and the real possibility (which I consider likely) of it having been under state control.

Second, my response to Griffin's Four Words (as mentioned above – my own term for it) would be:

**Solidarity** instead of 'Freedom'.

**Community** instead of 'Democracy'.

**Race** instead of 'Identity'

**Safety** instead of 'Security'.

I'll call that 'the New Four Words', but it's something that needs work. It's just a start. The point is that any messages we adopt should achieve the balance of being appealing to those sections of the population we can realistically hope to attract, but also true to our core beliefs and loyalties. We should not try to argue on our enemy's own terms just for the sake of hoped-for electoral success, which can only be short-term and transient anyway and will not lead to meaningful reform.

## 3.6.

## The Dumbest People Ever: the nazification of whiteness[22]

The latest emotional spasm in the media over Gaza is nothing new. The matter of Israeli brutality (which is largely beyond doubt) and the resultant, pre-programmed outrage from the usual quarters, is so recurrent and predicable that it has practically become a Western tradition in its own right, with its own coded language and ritual and putative 'outsiders' who 'don't get it'. Criticism of Israel and Zionists is of course perfectly understandable and, if I were required to make the choice, Anti-Zionism is the only position I would be prepared to take. However, I have found that there is an additional, third option, which is simply to accept that each side, the Jews and the Arabs, have a right to fight for their existence. This is what is known as neutrality. It normally involves not making any outward assumptions about the legitimacy or moral superiority of one side or the other and simply letting them fight it out. Some people may be persuaded to reject neutrality in this matter on the basis that 'our' governments are aiding the Israelis with military technology and what not, but these are not 'our' governments. Western governments are largely under the influence of the Zionist lobby. If they wish to supply and lend favour to their client, Israel, that is a matter for them, but no imperative arises from this for white people to take one side or the other.

I recognise that my view on this matter is likely to be in the minority among White Nationalists, however in reality we can see that much of the vitriol and propaganda directed at Israel is based on a mixture of hyper-emotional responses and a conceit among people of varying ideological alignments that a calculated, Machiavellian response to Israel's actions that exploits an emotional facility among the public will somehow serve some political interest or other. I would like to suggest that these responses do nothing but serve the long-term ethnic interests of Jews, who have mastered the art of playing-off the two Western political extremes against each other. On the Left are the self-haters and the anti-white invaders, who either want to destroy the White Race or are indifferent to our genetic destruction and sneer at those who warn against this. Some of them are projecting their private hate of non-whites and working class whites outward onto those who hold a more or less truthful position on race and tell it how it is. Meanwhile, on the Right, you will see the more explicitly xenophobic type. The 'Other' may be white foreigners who arrive in my country to work or non-white immigrants. It may be Jews or liberal whites. It may be homosexuals. It doesn't particularly matter. They just want something to hate. At the moment, it is Jews who are the subject of the Ten Minute Hate, which is giving encouragement to the far-Right who think that the public are finally turning and 'seeing the Jews for what they are'. In fact, all that is happening is hate. Hate is an end in itself. It relieves the pressure of modernity, and provides an escapist target to distract from one's own personal and environmental inadequacies and anxieties. It is also the perfect manipulative tool for those who have an interest in mass social control: in this case, the Jewish-influenced media.

Zionism and Anti-Zionism are simply two sides of the same coin, used by nefarious influences in the West to manipulate us and keep us from seeing the European Gaza

---

[22] First published on 11th. August 2014 at http://www.johnlonden.com

that has been created on our doorsteps. Whether this 'Anti-Zionism' is fuelled by liberal racial supremacism (known by media codewords such as 'compassion' and 'human rights') or base antipathy towards Jews per se, it serves to ensure that the dog keeps staring at the finger (the Gaza in Palestine) and not at where the finger is pointing (the Gaza in Europe). That most whites appear not to see this is the ultimate testament and further proof – if it were needed – of a white penchant for altruistically serving the interests of others rather than our own kind. For the far-Right, white altruism over Gaza can be explained by a toxic alchemy of misplaced liberal racial supremacism (i.e. White Man's Burden), Realpolitik about the potential of geopolitical Islam as an ally and check on Zionist expansionism, and last, but by no means least, a boiling, primal antipathy among the white-conscious towards Jews per se. The far-Left, for their part – licensed by the media with a curious exemption that permits modish hatred of Jews at home and abroad – have an obvious ideological interest in attacking the notion of a Jewish ethno-state. Its continued existence is an affront to the liberal nostrums of internationalism and mixed-racialism. Not to mention that Palestinian Arabs, being brown-looking, are bound to attract the basic sympathy of soft-hearted liberal types.

Looking at this more objectively – i.e. without the Judaic distortion goggles handily provided by the media – if we can let go of our manipulated feelings of 'like' or 'dislike' for Jews, as the case may be, and simply observe the plain truth, what we see happening in Gaza is terrible and not something one would wish on these people, but for those of us in the West it is not our concern whether the Palestinians win out or the Zionist Jews manage to retain their sovereignty. By all means, civil aid can be provided to Palestinians who are suffering as a result of the Israeli onslaught. No humane person could argue with such efforts, and if people wish to boycott Israeli and Jewish goods and services, then that is all to the good and you will not hear any objection from me, but from a racial and political perspective, Gaza is simply none of our business. By pretending that it is, we are repeating the same mistakes that led us to the European Gaza we now face. We are allowing 'white altruism', our supposed compassion for others – which I would suggest is in fact just a mixture of narcissism and a sense of tacit racial supremacism – to cloud our understanding of what needs to be done to protect and preserve what is left of white communities.

The question begged is how we should advance a real white racial agenda? I think we have to start by deciding who we are and then, where we are going. Who we are may seem a curious point to begin, if not a little incongruous, and Nationalists especially are averse to disruptive heterodoxies, but unless we are willing to re-assess dynamically, from first principles, the aims and objects of white survival, then we risk ossification and irrelevance. One question might be: Are we still a White Race or are we now just a tribe of hyper-racially aware dissidents who need to separate from the culturally deracinated masses? I don't myself know the answer to that – it's a massive question in its own right – though I suspect the answer is the latter, and I for one no longer consider myself a 'Nationalist' as such in any case (though I still use the term occasionally for brevity). I began purposefully by discussing Jews and Israel, because those constructs are relevant to this question and are the source of how so many politicised whites, both on the Left and the Right, seem to define themselves. The Jewish identity seems to be the counterpoint of the white political identity. The white Left, expressing Jewish ethnic interests, are now consciously deracinated, if not conspicuously so, and believe that the rest of the world, including (ironically) Jews, should be like them, though they express this (self-) hate only tacitly and project psychologically by 'blaming' racially-aware whites, citing their 'hate'. Meanwhile, the white-conscious Right, affirming their 'unJewishness', aspire for the ethnically homogeneous state that the Jews are sustaining. Here an interesting disjuncture arises. Jewish interests seem to be promoting for whites in Western society ideas and values that, on the face of it, might ultimately threaten the Jews' own ethnic survival; while Nationalists spend a great deal of time attacking Jews for exercising the very right that they, Nationalists, demand for themselves – the right to fight for racial survival – with the possible consequence that, should the Jewish state fall, any notions of racial or ethnic sovereignty might fall with it. The apparent double contradiction is unravelled by realising that the Jews are playing us, not the other way round. Admittedly, it is a risky and dangerous strategy for them, but the stakes are high: if white people were to develop the kind of serious racial community that actually advanced the interests of whites instead of fake white altruism, Jewish influence (and lots more besides) would be threatened. Better to keep the 'dumb' whites distracted and manipulate what 'racial opposition' there is by giving Nationalists (and the far-Left dupes too) an easy target: the bandit Zionist State of Israel. White vitriol against Jews serves the purposes of Jews. It distracts from the real issue, which is Jewish control of our own societies. It also encourages needless emotional tension and paranoia between race conscious whites, who begin to obsess about Jewish influence and even start accusing each other of being Jewish or defending Jews. What is required isn't 'liking' or 'disliking' Jews, but a cold recognition of reality and then appropriate action.

In this respect, it is perfectly possible to like Jews individually, even collectively, if you so choose, while retaining a firm, unshakeable view about their influence in society. It is also possible to admire Jews for their ethnic loyalty, and in other respects retain a balanced perspective on all things to do with Jews, while at the same time denouncing the ways in which they are acting to harm white interests. It is, furthermore, possible to resist slipping into the Jewish genocide narrative while at the same time understanding clearly the difference between right and wrong and that the vigorous exercise of racial morality and intra-group loyalty needs to give way at some point to obvious notions of respect and decency. It is also possible to move beyond reacting to matters racial with simple emotional responses, such as hating, condemning, and narcissistic grandstanding, and to instead construct a positive narrative that advances white interests on our own terms. By hating, we are allowing our opponents – be they political Jews or whatever – to control us and dictate our agenda. By simply reacting, we allow our opponents to frame our agenda and even our very identity. The reactionary pathology is, however, deeply embedded in Nationalist political thought, largely I would suggest due to the dominance of the Right.

What is 'Racial Nationalism', when all is said and done? I would suggest it is neither Left nor Right in character. It is, if anything, an ideology and governing philosophy of 'radical centrism', simply an accentuated expression of what, anecdotally, we all know most normal people want: in this case, a community based on a shared identity. Another word for 'radical centrism' is fascism, and in truth, the former term is just a euphemism for the latter. For the white conscious, the objective is racial fascism in the sense that we would have a community that is, for all intents and purposes, an extended racial family, with all the policy and behavioural strictures that flow from this, and in which the individual is an integral part of the whole and subsumes important aspects of his interest and identity to the community. Most white people have been taught to instinctively recoil at the thought of a fascist society, yet what they do not realise is that they already live in one. What we live under today is mixed-racial fascism: or anti-white fascism, as it might be termed. This system is the expression of the wishes of a minority racial interest in society, the Jews, and the non-white footsoldiers they have brought into Europe to dominate us. Mixed-racial fascism is successfully presented as the opposite of fascistic, in that it promotes the propaganda of 'liberal democracy' and the notion that we are required to think of ourselves and each other purely as individuals, allowing a vacuum in which there is no private or community-level sphere of action and significant power can be drawn to a strong state. Another crucial aspect of the propaganda of the mixed-racial fascists is 'racial democracy', the idea that race is no longer (or should not be) considered a relevant factor in people's lives, except to the extent that it might be used as a basis for suppressing or frustrating whites. The individuation of mixed-racialism fascism is largely confined to white culture. Other, non-white, groups are permitted to retain their racial and ethnic cohesion to varying degrees.

We can see that now the shared identity of whites is being lost, all talk among the ordinary populace of 'democracy' is revealed for what it is: a superfluous, childish fantasy. There is no 'democracy' for an ethnic group that cannot exercise its own culture. Instead, the suppressed group has to start complying with the norms, values and rituals of the invading group. This is almost a law of nature. Where this invasion is carried out 'democratically', and is of a demographic and cultural character – as is the case in the mixed-racial fascism of Britain and most of Europe – initially the signs of racial alienation will be subtle and difficult to surmise, but in time the exorcism from the mainstream of the indigenous host culture, and its marginalisation, becomes obvious and blatant even to the most obtuse mind. And as the white European public become more and more vocal and angry in their objection to these developments, those who were responsible for this will be nowhere to be seen when it comes to accepting the blame, but they will not be difficult to find. They are your neighbours, your co-workers, your family – and the person you see in the mirror. We are all responsible for this mess, and the key to reversing it, or at least doing something worthwhile and constructive about it, still lies in our hands, if only we could see it.

Those of us in the 'reasoned middle' who recognise this, who are neither far-Right, nor far-Left, who note the good sense of a realistic attitude to race, who ask for an examination of alien racial influence in white societies – including that of Jews – who recognise that race is an essential precursor of culture and is the basis of all that is good and positive in our society, see 'Nationalism', such as it is, as a vehicle for the resurrection of a European civilisation. We are 'Nationalists by default', in that we rest on that creed for our survival and all that is decent, much like many of the intelligentsia in the former Soviet Union took refuge in free market Austrian School economics as a rebuttal to the excesses of Soviet state capitalism. But then nationalism is not necessarily an intellectual position. Its fodder is the emotional, reactionary flag-waving type who enjoys the comfort of being part of an identifiable sub-culture. Those among nationalists who do exhibit a more erudite or thoughtful disposition tend to emphasise a deeper, esoteric understanding of society and a sense of shared experience that is difficult for outsiders to grasp in a conventional, linear way. The intelligent non-racialist/non-nationalist looks on and wonders what the sense is in continuing to base one's politics on archaic ideas and constructs. It is, I would suggest, fundamentally a different mental attribute and character, rather than simply a difference in learning and experience, that leads to the nationalist intellectual rebelling against the canon. The intellectual nationalist simply does not want to live among other races, and constructs his reasoning retroactively from there. The difficulty is in intellectualising a position that cannot, and perhaps should not, be reasoned intelligently because in the end, this is about what is in one's gut. It's about who we are. I should not have to argue that I prefer to live among white people, nor engage in complicated academic discursions to justify what is, in reality, a natural position. The burden of proof should be on those who argue for, or allow, deracination.

In response to what is happening in society, the 'Nationalist by default' is focused on constructive activity and is not really interested in being part of a 'movement' or rebellious sub-culture. The accent is on 'doing something' rather than merely 'being something'. 'Doing something' is difficult. It involves complexity and mediation with the real world. 'Being something' is easy. It need not involve anything more complex than attending a demonstration and shouting slogans at people, or maybe posting a comment on an online forum. I would suggest that much (but not all) of Nationalism has become the latter, with many activists bogged down in emotional ghettoes, futile oppositional reflexes and antiquarian esotericism. The tendency reaches its zenith in the nagging persistence of overt, outright Hitler worship and Third Reich virtual tourism. It seems that some pockets of the movement have their own 'TINA' written into their political DNA: there is no alternative other than a visibly antiquated ideology that glorifies an Austrian-born German who shot himself in 1945.

The obsession manifests itself in different forms. There are the neo-Kuhnite North American White Nationalists with their paramilitary uniforms, black leather jackets, Hakenkreuz and Seig Heil salutes. There are websites that cater for them such as Daily Stormer, with its Teutonic imagery, recurrent wartime and Third Reich themes and repeated mentioning of Hitler. The great cruel irony of this odd sub-culture is that its portrayal of German 'Nazis' is fundamentally Judaic in nature and antagonistic to whites in that owes its genesis in the enemy portrayal of the Third Reich. One article on Daily Stormer describes German Third Reich military uniforms as 'cool'. Indeed they are – on Germans who lived in the 1930s and 1940s. This is the year 2014 and most of us aren't German. They don't look cool on us. They just look silly. It's as ridiculous as a group of syndicalists running a website on current affairs based on the imagery of Italian Fascism and the personality of Mussolini. It smacks of mental and emotional weakness, an aping of the Judaic-Nazi Myth of National Socialist Germany, invented by the Hollywood System and Jews. None of it has anything to do with the historicity of that era, or with national-socialism, Nationalism per se or white racial consciousness, as I understand these things. It is just street theatre, encouraged by people who are hostile to us, who wish to discredit us, and who want to dissuade normal, sensible white people from thinking racially by presenting those who do as deviants, 'weirdos' and outcasts. One also has to question the literacy of this 'Nazi' symbolism. If a form of American national-socialism were ever to be resurrected, it is much more likely to resemble something deeper in U.S. history than German-American nostalgia for National Socialists and a bunch of comic-opera thugs giving Roman salutes.

The whole basis of national-socialism (I use the term in its white racial sense) is that it must be culturally-consistent with its locality, otherwise it is not really 'national'. An American nation-socialism would be less Alfred Rosenberg and more Daniel Boone; less the Führerprinzip and more (perhaps) a Jeffersonian farmers' democracy, or reflective of some other indigenous European civic influence. A national-socialism for Britain, likewise, would be something different and more reflective of the British experience. I think this applies even if, like me, you reject nation-states as such and dislike the nativist perspective and think that the real nation is 'white'. Even in a less parochial, more 'internationalist' type of 'Racial Nationalism', the political, social and economic character of white sovereignty will reflect the varying ethnic peculiarities of local experience. Hitlerian National Socialism was a result of the specific circumstances in Germany and Europe at that time, just as Japanese national-socialism (run for the last 70 years under an ostensibly 'democratic' system) reflects the character of those unique people who live on an island off the Asian landmass and call themselves Japanese. Same with Chinese national-socialism – otherwise known as Maoism, or 'communism' to those who believe in fantasies. And so too with Jewish national-socialism – or 'Zionism' to you and me. That it is not to denigrate in any way the German experience, which is important and valuable and needs to be discussed because of its importance and relevance to our struggle now. It is simply to recognise it for what it is: a local expression of a larger, generic idea that has empirical validity for all peoples. We could call this generic idea 'national-socialism', 'fascism', 'democracy', or whatever you like, but the point is that to try and ape one specific example of it and turn it into our banner is not real politics and is not an intelligent response to mixed-racial fascism. It is, really, nothing more than an exercise in rebellious chic, a kind of indulgent fashion statement for the petulant – that makes you look ridiculous.

The 'nazification' of Nationalism and the perpetuation of the Judaic-Nazi Myth has been a gift to our enemies. It has allowed them to portray a moderate message as 'extremist' It has even opened the way for our enemies to nazify whiteness itself, to portray any overt expression of white consciousness or white interests as something vaguely relating to a particular period in history that everyone is taught not to like. This conflates the cure – white political action – with a completely unrelated toxin, discouraging whites from thinking as a group and allowing the mixed-racial poison to spread unhindered in the vacuum left by the absence of an appealing Popular Nationalism. Much of this nazification is a reflection of a lack of self-confidence in our substantive political message and with that a need to latch on to a historic period when, it is felt, National Socialism found full force and vigour. That itself is a myth, but the sense of anger and alienation among working class whites fuels the romantic retrospective, a pining for better times. We can also ascribe deeper psychological motivations to neo-Nazi chic. People of an immature disposition can be led into Nationalism because they want to rebel against society in some way, and what better or more effective way to do this than to adopt an ideology that is reviled in 'polite company'. Others attach themselves to causes that ameliorate their own inner insecurities, and this especially appeals to downtrodden whites, who want to feel that they are equal to, or even superior to, others, including other whites who they can pretend are not as far-seeing or visionary as they are.

We should also bear in mind the way Hitler is mythologised by White Nationalists. He supposedly represents white consciousness at the apex of society, strong and triumphant. His memory therefore appeals to whites who feel the very opposite of 'strong' and 'triumphant': in other words, weak and emotionally-dependent whites who see their group identity under continuous and permanent assault from nefarious forces in modern society and want to draw strength from old stories of military glory, Pathé reels and what not. It's a comfort for people who want to be passively led. Hitler was also in some ways an intentionally vacuous figure, as most really successful politicians are. White people can fill themselves into him and he personifies their greatest hopes and dreams, whatever they may be. In all of this, a simple fact can be overlooked: Hitler is dead. He has been dead for 70 years, so unless a necrocracy is being planned or a way of resurrecting the dead has been found, it's difficult to see his present relevance. We are alive and, unlike Hitler, we must confront the problems facing white people in the 21st. century. The answer for us is not to become more marginalised and end up ghettoising our views. The answer is to build a new White Alternative that appeals to ordinary white people. That means looking forward not backward, becoming active rather than passive, turning away from reactionary politics and all its accoutrements – including leaders, elections, attackable structures – and building an 'alternative politics' based on white autonomy. It means moving away from 'hating' others towards giving our fellow whites a positive message.

Some people think 'hate' is good or useful in that it is a weapon or forms the basis of some kind of membranous racial defensive values. I think these notions are misconceived. 'Hate' and 'Hitler' are just weapons in the ongoing psychological warfare against whites. They work most effectively when they are paired together, and when combined with 'Jews', they turn all whites-conscious people into a moving target, regardless of individual sophistication, moderacy or reasonableness. The target is easily hit with the trigger words that the media have invented specially for us. The reason the word 'hate' is invoked so much in a legal and political context is that it is acknowledged that to resort to hate is to admit that you have given in. It is a weakness, as it clouds reason. The accepted, legalistic definition of 'hate' is thus broadened out to all kinds of benign or relatively inoffensive behaviour and printed material so as to make it appear that racial arguments are insubstantial. If you hate Jews, then you are acknowledging that you are under the control of Jews.

The positive message has to be about white people. We can't complain about others misrepresenting us if we are so determined to misrepresent ourselves by adopting or alluding to neo-Nazi imagery and ideas. We ought to be able to laugh off the Nazi epithet and dismiss our opponents' jibes along these lines as ridiculous and exaggerated. We also ought to be able to ask our opponents:

*"Why are you always misrepresenting white people as Nazis"*

That would be a powerful question under the right circumstances, and it would be difficult for our opponents to respond to it, but we can't ask this because some Nationalists are still stuck in the neo-Nazi groove, and that is part of the problem. Casual neo-Nazi chic is pathological and runs deep in some pockets of Nationalism, but it also shows itself more subtly in the mainstream of the movement. The main online discussion forum for White Nationalism is called Stormfront, which is an interesting name, to say the least. I believe the name was chosen innocently, as an allusion to the idea of a counter-cultural front that would cleanse Western society of mixed-racial influence, etc., but in reality, to the ordinary white, the name is Teutonic and alludes to the cartoon Hollywood Judaic-Nazi caricature. Why should this be a problem? Well, to someone who has always been a White Nationalist, it won't be, but to an 'ordinary person', the site looks weird and extreme. What we whites need more than anything else is to mainstream our message while maintaining our core integrity.

Stormfront probably attracts a lot of curiosity from white people who are suffering from cognitive dissonance – otherwise known as maturity – and there's always a risk that the more independent-spirited among these ordinary folk will start to think for themselves, so the Teutonic imagery and the hostile character of sites like Stormfront hands a useful psychological weapon to our enemies, a Rubicon that acts as a barrier for dialogue between the 'race-aware' and those who are open to our message. Even the most critically-minded person will have difficulty getting past a name like 'Stormfront', as it conjures up all kinds of mental associations. If we are honest about this, presentation does matter. Of course, none of this would be a problem if 'Stormfront' was somehow a true reflection of who we are and what we are about. Is it? Is this the tone we want to set? What are we? What are we about? Here we come full circle, because these are the kinds of questions we need to ask and find answers to. Are we a comic opera company or a serious political movement?

Recently, Daily Stormer publicised an online poll for the Smartest Person In History, urging its readers to vote for Adolf Hitler. This was clearly an attempt to draw attention to the supposed qualities of a 70-odd year old corpse, but I am not sure why I should vote for Hitler or any other historical figure. Dragging Hitler up from the grave doesn't help us. We whites need to stop valorising these demagogues, both the dead and the alive ones, and start voting for ourselves. Instead of choosing between leaders who are dead and alive leaders who are brain dead, let's choose a White Alternative, in which – just for a change – we start building our own solutions and answers, from the ground up. I have no idea if Hitler was the Smartest Person In History, but the risk we run with this continued unhealthy obsession, not just with Hitler but with demagogues generally, is that for all our intelligence and achievements as a race, we are going to end up as the dumbest people ever. In a thousand years, no-one will remember white accomplishments unless there are intelligent white people around to speak of them. At this rate, all they will remember is that we were just another one of countless groups eradicated from the face of the Earth, or enslaved. That is what is really at stake. This is a fight for existence.

# 4.   What Should Be Done?

**4.1.**

**Bursting The Liberal Bubble[23]**

The Nationalist youth street activist group, National Action, has been the subject of much discussion lately on various White Nationalist forums, largely due to a recent successful demonstration against global capitalism in Liverpool. The above photograph, taken from a demonstration in London, has now gone viral. It shows members of the group posing next to the Mandela effigy in Parliament Square after having put a banana in the hand of the statue. This is young British men openly and publicly mocking the core of British liberal precepts.

My view on National Action is that they are an effective and cogent expression of National Socialism through white youth sub-culture. However, others within Nationalism take a different view and believe that the disruptive street tactics of National Action might be harmful to the general cause of White Nationalism.

Here's a contribution from one such sceptic, posted recently on a prominent White Nationalist discussion forum. The contributor appears to be defending the Mantra as an alternative to street activism:

*"The Mantra approach might not offer the same adrenaline rush as a torchlight parade down your local high street, but ultimately I believe it is the bread and butter approach that points out the lies and contradictions in the system and will ultimately trigger its mainstream collapse.*

*"I wish National Action well, but I hope they can come up with something original and don't fall into the trap of becoming the Hollywood Nazis that our enemies always love to portray us as."*

My response and take on all this, just posted to the same forum is below. In summary, I believe that street activism is an essential counterpoint to the other strategies and complements them. Where I think National Action does present a problem for the traditionalists is that it challenges their long-held pining for respectability and acceptance among the mainstream and also the notion that Nationalism should be hierarchical and 'right-wing' rather than a movement that rises-up as an expression of popular consciousness.

Here's what I said:

The 'Mantra' is good and I'm all for it. It's effective as far as it goes, but its limitations are that it's rhetorical and it's based around the internet. Like any good and effective method, it will only take us so far. Different strategies are needed. I think your point might be that these differing strategies ideally need to be complementary, not in friction, and should not weaken each other or distract from the overall aims. If so, I would agree that this is how it should work in the ideal world, and there is nothing about National Action to suggest that they are consciously trying to undermine us. Quite the opposite.

---

[23] First published on 17 June 2014 at http://www.johnlonden.com

Nationalism is not a hierarchy. If we are going to capture the consciousness of our people, then our movements and groups need to work from the ground-up and express the interests and values of real people in real society, not a bunch of internet warriors and the sombre suits and ties approach taken in pseudo-academic seminars and mock-serious political meetings.

I also think National Action is capturing the essence of something that is transcendent and emergent in society. I am by no means 'young' in the age sense, but I feel young politically and I am much more attracted to the style and approach of National Action than the suits and ties, plastic Union Flag and Pomp & Circumstance of more 'traditional' Nationalists.

I think some of us just have to accept that Nationalism itself has become somewhat 'liberal', 'kosher' and 'democratic', and bursting the liberal bubble might also involve, in a nice sort of way, challenging the sense of entitlement found among the 'far-Right' and ultra-Tory types who think they own Nationalism.

Nationalism belongs to all white people, not just people with nasty right-wing views.

## 4.2.

### Soon to be flotsam and jetsam: a rallying cry[24]

Mass non-white immigration into the West is treason, pure and simple. A Nation only has meaning if it has racial integrity. Change the racial and genetic basis of a Nation, and you change that Nation, irrevocably. Abolish the Race and you abolish the Nation. Mass non-white immigration involves the abolition of the indigenous peoples by a gradual process of miscegenation ('integration') and ideological indoctrination ('racial equality'). I consider these irrefutable facts.

If the non-white numbers entering the country were notional or tiny – say, under 10,000 per year – that would be a different discussion. It would still present a problem, but we could afford to adopt a more moderate and considered – even relaxed – approach in those circumstances. Alas, we do not have that luxury. The numbers entering annually are massive and will have a revolutionary effect on our society. This is not all the fault of the present government, and it is not the present government that initiated this unwise policy. The roots of this go back to the 1950s.

Mass non-white immigration was commenced decades ago without the consent of the indigenous white British people. Thus, the policy is unacceptable on democratic criteria alone, but even if it did carry 'democratic consent', it would still be treasonable conduct.

I think we can comfortably assert that no species on this Earth has ever consented to its own abolition. To campaign for one's own demise is perverse and unnatural. Those who do so are sick in the head. Mother Nature, who is unforgiving, must look on the White Race with scorn. All around us we see white people, some otherwise highly-intelligent, bending over backwards to accommodate peoples with whom they share no genetic affinity, nor any national, racial or cultural perspective. Unless we, the indigenous peoples, stand-up for our inherent right to a homeland, we will soon be the flotsam and jetsam of the planet, a trash people open for abuse and exploitation. Forgive my brutal honesty, but it's best we confront the reality of our peril.

No other race or species on the planet does what we are doing now. You don't hear 'liberal' elephants complaining about trunk supremacy. Elephants just get on with being trunk chauvinists. I've never heard of a 'liberal' wolf philosophising wanly over the natural supremacy of wolves and its super-predator position in its own environment. I've never heard of black bears in America lobbying Congress so as to promote greater rights for yellow jackets. Species prioritise their own survival. Elephants are supremacists. Wolves are supremacists. Bears are supremacists. For their own species. They have to be, or they wouldn't survive. I have yet to encounter a convincing argument as to why humans, or groups of humans, should be any different.

That is not to say I am a white 'superiorist' in the political sense of the term, but I do have a high opinion of white people compared with other peoples. Why? Well,

[24] First published on 26 June 2014 at http://www.johnlonden.com

because I am white. Do I really need to explain further? I also quite like living among people with whom I share a genetic affinity: that is, among white people. I apologise most sincerely if that offends you. Please sit down and take a deep breath. There was a time when my type of view was considered quite normal and not offensive at all. That is still the case everywhere in the world except Europe and North America. The contrary view would have found you locked in a padded cell, and still will in most parts of the world where sense still reigns. Now the tables have been turned, but only for white people it would seem.

My question: To what end?

**4.3.**

## John May Lives?[25]

You may be reading this soon after I type it, in July 2014, at a time when the struggle for a white nation seems lost. Or you may be reading this years in the future when, for all I know, our prospects may seem doubly bleak, if that is possible. Whoever, wherever, and whenever you are, I want to tell you that in our time we are only at the beginning of this struggle. The road ahead will be hard and rocky, but it is just a beginning, and each and every positive step we take towards a white independent nation – even the trivial, seemingly inconsequential things – is a step in the right direction and it will lead, in time, to our goal. We are building a new society, but entailed in that project is resistance against the existing society around us. Ours is a resistance movement, resistance to the here and now. That is what makes this difficult. And at some point, there is going to have to be a reckoning, a confrontation. There is no point soft-soaping this. It's in our genes. It is our destiny.

Getting down to practicalities, in order to progress we need a combination of methods. Central to everything is the 'New Tribe': racially-aware whites who are committed to building white conscious communities. The leading community-building project is White Independent Nation (WIN). I would urge any white person reading this to apply to WIN now and join the struggle. This is a collective endeavour and those who join us need to think about how they can help propagandise our aims so that our views become more widespread, first among the Nationalist community, then among the wider white community.

Part of the purpose of this blog is try and introduce Nationalists to subversive ideas and new ways of thinking about the issues. This is necessary because WIN is a difficult step for some Nationalists who remain wedded mentally to traditional electoral politics, leaders, and the Establishment's other methods of control. I have been around all the forums now, in various guises, and I have argued with Nationalists who, even in 2014, persist in blaming 'Establishment politicians', Jews, Cultural Marxists and so on for our plight. The harsh truth is that our situation is self-inflicted. We voted for these people, or we allowed them to continue in office, or we failed to convince the British public of the rightness of our cause – whichever, none of us have clean hands. It is time to acknowledge this and take control of our own Fate, rather than leaving it to gurus, mystics and avuncular stockbrokers.

Of course, that didactic plea applies as much to myself as anybody else. The activationist spirit that brought us into fringe politics is, at present, spent in the futile, plastic politics of UKIP, or for those – like myself – who reject electoral politics, in peripheral activities such as discussion and writing. As I sit here composing this blog, I know it is hardly an impactful activity. Political writing does have its place, but if we are to be an effective movement, it can only be the tip of a massive iceberg. On its own, 'virtual Nationalism' is not enough. It will not win the 'war'. Ultimately both I and others are going to have to take real action. In acknowledging this truth, let us not be too harsh on each other. This pause may be a necessary phase in our long-term struggle. The way I see it, at the moment Nationalists are just biding their

---

[25] First published on 8th. July 2014 at http://www.johnlonden.com

time, waiting. My articles try to steer people who are already race-conscious towards autonomy and rejection of leader cults. This is because those who join WIN need to be more receptive to a community-building strategy and less reliant on electoral politics, if their involvement is to be productive, but in the end only the individual can make the shift in thought – only you, the anonymous soul reading my words, can decide whether you want to aim for something bigger than the proxy victories of leaders who despise you.

Those who do make this necessary mental transition are rewarded by joining reality. The real world of actual political struggle is a cold, harsh place without ego and with little, if any, material reward – there is no comfort in real politics – but it is at least the real world, not the fantasy world of electioneering and civic gossip, conjured-up on the television. You will have noticed that some of the new-wave nationalist movements that have emerged with the demise of the BNP and BDP still operate within the parameters of the Jewish fantasy world. They ask you for money, or give vague hints that they need financial donations in order to make their plans work. They also talk about the need for structures and rigid hierarchies. They usually have leaders or guru-like figures. These are the failed 'business models' and scams that Nationalists have invested faith in time and again, only to suffer inevitable disappointment when it becomes clear that working within the existing system always brings the same results: failure.

We are not asking for money. We don't want it. It's not welcome. Apart from anything else, money creates problems – paper trails, organisational structures, expectations and promises that cannot be met. What we need is people: talent, energy and time. We need to work in the shadows. We need to forge new networks that are covert and hidden from the authorities. And aside from the community-building efforts of WIN, which are important in themselves, we also need to organise an underground: people who will meet secretly and work on the edges of legality to undermine the mixed-racial society. We need, in short, a kind of grassroots 'white resistance'. Not terrorists – at this stage, no violence is called for – but an army of saboteurs and civil resisters who will serve to motivate those who we need to join us and remind the Establishment that their genocide does not have the consent of all whites.

This radical activism will not appeal to everyone. Different approaches appeal to different people. Some people like the idea of getting involved in something exciting and edgy. For others, the cultural and intellectual approach will appeal [hence this blog]. Still others will want to focus on the more practical aspects of community politics, including business and cultural work on the ground. We need different ways of getting different people involved, perhaps involving lots of different organisations or groupings, but all working under the informal umbrella of the 'New Tribe' that WIN embodies. We also need to be patient with people and recognise that kosher outlets such as UKIP do have a positive side in that they might bring some people, both in and outside the nationalist community, round to our general way of thinking. Anyway, none of these UKIP supporters are going to eat humble pie when they are proved wrong, as is inevitable.

There is an old slogan I remember from my time on the Left, that originated in the New Social Movements of the Sixties: "the personal is political". The idea was that for feminists and other rights activists, politics was truly about their personal lives. I always shied away from quoting it, and I remain sceptical of its usefulness, even for the Left, as I tend towards the view that the personal is not (or should not or ought not to be) political. The radical social liberals have almost succeeded in their quest to destroy the traditional family at the formal legislative level, but traditional families remain in our society and decent (if not traditional) society can be revived again. That crucial lacuna has perhaps not been considered by the radical social engineers. In their shrewd assessment of the cultural battleground, they have perhaps not taken full account of basic geopolitical realities: one day, those of us who resist their poison will once again be the hegemony and that will be the true revolution.

But, to paraphrase a successful insurrectionist, Mao Tse Tung: a revolution is not a tea party. It is bloody, if only figuratively. The reality of the situation is that each of us is going to have to make a difficult decision here, even if only as a silent resolution in our private mental worlds. This is now a resistance movement. An active resistance is not something that can be raised out of thin air and it may take years to build a workable underground operation, but we are not going to get anywhere sat behind computer screens or other similar activities, hoping for some suited Saviour to rescue us from our self-inflicted plight. We are going to have to start taking risks – and that may include certain activities that make National Action look like a Sunday school outing.

*John May Lives?*

In the 1980s, in a rare exception to the usual rubbish, the Hollywood machine produced a miniseries that was quite literate. 'V' depicts the invasion and conquest of Earth by an acquisitive but highly-advanced lizard-like species of extra-terrestrials. It is common for fans and obsessives of the 'V' series to interpret the narrative arc through their own political or social views, whether left-wing or right-wing. There are certainly strong environmentalist and anti-capitalist messages, if nothing else – but the strongest allegory of the series is undoubtedly found in its feature of having aliens 'hide' their true identities as they live and work among the human population. Consciously or otherwise, this is a racial subtext that was interjected in the conflict between the Visitors and what they saw as their human cattle. This subtext became more of an explicit theme in the otherwise dreary 2009 re-make, which had the aliens plotting to eradicate humanity through inter-breeding and genetic engineering. Of course, it is probable that this was not the intended allegory (in so far as there was such). For one thing, the original series features a sympathetic Jewish character and there is a clear implication that the Visitors are 'fascist' authoritarian oppressors. But whatever the intention, as is often the case with narrative work – which is by its nature discursive, due to its complex range of influences – other interpretations are possible. The greedy, psychotic alien invaders were not simply brutal oppressors. They also waged a psychological war that was initially quite subtle. On revealing themselves to humanity, they sought to conceal their true nature and insinuate themselves among the cattle species, adopting their values and parroting their buzzwords while carefully working behind the scenes to control the media and academia. They also worked hard to gain emotional sympathy among the public, while demonising the resistance and (in the original series) accusing sceptical scientists of conspiring to destroy them. They achieved all this through a mixture of consent, acquiescence and fear, but it's also clear that they only got away with their diabolical plans for such a long time by hiding the extent to which they were truly alien. This was done by wearing grotesque suits of human skin, which prevented their human cattle from seeing them for what they really were: fundamentally 'different' from the human population. The parallel is clear: the Jews and capitalists who run our real world are the 'lizards'. Not literally: this is not some weird conspiracy theory – we have no time for such nonsense. They are 'lizards' in the figurative sense. They are human, but without any sense of humanity: almost animals in human form. To defeat them, we must, ironically, borrow some of their values: become tribal ourselves and let go of our 'humanity', which has weakened us and given us the slave morality that makes us vulnerable to predation. Conversely, while our enemy is powerful, cunning and seemingly omniscient, these strengths are also its Achilles' heel, and are the key to our ultimate victory. Just as in the Hollywood fantasy, in the real world this enemy can be beaten.

Over the last few days, our 'honest' media have faithfully reported to us that our country is run by a cabal of sexual perverts and their apologists. A dossier exists, or existed, detailing the names of paedophiles working from the highest echelons of power in this country. These stories give us a brief, teasing glimpse of the true 'Face' of our governing elite: they see us as cattle, and have no scruple or compunction about lying to us and thieving from us – even molesting white children in children's homes, and turning a blind eye to the abuse of white children in Asian communities. All of it done against a background of seediness, selfishness and profiteering, the same instincts that are stealing our birth right as a white European nation. The problem is that to most journalists, truth is just part of the news cycle. The 'revelations' are not revelations at all. They are part of a controlled agenda to trick, confuse, deceive and divert attention from the real issue: which is the fitness of this kakistocratic elite class (or any elite) to govern us. In due course, the 'revelations' will be forgotten, only to resurface again in some form at a later date, in a tightly-controlled way, so that the gullible and credulous can be deceived again. The dossier exists as a distraction, but what the 'dossier' (and other media events like it) should be is a consciousness-raising event. It should turn any thinking person towards a serious re-appraisal of revolutionary politics over the stale, populist, merry-go-round politics of UKIP, the Purple Tories, and similar parties.

We need a revolution. 'John May' was the fictional iconoclast of the 2009 re-imagination of the 'V' series. He was not alive. He was just a memory, but he acted as a symbol of the enduring reality of the resistance and the courage and indefatigability of its followers. Humans and rebel Fifth Column Visitors used the slogan 'John May Lives' unselfconsciously as a show of defiance and as a rallying cry. If we are going to win, we need that spirit in the real world. John May must live for the White Race.

**4.4.**

## The Lessons of Leith[26]

Nationalism in the modern sense was invented in the 17th. century during the break-up of the Holy Roman Empire, a multi-ethnic construct that dominated Central Europe (and that in fact was only formally dissolved in 1806). The Peace of Westphalia of 1648 established a new diplomatic system in the West based on the principle of non-interference in the domestic affairs of sovereign, nation-states. The nation-states that emerged in Western and Central Europe out of the new concept of Westphalian sovereignty developed vital, discrete national identities in their own right, that were to a large extent fictitious, but which served an important ulterior purpose in the management of emergent mercantile and industrial economic systems that required mass social control of populations. That is to say, Nationalism as both a concept and institutional reality divides the loyalties of working people internationally, so that a worker in France, let's say, does not recognise his common cause with a worker in Britain. When put like that, in bare terms, the ploy seems laughable, but it is obvious that it works: consider, for example, the aggressive rhetoric against Polish immigrants that permeates the British media. Poles, it is believed, have different interests to Britons. A moment's thought ought to tell us this assumption is flawed. In fact, the average Pole has much in common with the average Briton, not least the shared economic disenfranchisement that capitalism implies – and each has more in common with the other than with their own ethnic elite, in so far as these elites share the same ethnicity at all. But the ploy works, and this is why, though much-maligned, Nationalism in the narrow ethnic sense remains a useful tool for democracy in keeping the public virally dumb. (See my essay: Democracy Keeps Us Dumb).

Now and again, contradictions in the capitalist system emerge and become apparent (problems such as crime, poverty, homelessness, mad mullahs, and so on) and the usual pattern is for some populist party to emerge to assuage public discontent, normally via the use of scapegoats. At the moment, it's UKIP that fulfils this function, but it could be any set of con artists. In fact, it does not specially matter whether the distraction vehicle is putatively 'left-wing' or 'right-wing' or 'far-Right', or whatever. These designations are made-up anyway. The only criterion for the scam is that it should work in keeping the public stupefied, the most effective method being to reveal part of the truth in language that reflects whatever are the current, frenzied bigotries and prejudices, but without actually explaining anything. The aim is to co-opt the more critical but uncommitted in society to a harmless controlled opposition movement, while the real opposition is left with the 'weirdos' – i.e. the embittered, lonely, fanatical or hyper-critical, people who tend not to be very attractive or plausible anyway – even though they might be right – and so can be safely ignored. Mr. & Mrs. Dumb White Briton are happy because they get their consumer lifestyle and their kicks bashing gypsies, 'radical Muslims', PC-obsessed primary school teachers wearing sandals, man-hating feminists, homosexuals, or EU bureaucrats – or whichever is this month's Most Hated Group. Meanwhile, the real problems continue: among which are the economic inequality that threatens our civilisation but is never talked about and that is becoming worse. But our concern here is with the

---

[26] First published on 18th. July 2014 at http://www.johnlonden.com

non-white demographic column in Britain, that continues to expand at a pace, doing the work of Jewish capitalists, safe in the knowledge that the tried and trusted scapegoats are on hand, like Guy Fawkes dummies, for burning as and when needed. This has been going on now for at least 45 years, since the Birmingham speech of Enoch Powell. Indeed, it was Powell who, in that epic self-immolation, inaugurated the 'rinse and dry' tendency that has become the hallmark of the British right-wing. When Marx, borrowing from Hegel, postulated in The Eighteenth Brumaire of Louis Napoleon that history repeats itself, first as tragedy, then as farce, he was, if anything, understating the tendency. In fact, one explanation for the failure of the far-Right in Britain and elsewhere in Europe and North America, is that they represent ideas that are simply out-of-date, in no small part due to the single major event that defined Powell and his generation politically.

One thing that is often missed about the Second World War is that it sounded the real death knell for traditional Westphalian Nationalism. Before 1945, Nationalism was a major and significant philosophy in the West, with the power to move armies. Following the defeat of the German Third Reich, Nationalism in Britain, and other Western countries, slowly became a marginalised current that mainstream politicians would learn to pay lip-service to while pursuing a more internationalist outlook. Nationalism, as framed by the concept of Westphalia sovereignty established in the 17th. century, had become less useful in explaining a world in which the interests of capital demanded co-operation and synergies between competing national interests. But the space this left for what might have been a legitimate well-spring of popular working class consciousness against globalism became an unfilled void, which turned into a problem for the Establishment when mass non-white immigration began in the 1950s. In time the void was filled, but not by the working class movement that could have stopped the globalist attack on Britain, but instead by the so-called far-Right. This was in essence a reaction to the putative Cold War between Jewish neo-liberal state capitalism (the free market West) and Jewish Bolshevik state capitalism (the 'communist' East). Each type of capitalism – each Jewish political tribe – needed the certainty of an identifiable enemy, even if fictitious. To simplify: in Britain, as in the rest of the West, the Zionists captured power and influenced the direction of the country, while the far-Right, putatively anti-Zionist, filled the void left by the absence of anti-globalist opposition and in doing so borrowed and co-opted the symbols, token narratives and mythology of Westphalian Nationalism. This might be an indicator of the times, or it might be indicative of intellectual weakness, or it might even suggest that the putatively anti-Zionist far-Right has in fact been a tool of Zionist interests all along. We know that the Left, which might have provided the source for a genuine anti-globalist, White Racial Nationalist movement, was captured by Jewish interests. This factor is often-overlooked by Nationalists and far-Right types, who affect an aversion towards the Left. The aversion is misplaced and damaging, not to mention puzzling. It is the Jewish Bolsheviks who corrupted Marxism and socialism and evacuated it of meaning, twisting it against the West and the White Race.

Parallel to the rise of a so-called far-Right, and to an extent convergent with it, was the emergence of an underground neo-Nazi sub-culture. The far-Right rested its case to the British people on an appeal to the 'Old', pre-War Nationalism, attempting to link this with a case against mass immigration. The far-Right was not necessarily racial as such. Rather, it was, in the classic Tory sense, against immigration of any sort (or most sorts) and against any foreign intrusion on Britain, and in that sense, it could be said to have been indirectly racial – and it certainly often relied on racialist imagery and propaganda. We can see that due to its reliance on the out-dated predicate of pre-War Nationalism, and its lack of connection with the economic interests of working people – or indeed, even their racial interests – the far-Right could not appeal significantly beyond a small base of committed supporters, the type of people who felt, and still feel, a nostalgic or emotional attachment to the pre-War Nationalism of Britain as an insular country. The geopolitical, social, financial and economic realities of mass immigration, free markets and globalisation have rendered that viewpoint archaic and irrelevant. Against that background, the gradual marginalisation and failure of the far-Right over several decades is explicable. The result of this sad state of affairs was that the two groups of fellow travellers, the far-Right and neo-Nazis, became more closely associated with each other, identifying together as 'Nationalists' incestuously, finding solace in their shared exclusion from the mainstream politic, and each attracting the type of people who are themselves excluded in different ways, thus reinforcing this sense of exclusion. This is what gave rise to the pathological secrecy and exclusivity of what has become known as political 'Nationalism', and it is that which I will now discuss.

We can see in hindsight that the political narrative of the far-Right during the 20th. century was really a narrative formulated by British Zionists – the enemies were 'Reds' and 'socialist', reflecting Cold War paranoia and second-hand ideas about socialism and Marxism; there were 'spies' and 'infiltrators' everywhere; and, the Jews controlled everything and were to blame. The latter, of course, was to some extent true, but when used to turn the Jews into scapegoats, it was not helpful and only served the Jewish interest of appearing to be victimised by whites. Rather than live up to their name and reach out across the political spectrum with the aim of becoming a genuinely National movement, these co-called 'Nationalists' turned in on themselves and developed into a cult, obsessed with secrecy and the dangers of infiltration, inward-looking, paranoid and suspicious of new faces. These attributes have, time and again, been used against Nationalism and undermined its public presentation in the Jewish media.

When we look across the North Atlantic and recall the fiasco of Leith, we can see that the public and visible failure of the PLE concept in North Dakota was not just down to the mistakes of individuals. It had deeper roots in pathologies among North American White Nationalists that are comparable to those that afflict British Nationalists. The Leith activists were steeped in the neo-Nazi Kuhnite fanaticism that has been a feature of American White Nationalism since the Second World War – i.e. paramilitary uniforms, Hitler-worship, neo-Nazi cultism, Teutonic symbolism, MidWest American feeling for Germanic ethnicity, etc.. But Leith was also the natural and inevitable reaction of a committed sub-culture to its targeted, organised suppression and marginalisation at the hands of a hostile (Jewish) media. If people are silenced, ridiculed and poked like bears in a cage, then at some point, if they are strong, rather than cower they will turn on their oppressor in anger and defiance. That was what Leith really was about. These people weren't tools of the media. They were heroes in a useless Quixotic sense who, having been pushed too far, felt the need to declare their allegiance to a disruptive, revolutionary creed in defiance of their oppressors. It was what the Left and Jews wanted, but it was also what Cobb and his followers wanted. It was a mental release. What happened next to Cobb is a disturbing example of how an authoritarian system can manipulate dissenters psychologically into turning and becoming unwilling tools of the system. A kind of self-negation is a requirement for anyone who appears in the Jewish media and Cobb was required to appear at the confessional and cleanse himself of anti-liberal sinning. Without this, he might have thought that he could not be given a fair hearing.

Something similar to Leith has also been seen in the UK, especially since the rise of the New (post-Tyndall) BNP. Only, here due to the lack of a First Amendment, and due to the organised and institutionalised repression and suffocation of Nationalism and denial of access to the media, British Nationalist 'Leithianism' has taken on a much more twisted, and if anything, more invidious form. The strange ubiquity of reality TV in British culture also accounts for some of the embarrassment. We've had Collett (RE:Brand and Young, Nazi and Proud), I think there was also a documentary on BNP wives (I forget the name of it, not that it matters much), and various other media vehicles of different sorts, in which far-Right idiots posing as Nationalists draw attention to themselves in the manner of narcissistic Jews. This all really started in the late 1970s, when the media began its campaign against anything remotely resembling Racial Nationalism, using documentaries as a political tool. There was, for instance, the 1978 World In Action documentary, The Nazi Party, a hysterical piece that took advantage of the far-Right/neo-Nazi confluence to monsterise the National Front and discredit it as an electoral force at a time of genuine popularity, and also by implication, to warn off anyone else who dared to question or challenge mixed-racialism. In the paranoid climate of the 1970s, the National Front was perfect copy for sinister scare stories about police informants, neo-Nazi plots and so on, and this fed the egos of those involved in what remained an archaic pre-War style of 'Nationalism'. But it wasn't just ego. That would be too simple and would not serve as a satisfactory explanation, especially when we consider how thoroughly ideological Nationalism became during the 1970s, with the involvement of figures like Tyndall, who had come out of the neo-Kuhnite Greater Britain Movement. For Tyndall, his beliefs were akin to a religion, yet in order to popularise the National Front during the 1970s, he had to pursue a strategy that downplayed his own ideological commitment. We should consider here the basic psychological features of such a person: the contradictory urges at work, especially when he is placed in the position that he is 'against' the society and is some kind of specter hiding threateningly in the shadows. There is perhaps a degree of frustration, a need for mental release, a need to lay bare, to expose oneself – a kind of implicit narcissism that develops over time and ultimately consumes the personality, so that what begins as a negation of liberal society and its financial prostitution, flattery, manipulation and control becomes an accommodation with it and thus a self-negation, a kind of confessional of anti-liberal sinning. I would argue that Leith, and other neo-Leithian fiascos on both sides of the Atlantic, are simply the logical extension of a masochistic media culture in Nationalism that involves a need to parade one's own negation. It includes the BNP and its ridiculous, amateur media stunts that are still ongoing. People who feel guilty about something often find a way to parade their guilt, often unconsciously. Cobb, Collett, the BNP wives, lived in a society in which they were constantly attacked and made to feel guilt in all kinds of explicit and implicit ways. To bend at the altar of the Jewish media is a kind of cleansing mea culpa.

There is also perhaps a more circumstantial explanation for Nationalist attachment to the Jewish media. Among all politicians and indeed celebrity types, there is a reliance placed on media that is clearly materialist and opportunist and this extends into the mainstream. It's not that hard to imagine Nigel Farage or some other high-profile UKIP leader appearing on Big Brother or some other mindless TV distraction. These people are part of the media culture. They have bought into it, and their problem is that they are dependent on it. No doubt one of the reasons why George Galloway appeared on Big Brother was 'political', in that he wanted to attract attention to himself and his radical causes, but part of the reason for Galloway's success is also that he has good basic business savvy and a keen sense for how politics can be turned into a commercial opportunity. Or to put it bluntly: he did it for the money, capitalising on his profile as a radical politician. If we are honest, and perhaps if Galloway were really honest about this, the reason for his media profile isn't so much that people agree with him, or even understand him, but rather due to his personality and the fact that he can be entertaining. Although he is not physically-attractive, he has nevertheless found a way to be telegenic: that is to say, he appeals to his audience through the sheer force of his personality. Of course, what also helps is that his far Left views are given a free pass because they are seen as non-threatening by the Jewish media. Another example of this kind of media phenomenon would be Russell Brand, who in a strange way manages to make unattractiveness attractive and appealing. However Brand's approach is typical liberal self-negation, using a humorous persona that in fact implies childishness and immaturity – and is in a sense a parody of Brand himself – to attack a fictitious received reality.

Nationalists – i.e. what the far-Right like to call themselves – do not have a strong 'Galloway' figure among their number, and this does partly account for why the far-Right has been unable to generate serious appeal on the media's terms outside its own narrow philosophical premise, with the consequence that what is seen as 'Nationalism' is – quite rightly – something vaguely connected in the public's mind with Little Englanders. However, Nationalism does have its own 'Russell Brands' a plenty – people like Griffin or Cobb or Collett – clowns, in other words, who have tried to become sympathetic 'personalities' fawning at the Jewish media alter, confessing their anti-liberal sinning, but who have adopted approaches that betray the same style as Brand – outraged self-negation. They have failed where Brand has 'succeeded' because whereas Brand understands the need to connect what he says to the lives of real people, the 'Nationalist' ferment that Griffin, Cobb et al have emerged from has no appeal beyond a very narrow section of the population.

That said, those who consider themselves 'moderate' and 'sensible' and sneer at Cobb and his Leith venture should ask why they might support Farage and his clown-like antics in the European Parliament. When Farage makes his rare appearances in the chamber to fulminate against some unpopular bureaucrat, or when UKIP members turn up in colourful suits or fancy dress to make a mockery of the institution they were elected to, these juvenile antics are only one step from Leith (and indeed, not dissimilar from doing a Galloway and playing the pussy cat on Big Brother). It's a show, a circus, and it is made to appear like the only game in town. That's because it is all in the service of Jews. But it isn't the only alternative. There is another way, that requires an end to this narcissism, and to an extent an end to the suits and ties and pseudo-respectability as well. The alternative I refer to is not for everyone.  It requires the application of patience and years, perhaps many decades, of quiet work and waiting.  It means that we adopt a community-building strategy based on the precepts of PLE.  Not Leith, which was a corruption of PLE, but real PLE and its UK application, White Independent Nation (WIN).  In order to be successful, PLEs/WIN will need to look outwards from Nationalism into the wider white community, and find ways of attracting the best of the whites around us.  This requires that we develop suitable constructs that reflect the wishful abstractions of ordinary whites back at them.  Whether it is the need for community in the post-industrial North or the wish for a restoration of pastoral civic life in rural areas of the south and west, or whatever.  Direct racial messaging will not work in winning whites into a singular tribal community, nor will the traditional Nationalist appeal to self-abnegation.  Rather, what works will be whatever it is outside the Jewish mainstream culture that holds appeal to ordinary people.

Due to the political environment we are working in and its hostility to Nationalism, any community-building group is vulnerable to infiltration, exposure and sabotage.  For that reason, there is a need for secrecy and discretion, and one question for PLE/WIN organisers is how to deal with the Leithian, narcissistic culture that has grown within Nationalism as a reflection of modern life and that seeks attention and self-negating worship at the alter of media victimhood.  I would argue that this is a culture that has infected a significant part of Nationalism – not just the recognisable names, but ordinary activists as well, some of whom have created blogs to launch personal attacks on fellow Nationalists and have engaged in similar disruptive activities that are essentially a projection of their own insecurity and narcissism.  The fear is that some of these people might compromise PLEs through their need to make public proclamations or draw attention to themselves in some way.  Many of these elements will display other character flaws – for instance, a tendency for violence – or be practising homosexuals, or whatever.  There are also the kosher nationalists to consider.  Such people can be useful in that they may present well publicly and will be useful, provided they can understand the need for discipline and to exercise care with anything that brings us into contact with the media, and preferably to avoid such avenues altogether.

One method of addressing the problem is accommodation, a suggestion made in H. Michael Barrett's The PLE Prospectus.  The idea is that far from rejecting the 'undesirables', we should welcome them as they are, after all, race-conscious and carry the necessary white genes.  As such, they need not be part of the controlling group or even be located in the specific target area of the community, but can be part of the general 'Uncontrolled White Nationalist Culture' that emerges from the PLE or white conscious community, providing a ballast for the white community in whatever region of the country is selected.  Such people can also serve as a valuable 'internal opposition', giving the white community credibility as something diverse, and as such, they may be vital in presenting the new emerging white conscious culture as inclusive.  The alternative to inclusiveness is to reject altogether Nationalists as such, and involve only those who are fully committed to the racial cause per se and who do not display any of the dysfunctional personal characteristics that have plagued Nationalist efforts in the past.  This does have the advantage that any ensuing project will be more focused and without the risk of sabotage or exposure, and the group can always be widened at a later stage to embrace peripheral involvement, perhaps a few years down the line, once the necessary foundations are in place. However, this approach does carry the risk that any such group will wind up as nothing more than an exclusivist sect that does nothing.

Another possible solution might be found in the example of the Northwest Front. This is a National Socialist organisation, but as far as I can see, it is simply a website; however; there is some merit in the strategy adopted by its founder, the author Harold Covington. The idea seems to be to push for a general white racial community in the north-west of the Continental United States, without any selectivity or exclusivity – provided that it is a white migration. The ultimate aim is for the establishment of a Northwest Republic, which it is believed will come about organically as race-conscious whites concentrate in that region. Something similar to this might be possible in the UK or Continental Europe, and a project of this kind could be pursued either in combination with or separately to projects like WIN. The Northwest Front is perhaps marred by the domination of one personality – Covington – who, though brilliant, is also unpopular with many White Nationalists. That's just further illustration of the problem with the 'leader principle', in that it will always be the case that people will associate the cause with the personality, and muddle the two, and there will always be some that don't like the leader, while others will worship or valorise the leader unmeritoriously or unjustly. A preoccupation with selecting leaders is perhaps also an explanation for why the Nationalist movement has suffered so much fragmentation. Nevertheless, I think there is some merit in the general concept of the Northwest Front in that a racial community could be formed by migration to a particular region of the UK, and this could be complementary to other efforts. It would require general fronts to encourage migration to the selected region, in the hope that demographics would take care of the rest. This is how I would separate WIN from the general concept of a racial community. The latter is organic, while WIN is exclusive. A racial community (a Northwest Republic) is to an extent unplanned and dependent purely on evolving demographics whereas WIN is a concerted, planned strategy for taking over a community and re-modelling it as a white conscious community. The strength of the Northwest Front movement is its conceptual nature – no secrecy is necessary, as discovery does not stop it and there is no organisation or structure. PLEs, on the other hand, are at present vulnerable to discovery and need secrecy. It is not inconceivable that we could work for a 'North East Republic' in the UK, in conjunction with more disciplined PLE projects for white conscious communities. The PLE would be more advanced and specific to a local community, whereas the North East Republic project would cover a wider geographic area and simply encourage general migration of whites to the selected region. I mention all this because a North East Republic could be the answer to the 'Leith Dilemma', as it might bring the 'undesirable' Nationalists to the fold without compromising WIN or similar projects. It's a thought, but the idea needs more work no doubt.

These are not easy questions and our position right now is unenviable. It feels as if we are stood at a cross-roads, one road towards the same old solutions, the old pre-War style of Nationalism and electoral failure, which sadly many Nationalists still cling to. The other route towards a different strategy of building Nationalism from the ground-up, through the people, but with all the perils in the initial stages of popular involvement in a hostile and repressive political environment. What we do know is that things have to change within Nationalism. We do not have much time; the non-white column is growing in this country. The narcissism of the pre-War style Nationalism and its media obsessions are not wanted or needed, but nor are its two opposites, one of which is hiding and becoming an unknown, invisible, sterile sect of 'exclusive' members who are ideologically and socially pure but ineffective; the other is the opposite of narcissism, or its counterpart to be more precise: the 'inverted narcissism' of dependency on guru-type leaders that is still a feature of the far-Right, even after 70 years. Whether your preferred guru mystic Wise One is Nigel Farage or Craig Cobb, John Tyndall or indeed Enoch Powell, I would say to you that it is time to critically re-assess these predecessor and incumbent leaders and place them in their proper light: as ordinary human beings, with strengths and flaws. And it is for each of us, individually, and combining collectively, to take back Nationalism. If we continue to devote a large part of our psychic energy to voting and the electoral machine, escapist diversions such as the EDL and media stunts like Leith, we will continue to fail. It's one reason why we face two battles: taking back this country or inventing a new one is only half of it. The first battle is to establish Nationalism as what it should have been all along – a revolutionary struggle against the Jewish owning class, rather than some vague bunch of little Englanders talking the received language of Zion. That means we Racial Nationalists need to separate ourselves from the far-Right and make it clear that right-wingers no longer hold an exclusive ideological or philosophical franchise on Nationalist thought. Nationalism does not belong to the Left or the Right. It is its own ideology and philosophy, revolutionary in intent, and for all white people. Most white people may not accept this, or us, at the moment, but whether they accept us or not, we accept them.

**4.5.**

### Down with Britain![27]

In a previous essay ('The Lessons of Leith'), I outlined how political Nationalism in Europe and North America remains stuck in a kind of First Wave, in which the preoccupation is with traditional-style loyalty to old nation-states that are now all-but defunct for racial purposes. The First Wave Nationalists cannot face reality. They still cling to the ideas and concepts of a diplomatic system that originated with the Peace of Westphalia of 1648 and that ended for all practical purposes in 1945 at the conclusion of the Second World War. What was needed in the 1950s was a working class race-conscious Nationalist movement, grounded in socialism and labourism, and opposed to globalism. Instead, what filled the void was the legacy concept of Westphalian sovereigntism, which staggered on in the shape of various far-Right movements, in defiance of popular views and attitudes and economic and geopolitical reality. The far-Right assumed an exclusive franchise on Nationalism, and introduced a Zionist perspective and various Cold War-era pathologies. The result has been 70 years of stagnation and false victories, to the detriment of the White Race and Western civilisation as a whole. Rather than becoming the popular movement it should have been and had every right to be, Nationalism became associated with various marginal ideas that have no relationship to the interests of ordinary people.

The UKIP of Farage is just the latest unwelcome reincarnation of First Wave Nationalism, with its naive, xenophobic pre-War conceptualisation of 'Britain' as a rugged, independent nation-state. Not that UKIP is actually a Nationalist party. It just pretends to be when it suits. In fact, it can be observed that, in reality, UKIP is – by its own admission – a neo-thatcherite free trade party. The apparent paradox is unravelled when one examines closely who UKIP really are and who they represent. UKIP is a vehicle for a revived Tory Right, with pro-capitalist, pro-business, pro-immigration, pro-globalist, pro-Zionist policies. UKIP's co-option of First Wave Nationalists is a familiar tactic designed to suffocate real race conscious opposition. Its commitment to anything remotely nationalistic is superficial; its policy of 'no more uncontrolled immigration' is simply code for more immigration; its policy of free trade is code for more foreign intrusion into Britain, including cheap, non-unionised labour; and, its policy of withdrawal from the EU is a deceit: UKIP know that, even after ratification of secession in a referendum, it would take years for the UK to formally leave the EU, if not decades, and the single market would in any case remain a powerful and decisive influence for British exporters. UKIP is an example of what George Orwell referred to as 'wind given solidity'.

When people ask me whether I am 'FOR' or 'AGAINST' UK membership of the EU, my response is normally something like this: DON'T CARE. It's an argument for the elites (i.e. Jews and capitalists). I have no interest in their interests. I am only interested in my interests and those of my Race. If a sufficient conscious white majority were ever to arise in this country, then I have no doubt that the decision would be whatever is in the interests of the Race, that being all European people with whom we share kinship. The rest of it is just propaganda. In? Out? I'll toss a

---

[27] First published on 20th. July 2014 at http://www.johnlonden.com

coin if you like. Won't make any difference to immigration. Not one iota of difference. I'm voting for myself, not your media fictions.

In the real world, if the White Race is to survive then we have to abandon our altruistic concern for the racial and economic interests of others. It's nice that ordinary whites are concerned for the economic interests of Jews, but we have no stake in whether the UK is 'in' or 'out' of the EU. We must start acting as a Race again, this time under the auspices of a Second Wave Nationalism: not based on parties, demagogues and personalities, but on nothing more nor less than racial unity and integrity, the Race as Nation. What we need is a Race Conscious Revolution. This Revolution will not be a single incident. It will not be traceable to any particular group of people, nor to a particular time or place. It will not be founded on any specific ideology or set of texts. It will be a gradual, imperceptible shift in consciousness, maybe over decades, even centuries. Much like the agricultural revolution, or the industrial revolution, it will mark the movement of European civilisation away from Jewish supremacy towards true white sovereignty.

I was born in Britain. I was brought up in Britain. I have spent the majority of my life here. I am 'British', however I no longer accept that I belong to this made-up collective identity, 'British', that has been gradually deracinated into a set of meaningless buzz words and catchphrases. So you can stick your Union Jack. To me, it is fit to be burnt on the streets. And you can keep your monarchy, common law, Magna Carta and all the other accoutrements of being 'British'. I reject them. Not out of self-hatred or hatred for Britain as a place, but from a realisation of what Britain is racially and geopolitically. It has become clear to me that Britain is controlled by Jews and collaborators with Jews – specifically, Zionists. 'British values' mean Jewish values. 'British interests' mean Jewish interests. Even our opposition groups are under the control of Zionists and pursue Zionist agendas: some Nationalists have, in effect, become ultra-Zionists in that they believe in removal of Jews to Israel. I, too, want the removal of Jews from my society, but I have no concern as to what happens to them after that or where they go. That is their concern. As long as Jews exist, the British state, in common with all Western nation-states, is a treason state and will remain in the control of a racial group other than whites, to the detriment of whites. It does not deserve the loyalty of race-conscious whites. But the solution is not to eradicate Jews or Judaism, nor to interfere in what happens in Palestine. The solution is a New Europe: racial separation, once and for all. That is why I say: Down with Britain! Hail the White Republic! Long Live The White Race!

**4.6.**

### The Necessity of White Resistance[28]

The existing political system relies on the passivity of the masses. People vote for leaders and parties largely based on populist scaremongering and personality considerations. There is no credible racial nationalist alternative to speak of. The two options on offer – the BNP and the National Front – are both dominated by the kosher Right, and despite the rhetoric of the anti-Griffinites, there is little to choose between them. The answer is that we need to stop voting for these traitors and start voting for ourselves, and the first step is self-organisation. White Independent Nation (WIN) is an important development in that direction, and anyone reading this who is not already a member should put in an application to join WIN.

However, not everyone can transit to a white conscious community immediately, and there is also a need to mount a planned and concerted street-by-street resistance against what is, in reality, a foreign occupation. A civil resistance strategy encourages whites to start thinking and acting as a racial bloc and to channel their frustration and anger in a positive and lawful direction. Therefore, in addition to white conscious community-building, we also need to start organising Local Resistance Zones [credit to 'Charlie Wax' on Stormfront for this idea] in the areas where we already live. This applies whether or not they have been intruded by large numbers of non-whites, because the alien anti-white invasion is cultural and intellectual as much as demographic.

In my view, what is required is a White Resistance Movement – which will be lawful and non-violent, and leaderless, and will provide a focal point and resource for people looking to organise on a cell basis in their local areas. Resistance activities could certainly include infiltration of local politics – for instance, and to be fair to UKIP, it appears some of their councillors have campaigned against mosques; many Labour people are natural 'nationalists' and against immigration but dare not speak out; Conservatives tend to be anti-immigration but likewise have been silenced, but infiltration is only a small part of what we can do within the law. The point as I see it is that Nationalism needs to enter a new phase.

We need a Second Wave that rejects conventional party politics, as such, and focuses on concrete work to challenge and undermine the system in different ways. I know it means a lot of work and there will be set-backs, humiliations and disappointments, but if we keep pinning our hopes on these leaders – be it Adam Walker or Nigel Farage – then we will keep being disappointed. All we are doing at the moment is suffering a slow, polonged racial death. Passivity needs to be replaced by activity.

---

[28] First published on 23rd. July 2014 at http://www.johnlonden.com

## 4.7.

### The Mechanics of Virtual Resistance[29]

I think it is in the nature of things for human beings to try and simplify a subtle and complicated idea in an attempt to understand it. This stems in part from an innate pragmatism. It's not so much an exercise in understanding as a need for practical brevity, because true understanding is costly in terms of time and effort. This is probably just the way our minds have evolved. In any political debate or discussion, whether online or off-line, it is a signal achievement if the two sides have even understood each other, let alone progressed to the stage of 'winning' or 'losing'. In a genuine debate, 'winning' is a false objective anyway. Unfortunately, too often discussion turns into an exchange of didactic rhetoric rather than a process of enlightenment in which one side learns from the other. We also have an innate tendency to relate what is being communicated exoterically to our own experience and the received knowledge available to us, and interpret it accordingly. This is understandable, but the process too often becomes stale and exhibits a repetitive cycle of rejecting ideas because they have been 'tried before' or 'won't work' for various reasons that appear to us cogent, but are in fact just excuses for inertia and non-action. It is this fatalistic exotericism that encourages the process of simplification, in that a new idea, irrespective of its novelty or usefulness, is reduced to a series of objections based on a limited comprehension of the idea itself. Any practical action that emerges at the other end is often a twisted or bastardised version of the original author's intentions and is often designed in such a way as to kill the idea before it can be implemented in a way that might do it justice. An example of the fatalistic simplification tendency is the reception in the Nationalist community of PLE. When serious online discussion began a few years ago about the PLE concept, the idea was often framed in terms of objections that, more often than not, represented simplifications of the concept itself. We still have some Nationalists who believe that PLEs are about white people running away and hiding somewhere and that the existence of significant PLE communities will just make it easier for state forces to sweep-up dissident whites. These 'objections' are just misrepresentations. They reflect what I would contend is a normal human tendency towards simplification and an aversion from understanding complexity.

Radical ideas are also a threat to a movement that is innately conservative and wedded to society's social and economic precepts. White Nationalists are perhaps the last people who would think of engaging in activity that threatens the existing society in any way. Not that PLE is itself a radical idea. It is in fact a deeply conservative and reactionary response specifically tailored to the context of the North American political scene, yet to many Nationalists the notion of re-engineering society as a race-conscious community seems radical. It may not be obvious to the average onlooker, but in reality White Nationalism and its most prominent sub-culture, neo-Nazism, is essentially a style trip and a form of escapism for the alienated and disaffected: mostly young men, who will often 'grow out' of it after a few months or years. It is not a serious political movement. Older White Nationalists know party politics is pointless as the existing system does not even begin to address the need for a racial community, and they are also often the type of people

---

[29] First published on 28th. July 2014 at http://www.johnlonden.com

who are not good at getting things done in the real world and fail to understand the complex personal dynamics involved in doing anything of practical value. So they find refuge in online forums and social media – their own little isolated corner, away from reality – where, in classic reactionary style, they let off steam against the Establishment, thus assisting in the continuation of the very society they affect to despise. In truth, their position is often bigoted or misanthropic more than racial, but it is the innate trait of conservatism – which is in fact liberalism by another name – that has been the central weak point in the First Wave Nationalism. These Nationalists take exception at being labelled Zionists by default (see my previous essay: 'The Far-Right: conning us since 1945'), yet their entire political lives have been spent propping up the system implicitly, obeying its rules and parroting its language, and in a paranoiac Cold War twist, denouncing all and sundry as spies, infiltrators and traitors. It is a movement turned-in on itself.

The truth that they cannot face (and to be fair, what the public seems oblivious to as well) is that this struggle has never been about flags, elections and parliamentary seats. This is about Race. The conformist, slave-like rhetoric of the far-Right does not threaten the Establishment. To the contrary, it is an expression of the Establishment's own values, albeit in more radical form. Had Nationalism as a movement paid greater attention to its origins on the Left and worked to become an expression of popular consciousness, rather than a mouthpiece for the Establishment, then things might have been different, and the West might still be white, or at least, less non-white. But we are where we are. Those of us who are part of the Second Wave, who reject parties, institutions, demagogues and leader cults, need to assess our situation pragmatically. What would threaten the Establishment and this liberal society is the formation of a genuine racial community: a solid race-conscious bloc that stands against mixed-racialism. That is what the Establishment fear. For the National Front and Griffin's BNP, their chosen method of building race-consciousness – parroting 'friendly' liberal jargon and standing in elections – did not work. It can't. The Front Nationale of France demonstrates this. The FN is the high watermark of the 'normalisation' strategy, having taken advantage of certain historical and geopolitical factors peculiar to France to gain local, regional and national prominence in that country – yet Le Pen's Party remains powerless to halt non-white mass immigration and the relentless and ongoing mongrelisation of France. Even if they took power, the eradication of white France would continue apace. That said, there is also much to be said for the FN model. Although it has failed in its real objectives, there are still some positive aspects to it which, if applied correctly, in a way that fits the local social and political environment, could form the basis of a white nationalist resurgence in Europe. Ironically, it was Griffin himself who was closest to the truth when, on the night of the May 2010 general election, he talked about the development of the BNP into a cultural association. What is needed is a Second Wave Nationalism that sets out to build a popular race-conscious opposition from the ground-up.

In that respect, I have written already about the Necessity of White Resistance. The term 'Resistance' is, admittedly, problematic in that it carries with it connotations of violence and illegality. This misunderstanding is part of a special hermeneutical problem that plagues any liberal society. Political language is given a distorted, positivistic meaning that serves the interests of the liberal elite. In this case, resistance is rightly identified for what it is: the overthrow of the present civil order –

but its proposed methods are misrepresented so as to narrow the range of perceivable options available to those who might legitimately oppose the way things are and seek a revamp. White Resistance need not be violent, and indeed should not be; it need not be confrontational either, and at least initially does not have to be; and there is no suggestion that White Resistance should be anything other than lawful. Used in the broadest sense of resisting and repelling non-white invasion, using non-violent means, what we are referring to here is a form of civil resistance. Among white conscious individuals and groups, that means the creation of embryonic Local Resistance Zones ('LRZs') (the idea of Charlie Wax), which will over time repel and evacuate non-whites from local communities using lawful methods, and – it is hoped – will pave the way for white conscious communities or significant white migration to other suitable areas. The inherent difficulty we face is establishing momentum, which in turns depends on trust and security among those involved. The solution to that difficulty is, I hope, now slowly taking shape in the form of a White Resistance Movement, initially a discussion and planning group on Facebook. The idea behind the Facebook group is to provide an online presence for a Central Resistance that will be a focal point for 'resistance education' and the exchange of ideas among LRZ groups. Some people will have reservations about using Facebook for this purpose, but the way I see it is that we must use the tools at our disposal, and the reality is that Facebook – a free gift provided to us by the Establishment – is an ideal mechanism for bringing together a large number of people on an anonymous basis to discuss political action. That said, we shouldn't look the gift horse in the mouth: Facebook has its own risks and limitations, which is why the scope of the central White Resistance, in whatever web or social media format it takes, will be deliberately narrow. It will not be an organisation or structure in its own right, it will not have leaders and, given that everyone who participates will be joining anonymously under an alias, it will not have a formal membership list.

Anyone who broadly shares our aims is welcome to join. The Resistance will be lawful and non-violent. The explicit aim will be to form Local Resistance Zones that are hostile to non-whites, so the actual activity of resistance will happen locally, under the initiative of local activists in each area. This decentralised structure is designed to reduce risk, but obviously in any endeavour of this kind there will be infiltrators. In my view, that in itself is not a valid objection to participation. Infiltration can't be prevented entirely. The issue is managing the risk, not preventing it – any attempt to do the latter would kill all initiative. It is also the case that some of us can expect to come to the attention of the authorities, and we may face arrest and detention. It is a choice that each of us must make. I believe the choice is between activity and passivity. Sometimes passivity is the smart option, but Nationalism has dwelt in passivity for too long now, relying on leaders as our surrogates to take the risks that we dare not undertake ourselves. The reality is that if we keep going down this road of worrying about what people might see online, or worrying about coming to the attention of the authorities, we are never going to organise anything and we may as well sit at home. These are in any case exaggerated fears based on a kind of Walter Mittyism. The risks are real, and the consequences are real, but these things need to be kept in proportion. The Resistance, remember, will be explicitly lawful and non-violent. The risks of activity also need to be weighed against the risks of continuing passivity. Some people do firmly fall into the category of passivity in that they are happy to vent online or attend pointless marches or meetings, but when it comes to the complex process of thought, discussion, planning and collaboration necessary to get real things done, they back down, and in the process, implicitly bow down to authority. This is not the road to change. It's the road to slavery. We need individuals with the iron will and determination to stand up to authority, and with an understanding of how to get things done – which requires pragmatism, intelligence, tenacity and courage in equal measure. The process begins with a meditative stage of thought, discussion and planning, and that is why we need this online 'talking shop', a space where we can work out a strategy. I also hope the Facebook Group – or something like it elsewhere on the web – will become a permanent space online giving people the opportunity to share ideas. The accent however must be on local organisation. This will not be a traditional political activist group which expects its members to travel across the country to keynote events. This will, rather, be a network of independent, decentralised resistance groups that work covertly to change their local communities, at first in small, seemingly insignificant ways, but with gradual effectiveness and prominence. Admittedly, the organisational tensions are in contradiction: we cannot stay on the margins, meeting in front rooms and the backrooms of pubs, etc., but we also need to tread carefully and work covertly and quietly to organise against what is a hostile Establishment, but the overarching point is that we must leave behind our conformism and passivity and start to act, or we will be consigned to irrelevancy and racial death.

As the mechanics of virtual resistance for the White Race develop, whether in this form or others yet unanticipated and unseen, our strategies, means and methods must also evolve. Facebook creates an environment in which disparate white people can come together and collaborate using the relative protection of online pseudo-anonymity. This presages and forms a response and influences our strategy: the web is as much a terrain for geopolitical battle as the jungle was the terrain of the Viet Cong resisters. The Viet Cong defeated the Americans by taking advantage of the tools available to them: chiefly, the native environment, which they knew intimately, and which they used to hide and made their base to mount a vicious resistance against the Americans. In mounting our civil resistance, we must learn from this example and the successful and unsuccessful examples of other resistance groups, past and present. The web is a ready tool, available for our use. It's part of our native environment. It is not the be-all and end-all of the matter, because real resistance takes place on the ground, in the off-line world, and that is where we should our concentrate our efforts, but the web is the rallying point, for now, and our main communications tool and can be used to bring our message to a mass audience, in various guises: not just as a White Resistance, but also in the guise of alternative news media, and for the dissemination of new cultural and intellectual perspectives, and to promote pro-white propaganda. The advantage of the virtual resistance – that is to say, a resistance without a structure, 'space' or organisation, in other words, a phantom – is that there is no need for a hierarchy or the other accoutrements that make any such endeavour vulnerable to the state. Nationalists traditionally seem to be obsessed with hierarchy and often speak of it, but what we really need is 'direction'. We need a mass of race conscious whites, active under different civic and business fronts and brands, but with a definite mission. The last thing we need is leaders and structures and bank accounts, which are vulnerable to official intervention (arrests, detention and sequestration, etc.) and media vilification, making the whole organisation vulnerable. Hierarchy is, in any case, just a particular kind of structure that serves a purpose, and the important thing is the purpose and the eventual goal. We should not be averse to the idea of having a hierarchy and a 'leader' or a leadership of some kind if it serves the purpose well. The point is that in this instance, it won't. What we do need is direction. That's where the tools that social media offer can help us. They are not ideal, and may need to be re-considered, and – I hope – as we gain physical control of 'national spaces', the strategy and the micro-tactics will change and we will reform and upgrade our means and methods according to circumstances and the changing social and political climate. One thing is for certain: we need tools of activity, not passivity. The virtual Resistance is a means to an end, not the end in itself: we cannot stand still and we cannot continue hiding in the corner.

**4.8.**

### The New Four Words[30]

In April 2000, Nick Griffin spoke at a Texas conference of the American Friends of the BNP. During his speech, he referred to four saleable words that the BNP would use to persuade the British electorate of its message: Freedom, Democracy, Identity and Security. I call these 'Griffin's Four Words'.

Whatever the issues may have been with Griffin, I would like to propose that there was nothing fundamentally wrong with his idea. The problem was in the strategy. By adopting the political language of our opponents and attempting to 'liberalise' the BNP, Griffin positioned the argument firmly in enemy territory, using the enemy's propaganda and weaponry. No doubt the idea was to turn our opponent's own words against them – which is an understandable enough strategy, and in its own way clever – but the end result was to simply concretise multi-culturalism, not just in wider British society, but even within the far-Right itself.

My central contention is that any attempt Nationalists make to roll-back the existing mixed-racial culture is going to fail and is a waste of time. Griffin's Four Words were based on this mistaken predicate. It was and is an understandable position, especially at the time it was developed – I am not suggesting Griffin was stupid – but now more than ever we need to understand that this approach to politics doesn't and cannot work.

We need to adopt a different strategy that (in my view) involves rejecting leaders (but not leadership), democracy (but not democratic mechanisms when they suit us), elections (but not electoral ratification as a vehicle for affirming public consent), and political parties (but not as a vehicle for achieving reasoned and sound aims and objectives).

In my opinion, we cannot hope to win over the majority of whites, who are either lost to us ideologically or simply spineless. The goal, then, will be the preservation of the White Race in the form of a New Tribe, as suggested by White Independent Nation (WIN) - in whatever social, spiritual and geopolitical form future generations deem appropriate. Time will tell.

For now, I think our aim should be to re-connect white racial consciousness with white people. We can do that by encouraging community-based resistance and by making people aware of our message. To do this we must develop our own 'New Tribe' political language independently of the mainstream.

In response to Griffin's Four Words, I would propose The New Four Words, as follows. These emphasise the communal nature of what we are doing and the shift in our focus away from mainstream politics – elections, political parties, personalities, etc. – to building education, propaganda, community work and racial consciousness outside the mainstream.

---

[30] First published on 5th. August 2014 at http://www.johnlonden.com

## RACE
We believe in the permanency and sovereignty of the White Race.

## SOLIDARITY
We believe that all White People should and must stand together, irrespective of class, gender, nationality, ethnicity and other factors.

## COMMUNITY
We wish to live according to common values, which we share as a White Racial Community and that we seek to apply on a local level in white conscious communities.

## SAFETY
We believe that all White People have the right to live and work in areas that are safe for them, without intrusion from influences harmful to white racial consciousness or which might impede the propagation and flourishing of the White Race.

## 4.9.

### TIAWA: There Is A White Alternative[31]

Talk of a need for consensus is fashionable among mainstream politicians and the broader social and cultural elites, who, in order to effectively pursue their interests against the rest of society, need to think and act as a more or less coherent class with a broadly shared understanding of the world. In the 1980s, the Tory party under Margaret Thatcher, borrowing from a classical liberal thinker of the 19th. century, Herbert Spencer, used the term: There Is No Alternative – 'TINA' – to encapsulate the determination of the elite that there should be no serious consideration of policy alternatives outside of economic neo-liberalism. In 1992, a book by political scientist Francis Fukuyama, 'The End of History and the Last Man' (expending on a 1989 essay, 'The End of History?') argued that with the collapse of what was erroneously known as 'communism', liberal democracy had become the dominant and final system of political and social organisation for humanity.

The actuality of this consensus is a little more complicated. Even the elites are sometimes undermined by rebels and dissenters who stand for variations of the existing order. Meanwhile, those involved in marginal and fringe politics and who, ostensibly, stand for a New Order, seem to thrive on the opposite of consensus: what passes for Nationalism is riven by splits, sectarianism and internecine ideological and philosophical conflict. If the opposition cannot unite and get its act together, and if all that the people have by way of political 'choices' are the non-choices of a liberal consensus, with its mindless, decadent celebration of the 'Last Man' and zero-conscious culture, then apathy will begin to permeate through society and there will be a feeling of hopelessness about the political process. Many putatively anti-Establishment politicians and modern oppositional commentators have found ways to articulate this sense of apathy and lack of hope in a kind of 'knowing cynicism' that acknowledges the political system is morally and functionally bankrupt but seems to offer no genuine alternatives or solutions other than petulant outrage and name-calling. The dots are frequently joined, but the solutions, while sometimes hinted at, are never presented coherently or in a way that might encourage an activationist response that gives meaning to people's lives. Thus, instead of an environment of criticism and enlightenment, we have a climate of alienation in which ordinary people can only find expression and meaning in dead-end pursuits: TV-watching, football clubs, Sky Gods, self-gratification and sadism. Sometimes the apathy masquerades as action: the type of action that is actually just escapism, such as the futile and endless marching of the EDL or the pointless, circular party games of the far-Right and UKIP. We live in the era of passivity, whose slogan is the pounding, demoralising, drum-like mantra of every Leviathan and that reverberates down through history – TINA: There Is No Alternative. We are discouraged from looking outside TINA, and the forces at work for TINA-compliance are powerful in society, stretching from the halls of academia to local newspaper offices and into the workplace and the home, but if we are to have hope, then we must escape from the Lotus of repression and controlled opposition and begin to recognise our true role, not as the figurative Last Man, but as the Superman, at whose feet are the great open plains of both history and future, stretching out

---

[31] First published on 7th. August 2014 at http://www.johnlonden.com

infinitesimally and rendering utterly significant the TINA 'reality' and its restrictive demarcations of knowledge and consciousness.

A radical step-change is needed, and ironically, white-conscious people have to begin by emulating the masses around us. We have to leave Nationalism behind: lock, stock and barrel. Except in the very generic sense of white nationhood and racial unity, Nationalism as a movement is redundant, largely because of underlying social and technological changes that have created a global interdependency among nations and peoples and weakened the relevancy of the nation-state. The decline and fall of Nationalism was really marked by one single historical event, the end of the Second World War – the victory of internationalists over national-socialists – the rights and wrongs of which can be debated, but the impact of which was and remains undeniable. Nationalism as a political concept was already dead in 1945. In the mono-racial societies that existed prior to the War, the motive force of Nationalism was simple patriotism: that is to say, loyalty to Queen, flag and country. There was no particular need to emphasise the racial aspects – real Nationalism – since society was racially-homogeneous. Indeed, it was once the case that an appeal to simplistic patriotism – fake nationalism – could move armies, but after the War a more internationalist climate began to emerge that undermined the diplomatic, economic, and financial systems on which nation-states had rested for their legitimacy. Thus, the old John Bull-style patriotism began to lose its effectiveness in defending racial integrity. At the same time, any efforts to promote actual Nationalism – i.e. Racialism – which was and remains the real opposition to globalism and mixed-racialism, was successfully marginalised by the diabolical, dishonest propaganda of the Establishment and a complicit media.

As I have explained in previous essays (see, for instance, 'The Lessons of Leith'), Nationalism in the ossified sense of patriotic Revanchism has no social or political potency, and is in fact decades out-of-date. What ought to have happened, and what remains lamentable, is the absence of a 'far-Left Racial Nationalism', which should have emerged in the post-War period. The Left mysteriously turned to globalism instead. This opened the way for the dominance of the far-Right in Nationalism, in conjunction with the rather odd post-War reactionary sub-cultures of neo-Nazism and Hitlerism. The damning legacy of the Right is a failure to connect their watered-down type of Racial Nationalism, such as it was, to the everyday concerns of the white working class. Now the brand is toxic, not just due to its media-inspired demonised status and its intellectual and practical putrefaction, but also because the very essence of being a Nationalist (at least in the racial and nativist contexts) has become a by-word for inaction, passivity and leader worship, punctuated by sporadic escapism and the occasional reactionary diversion.

All whites – not just the race conscious but also the unconscious in wider society – need to re-discover self-directed political practices: that is, self-organisation and community activism. We have to develop an entirely new political identity with its own alternative language and sub-culture. In short, we must re-invent ourselves and build a genuine White Alternative. This Second Wave needs to return to the roots of what it means to be a nationalist, and in that sense, paradoxically, it must represent a kind of Anti-Nationalism or Post-Nationalism: a refutation of what has gone on before while embracing the authentic historical roots of Nationalism as an expression of the shared political consciousness of our people. In embarking on this difficult mission, right from the start we should acknowledge the need for an academic phase of thinking and ideas. An intellectual exercise should always precede planning, and thoughtful planning should always precede action. Some far-seeing 'Post-Nationalists' have already reached the action stage: White Independent Nation (WIN) and its concept of the New Tribe is an important, pioneering example of the type of new thinking and practices that we need in the Second Wave, in this case applied to community-building. These laudable initiatives need to form part of a larger attempt among white conscious activists to build an alternative sub-culture, consisting of new structures for discussion, belief, activism and opposition, and other aspects of everyday life, with its own political language. We must reject TINA and embrace TIAWA: There Is A White Alternative: which needs to be created by us, not handed-down to us by demagogues and the state.

In a previous article, 'The New Four Words', I talked about how the revisionist Griffin leadership of the BNP had set out at the cusp of the 21st. century with the correct basic idea: in order to appeal to the British public, both the message and its delivery and style need to be couched in attractive terms. However, the strategy selected by the BNP was misconceived. The BNP sought to co-opt the language and conceptualisations of the enemy, borrowing the enemy's tools to advance Nationalist iconoclasm. While this approach to things was entirely appropriate for what is known as 'far-Right Nationalism', with its objective of winning elections, it was wholly inappropriate for achieving the objective of a racially-homogeneous society. What in reality has happened is that the far-Right has itself been slowly deracinated and multi-culturalised on liberal terms – to the extent that we even now have the spectacle of BNP activists on the web going round accusing other Nationalists of 'racism' and questioning what race has to do with Nationalist activity. This is what happens when means become the ends and when power is sought as an objective in its own right. This is based on the flawed belief that the problem is politicians and that power can be won by 'convincing the masses' who, given the opportunity, will one day turf out the corrupt elite. What people who think this fail to understand is that power is, and always has been, with the masses themselves. Any attempt to 'convince' the masses leads to intellectual cowardice and expediency, qualities that the Right has in abundance. It prioritises 'not causing offence' and being semitically-correct in order to win over thoughtless idiots, when in fact what we should be doing is telling the truth in order to win over that minority of the population who are actually valuable to us.

Of course, there is room for discussion about presentation and making our message attractive – these concerns should not be ignored or sidelined – but we should always remember that democratic means are merely a tool to be used when it suits us, not an end in themselves. We must resist the temptation of 'respectability' and we must not fall into the trap of adopting the liberal mindset, which restricts the scope for resistance and useful activity. In some respects, we will have to mirror the Left's tactics, which were to work quietly to spread an alternative cultural message through society, both politically and non-politically, but always with political goals in mind. Only, ours is a very different objective, so we must evaluate our tactics and methods with the uniqueness of our goals in mind and consider a different linearity. It is a mistake to believe that we can roll-back the mixed-racial society and the deracination of Britain and the West. What we need to do instead is create an alternative society.

Building a White Alternative does not mean opting-out of the mainstream or becoming a drop-out. It just means that as white people we should start to think as a racial community and build a nascent alternative sub-culture that supports whites and repels non-whites. That's the only way we will see change. If we keep relying on others to change things for us, we will get nowhere. So we must ditch the traditional, party-centred, hierarchical approach of the Right and embrace more anarchical, community-based solutions that emphasise activity rather than passivity, community rather than democracy, and self-help and self-organisation rather than leaders and parties. In other words, a return to authenticity and the very roots of the movement. As mentioned already, this White Alternative is already being put into practice with a community-building group, White Independent Nation (WIN). We also need a civil resistance movement, which will work at a local level to create Local Resistance Zones. A group has been formed to plan and discuss this, and efforts are under a way to turn lawful, non-violent white resistance into a reality, including an exploration of the potential in the cutting-edge possibilities of the web and its Creative Commons. We will build a new kind of resistance movement that the Establishment cannot stop. (For further discussion on this, see also my essay: 'The Mechanics of Virtual Resistance').

We also need a new political party that rejects the right-wing model and works without leaders, without a membership list and without formal structures and acts as a unifying banner that any white person anywhere in the world can align themselves with. This new party will provide crowd-funding mechanisms so that white-conscious people can stand for elections as Independents (and even under the new party's banner, when and where appropriate). We need an alternative media, a legal support network, an intelligence and rebuttal organisation, the list could go on. All of this should be done in a way that is next-to impossible for the authorities to attack, with no identifiable leaders, structure or membership lists.

It is important to understand that none of these initiatives will be the finished product or the final destination. They are a means to an end. Some of the more frivolous and ill-thought-out efforts will fail and lessons will have to be learned; some of what we do will peter out for natural reasons; and, objectives and goals will be missed due to ill-starred chance and circumstance. The point is that we must try. We must go on fighting. That is the only right, it is our right, and it is why we are here.

The White Alternative is not a retreat. It is a new beginning, an intelligent re-alignment of human resources towards tactics and methods that are more suitable to the operating environment. The White Race will only survive through this kind of intelligent adaptation. Unfortunately the Right will not understand this message, and its sterile, devolutionary politics will go on for some time yet. The far-Right, in particular, has so far managed to trick Nationalists by presenting itself as an 'opposition' when it is nothing of the kind, and even by presenting 'false alternatives' – for instance, the Alternative Right/Alt Right, which is just a bunch of academic 'racist' conservatives. I have already discussed at length in other essays the problem of UKIP as a controlled opposition: see, for instance, 'UKIP and the Enoch Powell Cult'. We need a White Alternative – a completely different way of thinking and organising in which ordinary white people reject leaders and demagogues and instead build trust and confidence among themselves to self-organise and act as a racial community outside the sphere of mainstream politics.

You can help start the White Alternative right now. Stop using the word 'Nationalist' to describe your political beliefs. Start referring to yourself by your proper moniker – you are a White Neo-Tribalist. You are one of the New Tribe. Welcome! We are, if anything, Anti-Nationalists. We reject the old ways and the hierarchies; the pride and the hate; the endless party games; the Hitler worship and so on. Instead, we look positively to the future and seek to fashion a creative synergy online, and off-line, in which we as the New Tribe work to build a movement, resist oppression, learn and propagandise, and above all, educate those of our fellow whites who still have the potential to see the truth and reach for the stars.

### _End Note:_ **TOWARDS A CREDO FOR THE WHITE ALTERNATIVE**

Here I set out, roughly, a possible starting point in developing a Credo for The White Alternative:

Our ideology/position is White Neo-Tribalism. Our aim is the fashioning of a New Tribe and true white racial sovereignty, embracing social and economic liberation for all white people.

We adopt The New Four Words as our political message: Race, Solidarity, Community, Safety.

Our allegiance is only to New Tribe-aligned groups -

White Independent Nation (WIN) – for community-building.

The White Resistance Movement – for lawful, non-violent civil resistance by whites in their existing communities on the LRZ model. Depending on local circumstances, this is as either a precursor to, or part of an evolving attempt to form, a PLE community in the resistance zone, or as a stop-gap for individuals and families before moving to the WIN region.

A new political party is needed based on an 'alternative politics' model. We'll hypothetically call it the 'White Homeland Party' – a leaderless political party that any race-conscious white person can join. The party's purpose would be to help whites mount a political/electoral attack on mixed-racialism by providing information and guidance on the political system and by supporting white-conscious individuals who wish to stand as Independent candidates (or under the party banner if the individual is already publicly-known as a 'racist'). The party could provide a crowd-sourcing platform to help fund the election expenses of candidates.

We need some kind of 'White Opposition', to counter the work of anti-racists and anti-fascists like Searchlight, the UAF and Hope Not Hate and to provide us with an operational and tactical intelligence capacity. This is, after all, a war.

We need a legal assistance network modelled on Amnesty International to campaign against and raise awareness of civil liberties abuses against race-aware whites.

We need to look into the possibility of building white business networks and the feasibility of local community trusts of white people which will guard local, socially-important assets such as community centres and churches from development by non-whites and traitorous whites alike.

These are just rough ideas. The accent needs to be on us, as whites, organising things for ourselves and working together locally rather than relying on leaders and structures. That's the approach that best suits the environment we face at the moment.

# 5. Miscellaneous Subjects

## 5.1.

### 'Literary' Nationalism: thoughts on the geography and politics of George Orwell and Jack London[32]

For brutally instrumental reasons, it has to be recognised that part of the price we will have to pay for white survival is the end of any meaningful English culture and its likely supplantation with a single, Americanised white culture.

My favourite writer, George Orwell, contributed a lot on the subject of Englishness – read England, Your England and The Lion and the Unicorn. I also like Thoughts on the Common Toad. What's interesting is that despite the heavy element of class in English life, Orwell still managed to capture something 'English' that transcends social differences and that most of us can recognise instantly. The loss of that identity would upset me, but my background as a socialist perhaps helps – 'grist to the hard wheel of history' and all that. This is the point where Nationalism Socialism, which is slightly marxian and rationalist-materialist, parts company with woolly romantic nationalism. Many Nationalists reject the class concept altogether, whereas I cannot shake it off.

When Orwell was writing about Englishness, what he really wanted to appeal to was patriotism: i.e. loyalty to a particular place and time and way of life. You will, I hope, recognise immediately how that is fundamentally different to Nationalism. Orwell deals with this subject well in his Notes on Nationalism. If Orwell were around today, I think he would sympathise greatly with a lot of what White Nationalists are saying, but in the end he was a patriot not a Nationalist. On balance, he would have opposed us (though he was well-meaning). I think this was due to his own social background. It's that dirty word, class, again – albeit applied in a less rigorous sense, more as a cultural and less as a scientific phenomenon: Orwell was the product of colonial India and English public schooling and held a typically patronising view of 'ordinary folk'. He explicitly rejected the idea of racialising human beings, something he regarded as akin to classifying insects, if I recall correctly.

Now, my view is that class and race go hand-in-hand, and unless you allow for a class understanding of things, there is always going to be a danger of rhetorical slippage into empty romanticism – but that's maybe an argument for another day. For now, the observation I would make is that an 'Americanised' white/European culture – whatever its desirability – can only really work racially-culturally if it also works economically. If it's just going to be a society that replicates capitalism, then I share the worries and fears of the ethno-nationalists about a hollowed-out culture and a lack of ethno-identity. Such fears should not be underestimated, as they can be crystallised in real problems – not least because the racial basis of capitalism is demonstrably shaky. On the other hand, if our aim is for a 'democratic' white society (I use the term 'democratic' in its purer sense – i.e. a society which is co-operative and in which everyone has the chance to flourish), then the considerations of culture become emptier and less relevant because the racial basis of the society is assured.

A useful literary contrast with Orwell's well-meaning English patriotism is found in the

---

[32] First published at http://www.johnlonden.com on 24 June 2014.

writings of Jack London, who I think was in many ways a White Nationalist. Whereas Orwell, struggling with a deep-seated intellectual ambivalence, came up with the muddled patriotic twaddle of the Lion and the Unicorn, London wrote stridently racialist works such as White Fang and Call of the Wild, fictional allegorical defences of White Nationhood as a natural and inevitable phenomenon. I think there is some significance in London's 'American' identity. It is not difficult to see how the idea of 'white' as a single identity arose in a European colonial society that had to defend itself against non-European natives on a geographically vast Continent. The Europeans of the New World needed a cohesive identity, which inevitably was 'white'. We in the Old World, Europe proper, now find ourselves in an analogous position.

## 5.2.

## Nationalism and the Hermeneutical Dilemma: some brief thoughts[33]

Some people apply what they think is a literal meaning to the word 'superiority', but the word itself has different shades of meaning and need not imply strict superiorism. In my case, it merely implies a preference: specifically a sexual preference, which is at the root of everything we are talking about.

Admittedly that's a crude and base notion, and one way some people like to add a patina of respectability in these political discussions is to pretend that 'racialism' (and, ergo, Nationalism) is something high and noble. What's argued is that the base imperative of self-preservation that so often overrides all else is mostly a feature of primitive life forms, whereas group identity and selection are markers of civility. In that way, Nationalism is seen as something that transcends material or genetic considerations and is in fact a signifier of high culture.

This very 19th. century perspective has been subverted by our understanding of the natural world, which has been shaped by the modern genetics and ethology that started with Darwin and the other Victorian evolutionary biologists. Even the most basic and uncomplex life forms – let's say, viruses – have and exhibit group identity and adaptability. The socio-biological perspective may have become gauche now, but I still think there is a lot in it. We are not just animals, but we are animals nonetheless and must betray our evolutionary markers at some point. This opens the way for a materialist basis to Nationalism.

Cautious Nationalists are of course wise when they say that it is better not to use the Right's own 's'-word – supremacy – in dialogue with people who are not specially race-conscious. My blog is aimed more at those who are already race conscious but wish to develop politically and better their understanding (as we all need to do). Frankly, anyone who is not race-conscious would struggle to understand my political writing anyway. For instance, on seeing the term: 'White Nationalist' at the top of this blog, they would immediately jump to certain conclusions – mostly inaccurate and wrong – about myself and what I think. The term 'superiority', when deployed, offers a more extreme example of that type of Pavlovian-like response to political language. Likewise, some will not understand how conscious and literate discussion about 'race' can sit alongside advocacy of materialist/scientific socialism.

In fact, the whole topic of how canonical meaning influences political thought and ideas interests me greatly. I actually think what might be termed 'the hermeneutical dilemma' is a major factor in our struggle. Needless arguments among Nationalists about the application and relevancy of terms such as 'supremacy' and 'supremacism' provide an example of how hermeneutical difference can lead to friction and division. Here a study of Gidden's 'double hermeneutic' can be helpful. The Victorian evolutionists may have helped to shape our understanding of the natural world, but it is the social and political language that is the key influence on canonical thought and meaning. In science, there can only be one hermeneutic (a single meaning). What is disturbing is how the interpretation of science can be corrupted, because it is the

---

[33] First published on 27 June 2014 at http://www.johnlonden.com

social environment that shapes scientific understanding, and thus the concept of racial difference has been evacuated of its rigorous science. But that is really politics – social science – to which the precept of Gidden's 'double hermeneutic' applies. In the end the truth is there for those who are diligent enough to search for it using open sources: i.e. the web. To a modern lay reader, 'racial supremacy' is something 'Nazified' and vile. To a scientist, 'racial supremacy' is simply biology.

## 5.3.

### Democracy Keeps Us Dumb[34]

The archetypal complaint of the media's own Devil creature – the bar-room reactionary – is encapsulated in the refrain: "We were never asked." This is repeated in different forms among the real-life ultra-Tories who lament figuratively that if only the British people had been "asked", then we would never have had mass immigration/joined the EU/introduced human rights/abolished capital punishment/abolished corporal punishment* [*delete as applicable, according to your own prejudices].

What underlines the complaint isn't some faith in the British public who, "if only we had been asked", would have miraculously made the right choices all along. Paradoxically, in his or her complaint of patrician insensitivity to populism, the reactionary seeks to re-affirm his faith in the very patrician tendency that he claims to despise. This is the 'leader syndrome': i.e. the same phenomenon I referred to a few posts ago (see 'Escaping the Lotus: democracy and the 'leader syndrome'). The leader syndrome is an obsession with finding leaders, mystics, gurus and so forth, who will lead us to some kind of 'salvation'. Among right-wingers, traditionalists and Tories (reactionaries) – the type of people who are attracted to hierarchies – it tends to find expression in a worship of Enoch Powell, and his contemporary incarnation: Nigel Farage.

Mr. Farage has recently decided to boost his democratic credentials by announcing a UKIP policy on the use of referendums and direct democracy. A future UKIP government will use referenda and other forms of direct voting (such as constituency recall) to involve the public in key decision-making (UKIP backs direct democracy and use of referendums). This illiterate proposal underscores how desperate and populist, and thus insincere, UKIP really are. UKIP is a form of escapism, not real politics. It's like a Moonie cult, just not as entertaining or sociologically-interesting. The democratic system that we now have relies on these empty 'media' parties that reduce politics into an alienated form of 'lifestyle' protest. This has its left-wing versions as well: the obnoxious Trotskyites obsessed with equalities and political correctness. It's an example of how this democracy has gradually degenerated.

Unable to satiate the revolutionary uprisings of British workers during the 19th. century, the Establishment resorted to force of arms to suppress socialism and trade unionism. During the 20th. century, the methodology of control of a now-subdued population shifted to psychological techniques: various mass-market ideologies (replacing loyalty to feudal statehood and religion with loyalty to new abstractions); mass media and advertising; informational propaganda; state schooling; welfare and prisons; various New Social Movements; football clubs and other religious crazes – the mechanisms are in place to control and shape public opinion so that the average working man and woman is distracted, never demands their fair share, but instead accepts their lot in life. In short, the war between capitalism and democracy, the class war, has so far been won by capitalism – and the true purpose of this 'democracy' is to keep the public ignorant and dumb.

---

[34] First published on 29 June 2014 at http://www.johnlonden.com

I actually like Americanisms such as 'dumb'. I am one of these unusual Englishmen who prefers 'Fall' over 'autumn'. Fall is more evocative. It's Old English. It's pithy and tells you exactly what happens in September and early October, much better than the Old French word with its metrological corruption. Likewise, 'dumb' expresses things very well – much better than 'stupid'. It's very English, quintessentially Saxon in fact. 'Stupefied' would be a fitting expression for it too. The public – that is, you and me – have been stupefied in the following ways.

Taking the issue of mass immigration. The protest normally seems to have a materialist basis – i.e. the complaint is that letting in all these immigrants puts a strain on services. This in itself should be a clue that the reactionaries are either confused or cowardly. It is capitalism that causes mass immigration of Third World populations to the West. The need is for cheap, pliable labour and the immigrant populations provide it. At the same time, the sending countries are mostly glad to let the migrants leave as it avoids significant social unrest in those countries. It is true that we were never presented with the options that the bar-room reactionaries talk of, but even if some kind of referendum law had been in place, the choice would never have been presented to us on the terms that the reactionaries specify, just as it was not presented on those terms in reality – and the question would be meaningless anyway, even if asked, since the forces that drive mass immigration are the very material interests that the reactionaries claim to hold dear. In fact, UKIP could come to power or significant influence, in the same way the Conservatives did, and not make the slightest difference to the prospects for the White Race – indeed, they will probably make things worse because they will have smothered any vestige of true opposition to mixed-racialism, while advocating the very economic system that caused the problems in the first place, this time through 'free trade' outside the EU. The real issue is Race and it is that issue that UKIP will not, and cannot, address.

We should consider the historical context of UKIP. UKIP is just an updated example of Powellite Conservatism, or to put it a different way: a British example of the 'Republican problem' that American white nationalists face. In the United States, the Republicans have co-opted all ethno-nationalist symbols and messages to suffocate real opposition from race-conscious white people. UKIP are performing the same function here. In fact, it is politicians such as Enoch Powell who bear the most guilt historically for the problems we now face. It was Powell, and others of his generation, who initiated mass non-white immigration into the UK. The explanation for this worship of Enoch Powell and his ersatz, Nigel Farage, is a lingering reliance on the system that keeps us dumb.

UKIP supporters and other apologists for democracy seem to think that, given the chance, the British people will somehow 'vote' for Nationalism. I think this faith in the machinery of democracy is misplaced. For one thing, issues such as immigration are never presented so transparently. The British people were never asked whether they were 'For' or 'Against' mass immigration because no-one openly discussed it as mass immigration (a term that carries unmistakable racialist connotations). It was normally referred to as something else back in the 1950s and 1960s. We can see that in much the same way, the Powellites of today – UKIP – refer to mass non-white immigration as 'free trade' and 'leaving the EU'. It is just code for the expression of the mercantilist interests that are the real purpose of UKIP. Referendum questions are always framed for the 'right' result. That's because referenda are just an additional means of control and an example of how democracy, as presently conceived, does not work – or rather, only 'works' for the Jewish capitalist elite.

It is important that true democracy should ultimately win in the sense of a society in which all resources are owned in common. Much of the human strife that exists in the world today would find its answer in such a society, but that society – the vision of the 19th. century socialists – can only come about among people who are capable of democracy and who can accept the rights, duties and responsibilities that citizenship entails. That is not possible in the present society, with its degeneracy, dysgenics and enforced or fictionalised equality. We are being asked to ascribe democratic attributes to a society that is nothing more than an elective hierarchy and that is devoid and empty of meaning and justice.

Confronting us is the basic philosophic difference between a society that celebrates strength (fascism) and a society that celebrates the lowest common denominator (what is now mislabelled democracy). The way in which we have lost sight of that difference is an example of how political language can be turned on its head: we now live in a 'fascism of the weak', a contradiction in terms, a sick joke almost, but very real nonetheless – and democracy is nowhere in sight.

**5.4.**

**democracy versus Democracy, or Why the patient can't be restored[35]**

Nationalists often elevate the concept of fascism at the expense of democracy, as if the two concepts are mutually exclusive or locked in some kind of epic philosophic struggle for the soul of Man. In rough terms, the idea is that under fascism the strong predominate, while in a democracy it is the weak who dictate the direction of society. On first sight, this might seem an odd distinction. Wouldn't all societies tend by default to become 'fascist', since the strong will always naturally tend to dominate? That is certainly the case in what I would call a 'normal society', but this is where we come to the central Nationalist (fascist) critique of Western liberalism. The point is that in a democracy there is political equality (and perhaps economic equality as well) and it is this feature that tends to draw a democratic society towards the lowest common denominator and to weaken it – genetically, economically, socially, culturally, spiritually. That – in summary form – is why, to a Nationalist, democracy is abnormal and undesirable.

By contrast, a fascist society would have little or no regard for such liberal norms as 'equality', to which it would be diametrically-opposed, and which it would neither respect nor institutionalise. Instead, through the mechanism of a strong, militaristic state, it is the needs of society's more vigorous members that would predominate through various facets of the national community. That is the conventional view of fascism. Here I want to cast some doubt on that, or at least refine the concept a little to take account of what I see as an important development in society: the erosion of hierarchy and the emergence of democracy and autonomy; a future in which 'non-state fascism' (or socialism or democracy – I see these terms as interchangeables rather than opposites) will become the reality.

What Nationalists define as 'strong' – i.e. of value to the community – might not bear any relation to what is seen as 'strong' in the present liberal democratic society. In Western liberal democracies, the value of an individual is measured by his monetary or financial 'success' and perhaps also by certain aspects of his character (a la Martin Luther King, etc.). To the average liberal democratic mind of our time, the idea that people should be judged on their inheritable characteristics – i.e. race, ethnicity – is both odd and undesirable, even vile. Yet to a Nationalist, this is quite normal and desirable. Not out of nastiness, but because Race is considered a basic criteria for acceptance in society and it is believed that the best societies are homogenous.

An important difference between the two perspectives (liberal democracy and fascism) that needs to be appreciated is the counterfeit nature of the liberal democratic perspective contrasted with the cynicism of the fascist perspective. In truth, the strong can only ever dominate a society – that is the fascist cynical truth that capitalism imperfectly expresses – and so the earnest liberal democrat is left living in a fantasy world at best, and at worst is engaging in an organised deception. Mixed racialism and individualism are simply expressions that help to advance certain vested interests. Despite this, an interesting phenomenon found among

[35] First published on 1st. July 2014 at http://www.johnlonden.com

Western intellectuals (less prevalent in the Far East and Asia) is the support given to liberal precepts (i.e. various types of equality) on the basis of 'fairness' or 'compassion' – various altruistic-like justifications are given. This is often a symptom of a pseudo-positivist mindset – the classic liberal disposition of the priggish, especially the 'educated' middle class, who accept bourgeois concepts at their face-value – but it can also be a more or less naked expression of class interest. Consider how notions of 'racial equality' and so forth can be used to denigrate and attack the ordinary white working class.

It is the White Nationalist (fascist), respecting and understanding Man's true nature, who is most capable of recognising and confronting the political system for what it is, both good and bad. Entailed in this is a rejection of the capitalist and individualist mixed-racial society and an adoption of communalism and socialism as the basis of a racially-homogenous future. In a White National Community, true democracy (or socialism), in which the resources are shared and economic activity is co-operative, would be the optimal form of social organisation for maintaining racial integrity. A contemporary example of how a similar society could work is provided by the Hutterites: a white community in the northwestern United States (similar to the Amish) that manages to live autonomously and applies a 'community of goods' concept. I am not suggesting that we should copy the Hutterites. Rather, I am suggesting that their model of society might be copyable by whites in Europe and elsewhere with adaptations for local conditions and local circumstances.

One of the mental blocks that prevents Nationalists from pursuing this kind of radical socialist thinking is a belief, or faith, that the existing Western system is democracy or, at worst, is some kind of 'democracy in bad health': corrupted by politicians, but nonetheless restorable. To understand why this is mistaken, it is necessary to appreciate what 'democracy' really is. Some people think it obvious that democracy is a system that expresses the will of the people. I would content this is gravely mistaken – indeed, it is this misconception that lies at the root of much of our problems. In fact, democracy has at least two valid, opposite meanings. Indeed, it can be seen as a double concept. There is the meaning that it carries in the West, and then there is its truer, more literal meaning.

The meaning that democracy carries in the West – its canonical meaning, if you like – is what most people would understand to be liberal democracy: vaguely some kind of representative system where politicians elected by us make decisions on our behalf roughly in line with our wishes. This is the sort of understanding that the average 'man and woman on the street' has. I would argue that the true meaning and purpose of Western democracy is something quite different. Democracy is a mechanism to keep us dumb because, in brief, it is a way of maintaining a hierarchy based on economic power. The issues and questions are decided in advance and everything is stage-managed. That's Western 'liberal democracy'. The truer, more faithful democracy – its non-canonical counterpart, if you like – bears no relation to this and is in most respects its diametric opposite and closer to the example of the Hutterites who I mention above.

The basis on which 'dumb' whites support UKIP and other traitor parties is the Western liberal Democracy I have outlined, rather than true democracy. This Western system requires people to live in a kind of abstract dream in which they somehow get what they want by putting an 'X' – the mark of an illiterate – in a box every few years, and in which political leaders mean what they say and say what they think. In this dream world, if we vote for something, then it will happen in the way presented. If UKIP say they want to 'freeze immigration', in the dream this means that immigration will reduce. It doesn't occur to anybody living in this dream world that 'freezing immigration' might mean that immigration actually increases, or that the immigrants might start coming from somewhere else. Pinch yourself and it might, but no-one will, because nobody really wants the dream to stop, for that would mean actually accepting responsibility for the world, instead of handing decisions over by proxy to remote politicians who we can call liars and other names when, predictably, they don't give us what we want.

When UKIP say they want to leave the EU, the dreamers swallow it because they think it means literally that. It doesn't occur to the Democratic dreamers that they are being diddled and that it might mean much the same relationship with the EU, in or out.

I regard the whole liberal democratic/positivistic world-view as a fairy tale. The contrast with the lives of the Hutterites could not be more stark. In the communal world of the Hutterites, or any similar group, true democracy is exercised, for both good and bad. The interests of the individual are subsumed to those of the community – there is no fantasy of selfish individualism – and the community has a common goal and a common identity.

Back in the dream world, the purpose of political parties is to uphold the existing economic system – which maintains the fantasy fiction of individualism – while controlling public opinion and suppressing dissent. Their role is to represent the interests of the powerful, i.e. people who own significant capital. They are not there to uphold the interests of the weak, i.e. us – though they will pretend to through the means of what they call democracy. That is the way the dream world works. This is never admitted, because no-one entertains the idea that 'democracy' is a double-concept. The reason no-one other than a few Marxists want to admit this is because that: (i). would involve some independent thought; and, (ii). would involve an admission that most of us (including you and I) have been fooled. No-one wants to admit they have been fooled, so we keep going with this merry-go-round of fake elections and leader cults....voting for Purple Tories instead of Blue Tories...and so on. It's like a bad soap opera: which is precisely how it is intended. It's meant to distract you AND alienate you from your true interests. It's not real politics. It's just fantasy.

However – and here is a note of consolation – the terms 'strong' and 'weak' are malleable. The only reason we are 'weak' is because we have been indoctrinated with that mentality. In reality, we are strong and the 'powerful' are in fact terrified of us. What is required is for people to reject these leader cults and wake up to their own strength. That is why when White Nationalists speak of rule by the strong, what they should remember is the quintessential democratic quality of the people's might.

**5.5.**

**Pervertocratic Pervocracy: the political science of child abuse**

The clouds have parted again and suddenly, out of nowhere, it is revealed that a dossier is missing that details paedophilic activity at Westminster and Whitehall during the 1980s. We know only a fragment of the history, in that the so-called 'dossier' was handed to then-Cabinet minister, the Jew Leon Brittan, in 1984 by Tory MP Geoffrey Dickens – at which point, a black hole emerges in the story. Brittan says he 'passed it on' to civil servants. Brittan is also being questioned by police over, as yet unproven, rape allegations involving a 19-year old – the alleged rape took place on a blind date, of all things. Mr. Brittan, who has the most appropriate surname possible for a Jew, given the racial strategy of that group, seems to be plagued by the most unfortunate bad luck.

Mysteriously, this dossier has not been made a fuss about previously in the media, but it surfaces now – after having been 'lost' by Brittan or his civil servants, fittingly in the year 1984, as if – just for japes – they were acting out a scene from George Orwell's famous [infamous?] novel. Civil servants are famed for their educated wit, if not a sense of humour, and I am half-expecting one of them to appear in the media and solipsistically claim that the dossier is not 'is' and therefore 'is' not 'was'. Don't worry – it's the sort of thing that requires a classical education, and is above us proles. The dossier emerges, but doesn't. It is, but isn't. It's as if out of the clear blue sky an alternate dimension has been revealed to us, from where truth is briefly glimpsed before the inter-dimensional door is frustratingly snapped shut.

What is the dossier? What's in it? What's its provenance? Why haven't the media given it such a high profile previously? Why is all this being discussed now? Why didn't the police initiate criminal investigations when Geoffrey Dickens was alive? Did Geoffrey Dickens go to the police? If not, why not? And if he didn't, does that cast doubt on the very existence of the dossier? Or to put it a different way – is the dossier just another diversionary tactic, a fiction? Is there only one dossier? Was there other correspondence with the Home Office during the tenure of Brittan and other Home Secretaries before and since?

The whole affair has a sense of hyper-reality about it, like an improbable plot from one of those bad novels written in the 1980s that you now find in charity shops. There is talk of a Westminster paedophile ring; Brittan himself is being questioned over the historic rape allegations; Simon Danczuk, a Labour MP, claims he was warned-off questioning Brittan about the dossier by a current Conservative Cabinet Minister; and there are also current allegations involving 'horrific' child abuse by an as-yet unnamed Labour peer and former Cabinet Minister. No doubt there will have been stories and hints of stories in the London media that have now disappeared down the memory hole, but why the sudden melodrama in the media over something they must have known about for decades?

As any successful gangster or organised criminal will tell you, answers to awkward questions like this need to be fronted-up by someone reassuring and credible: sometimes this might be a 'business' Face, other times it might be a grandfatherly figure. It depends on the scam, but all repressive, authoritarian social systems have such apparatchiks, and one of ours is 'Lord' Tebbit – a delusional psychotic and Tory ratchet man who, nevertheless, gives off the necessary air of senescence and kindliness for the benefit of 'dumb' whites who can't think for themselves.

Once again the clouds part, and 'Lord' Tebbit appears out of nowhere to dispense his pearls of wisdom. The usual tactic is the Big Lie. That's the tactic adopted by Mellor, who went on the radio and more or less denied there was even a dossier in the sense that has been alleged. That won't work this time – the scandal is too big. So Tebbit tried to 'lie by telling the truth': he admits there may well have been a cover-up. However…the 1980s, he tells us, was an era of official paranoia…need to protect the system….best intentions….no-one knew the seriousness of it…..different attitudes back then, etc., etc., blah, blah. Note the admission by Tebbit that the allegation of one or more cover-ups may be true. That is the crucial part which the media, to its credit, has focused on. Even so, my cynicism about the media heightens at times like this, and tangentially, I think of that famous, apt quote of 19th. century historian Thomas Macauley: "We know of no spectacle so ridiculous as the British public in one of its periodic fits of morality." There can be merit in the observation in so far as it applies to the British public, but the model of 'moral panic' can also be applied to the media. We are living in an era of manufactured media panics. To the lazy observer it might appear that, for once, the media is doing its job and adopting a relentless focus on truth-finding. The headlines talk of 'Westminster paedophile rings', yes, but it is also clear that the media are part of the cover-up. They must have known about all this for some time and so they are as much liars as the politicians, and they are taking us for fools, just like the politicians are.

The British public seem strangely mute about the whole matter. One explanation for this could be that they have, frankly, already had enough of Westminster politicians and their lying, fraud, thieving and promise-breaking. What's a grubby sex scandal? It's really come to something when our politicians are so venal, dishonest, seedy and corrupt that the public are actually bored by a potential child abuse scandal, having 'seen it all before': a sort of absurdist situation that would befit high-end satire. However, should any concrete evidence of organised paedophilia come to light, then the implications for public opinion and for any further public acquiesce in this fraudulent charade called democracy are unclear. Personally I would advocate the 'pitchforks and torches' approach: moral panics are a little abstract for my liking, and I think it's time to take matters in hand.

What is clear to anyone with multiple functioning brain cells is that we live in a kind of pervocracy – that is to say, a society that is governed by a social and political class who have subverted the normal, functioning institutions that keep a civilisation going – such as marriage – in favour of destructively permissive attitudes and lifestyles. It is now considered normal for men to have sex with men and even for men to live with other men in a state of matrimony or long-term partnership. How this squares with the need for society to continue through procreation is unclear, but then, what we are dealing with here is the propagation of official fictions, which all authoritarian societies – past and present – need as part of a machinery of formal 'consent'. Everyone knows the official fiction – that a society can be based on anything other than heterosexual relationships – is complete nonsense, but most people, understandably, dare not actually say as much, for fear of the official consequences: social ostracism, financial ruin, even criminal prosecution. That is the 'consent' that democracy relies on. Ignorance Is Strength, Authoritarianism Is Democracy, Fear Is Consent.

What most will not have not realised is the extent to which this pervocracy is also pervertocratic: which is to say, the elite classes seem to have been infiltrated to a significant extent by actual sexual perverts. Not only do we have perverted rule, we have rule by perverts too. The full scale of the infiltration can be ascertained by simply researching how many outed or suspected homosexuals exist in powerful or influential positions in Britain: across the media, business and corporate world, and especially in politics. The number represents a significant minority far out of proportion to the general population. Add to this the number of Jews and other ethnic minorities in key positions, and we begin to build up a picture of an elite class that no longer mirrors the indigenous white British whom it is meant to serve. Such facts provide a useful hint as to why so much legislation is now being passed that is actively interventionist and harmful in the private sphere of the family. The common explanation is that people who have 'interesting lifestyles' are pliable and susceptible to blackmail. Reference is made to the repressive agenda of Leveson Inquiry: the notion being that perverted politicians and celebrities want their behaviour concealed from public notice. There is certainly truth in these explanations, but where they are limited is that they provide only a keyhole to the larger truths that we need to understand. What the 'blackmail thesis' does not fully explain is the rapid and fundamental retreat of the British elite over the last five decades from its traditional institutions, and to understand that we need to shift our focus away from individuals to society at large, and even to a systemic analysis.

The decline in official morality is a reflection of increased liberalism, individualism and autonomy in society, trends that conflict with communal duty. The Gladstonian liberal economics of Heath, then Thatcher, complemented aptly the agenda of the post-War social liberals, while sitting uneasily with Thatcher's social moralism. Heath the homosexual (and suspected paedophile) would have found stifling the social communality of his post-War 'affluent working class' upbringing and would have been privately more at home in the emerging metropolitan climate of a liberal society, which was more welcoming to men like him who had lax sexual morals. Thatcher, by contrast the product of municipal lower-middle class respectability, would have been more uneasy and more ambivalent about this emerging new culture, hence the attempted retrenchment during the 1980s, during which the Conservatives introduced (among other things) the anti-homosexual Section 28, barring the promotion of homosexuality in schools. The retrenchment was destined to fail, not least because in common with the Labour Party, the Conservative Party boasted a considerable number of homosexuals and degenerate Jews. Whether Thatcher liked it or not, the metropolitan culture was here to stay. In an economy built on expansiveness, services and finance, libertine individualism was an important part of the cultural environment. People who are free of private restraints on their sexual behaviour, even if this is more perception than reality, make better consumers. It was this unintended ambivalence that marked the Thatcher era as fundamentally liberal in both the economic and social senses, so that whatever Thatcher's real intentions, hers was a left-wing government.

There are other features of the pervocracy worthy of note, comment and analysis. Parliament has been hollowed-out. It is no longer the country's substantive legislature: that role having been taken over by influential multi-nationals and an executive bureaucracy in Brussels. We should of course bear in mind that the Anglo-Saxon myth of popular sovereignty never existed. The present situation of Continental-style rule by technocrats based in Brussels who issue 'directives' [i.e. summary laws] is little different from the feudal rule to which Westminster had become accustomed before entry to the then-EEC. Careful observers should have little patience with pseudo-nationalists who pine romantically for a 'Westminster system' of 'democracy' that never in fact existed. Often the motive of such people is to replace one authoritarian system based in Brussels with another based back at Westminster, their only preference being that the people in charge be white British control freaks rather than white European control freaks. They hide this motive in fanciful rhetoric about how English constitutionalists respect liberty over democracy and how an unwritten constitution is the best type of system in the world, and other high-flown Burkean nonsense. Nevertheless, the power transference to Brussels served a purpose. The overt, official purpose was the modernisation of Britain as a country that looked more to a proximate, emerging powerful trading block: Heath and his contemporary rival, Wilson, shared this rhetorical obsession with turning Britain into a 'modern country', a theme that was to reoccur with Blair in the late 90s, save that the nature of Blair's obsession was primarily sociological rather than technological. The subversive, unofficial (but not hidden) purpose of British membership of the EEC was to undermine, but not end, parliamentary sovereignty, so that the political class would be able to control the population through a weakened domestic legislature, with the mechanisms for oversight and accountability removed to the Continent.

In contrast to the traditional Westminster system, the Brussels system has no meaningful legislative superintendence. Even today, after several reforming treaties, law-makers still cannot realistically challenge legislation from the Brussels commission or the Council of Ministers. Indeed, contrary to popular belief, the so-called European Parliament is really more of a 'consultative assembly'. The real legislature is the Council of Ministers. These arrangements reflect Continental political traditions, which emphasise a limited role for popular sentiment in law-making. Of course, none of this would necessarily be objectionable if the EU were a limited organisation concerned with only necessary areas of co-operation, rather than a federative state in the making. Personally, I have no particularly strong objection to a federal Europe, but that is only because I do not see it as relevant to the racial issues. The point here is that the Brussels system is entirely alien to the British, especially English, tradition of popular governance and common law, and whereas the Westminster system did not respect democracy, the Brussels system does not respect democracy at all and is quite open and unabashed about it.

The shift to technocratic, centralised decision-making serves a deliberate purpose: to reduce still further what little say the people across Europe have in government and law-making. There is nothing dishonest or criminal about this objective. It is the imperative, and prerogative of the elite. Romantic ethno-nationalists and naive conservatives who feign surprise at the idea of people with power wanting to keep the power to themselves really just deserve scorn and ridicule. Power is what people with power want – and more of it. That's the way the world works and it's the way people are. In this case, the trend manifests itself in increasingly interventionist legislation that allows government and officialdom a microscopic involvement in people's lives.  Countless new laws are passed which, due to their complicated nature and complex scope, are difficult for ordinary people to scrutinise and understand, thus alienating them further from the decisions that affect them.  Most of the decisions taken are the result not of some sinister conspiracy among Euro-communists, but rather pressure from multi-nationals and various types of lobbyists, including corporate lobbyists who have an interest in loading business costs on to small businesses and ordinary people through increased regulation.

This technocratic approach to government, which could be based as easily in Westminster as it is Brussels, lends itself more to a deeply commercial social environment: the bastardised result of post-War social liberalism and neo-thatcherism.  A feature of this commercial culture is that private and familial relationships, and the morals and values that uphold them and traditionally provided a ballast for civic and family life, have become subsumed by transactional relationships between people.  Increasingly we judge and value each other on the basis of money, physical appearance and financial worth.  This is the environment in which perverted values – including extremes such as paedophilia – are fermented and begin to spread.  Photoshopped models appear in magazines and on websites with flawless facial features, infantilising male sexual desires and creating unrealistic archetypes of feminine beauty.  A random example of the phenomenon could be the Australian model, Miranda Kerr, who regularly appears on the Mail Online site – they have something of an obsession with her – and whose seemingly flawless but impish features give her a juvenile, almost prepubescent, appearance.  Men who find that the flawless images do not translate into reality, and who develop a pictographic taste for the adolecentesque features of the contemporary female celebrity, may gradually turn to more exploitative, manipulative or predatory types of relational or sexual behaviour: especially as a way of releasing frustrated sexual avenues where the man cannot relate to women who are, perhaps, more assertive than they used to be.

The sexual abuse of children – the subject of the missing Westminster dossier – has to be the worst allegation that can be levelled at an individual.  However terms such as 'sexual abuse', 'exploitation' and 'paedophilia', while certainly reflecting real, disgusting behaviour, are now also being bandied around without necessarily any relationship to their plain meaning.  The relentless projection of these terms, the descent into cliché and empty moralising, in the tabloid media especially, and among unthinking people, is the hallmark of a society that is morally insecure and has lost its way and must run itself on fear as the necessary condition of consent: mainly fear, denigration and demonisation of white men.  Actual wrong-doing was ignored or covered-up and is only now revealed when it is too late.  What some naively thought were merely the misguided mores and norms of a strange, idealistic sexual revolution – a kind of historical oddity of a particular generation full of post-War angst – was in fact something altogether more sinister, and in fact criminal.  Paedophiles and child benders, gangsterism, evidence destruction, lying and, probably, blackmail, all of it in high places, even in the so-called 'Mother of Parliaments'.  But worse than that, the perversions of this elite are the result of a mentality that could not care less about the white working class and that will use us as cattle, whether it is take away our birth right as the inheritors of these islands, or even to sexually exploit white children.  That is why child abuse is more than a moral issue, a criticism of celebrity liberal whites with lax morals.  It is fundamentally a political issue.  The barbarism of men in the Asian community abusing white girls is one thing, and perhaps predictable, but when the same abuse is committed by a (mostly) white elite on its own children, then the political dimensions of the matter become clearer. This is a fight of white race conscious people against white traitors. The non-whites are just the more visible among our enemies, and therefore less dangerous. It is the traitorous whites who are the real obstacle to the restoration of a white society. They are the whites who are willing to betray us and debase us, whether through thought or deed. Child abuse is just one barbaric example of this white racial betrayal.

A rational observer, his consciousness raised by the strange, hyper-real events of the various child abuse scandals and the potential for more, might ask just what evil lies at the heart of our political system, even our society, and whether we need a different social system. He might ponder whether, in fact, it is time to burn not just the European treaties, but also the Magna Carta, the 'Mother of Parliaments' and the fraudulent system that is alienating and does not serve the interests of its people. The naive observer, by contrast, sentimentally seeks for individuals and groups to blame or looks to root out the corruption in the system. Perverts, nonces and paedos are a very effective scapegoat for the fundamental problems in society. His friend is the 'Eurosceptic' or the UKIP member, who with his feeble understanding, seeks the answer in the corrupt Westminster system rather than the corrupt Brussels system: the very same Westminster system that produced the mystery 'dossier'. But the naive observer cares not about that. He asks us to affirm the system, to place our faith in the pervocracy, for it must be made to work properly.

# 6. Essays from White Independent Nation

## 6.1.

*I wrote the below article in the summer of 2013 for the White Independent Nation website. I still hold to the views expressed in the article. My only quibble now would be over the terminology, in that I think the word 'Nationalist' and 'Nationalism' needs to be abandoned by white-conscious people if we are going to make progress.*

## A World of Meaning: Nationalism and New Europeans[36]

What vexes about Europe is not the notion of geopolitical unity itself – a goal most can support and subscribe to, if only in a vague sense – but rather why any Nationalist should oppose such a goal and instead maintain, against all evidence, adherence to the treasonous mixed-race nation-states that now govern the West.

I do not refer here, of course, to the more considered view expressed by some Nationalists that the European Union, as presently-constituted, is a detriment to our racial interest. While there are probative issues with this line of thinking and I doubt any serious discussion about cause and effect would bring clarity to the matter, the concern is entirely legitimate and understandable nonetheless. In blunt terms, it is said that the European Union is stripping the British nation of its long-held traditions of common law, liberty and popular sovereignty; that while the EU's Four Freedoms have their benefits, the increasing migration of European peoples into Britain in revolutionary numbers is socially- and culturally detrimental and undermines the economic interest of the indigenous population; and, that the erosion of legal and political nationhood reflects a broader, sinister, agenda to undermine human indigenous identities in the interests of Judeo-capitalism.

Let me join that chorus and make it clear that I, too, disapprove of the European institutions, and though my views on the European Union are not unequivocal because I see some positive aspects to it as well, I do not like the negative aspects any more than other Nationalists. The matter, however, is one of seeing things for what they really are. The E.U.'s modus, in its predicators, was a process of evolution, successively, from a collection of independent ethnic nation-states to a closely-integrated political and economic confederation, and that remains its goal and mode of action today. The line put about by British politicians in the 1960s and 1970s that the then-EEC was merely an international trade association was a simple, straight-forward lie, but simply to acknowledge that it was a lie does not promote any understanding and is not in itself an argument. The E.U. must be confronted for what it is. As a social and political experiment, it has demonstrated that a realistic consequence of serious, intensive co-operation at all governmental levels among closely-aligned nation-states is the incremental ceding of sovereignty, both informally through ad hoc social, cultural and economic relations, and formally and legalistically through legislative integration. This was to be expected, and could have been predicted, whatever the deceptions of the politicians. Sovereignty as an abstract may seem absolute, and it may manifest in absolute notions of state identity, but in reality sovereignty is necessarily relativistic in practice. The E.U. itself, and some of its apologist commentators, employ euphemisms such as 'sharing' or 'pooling' sovereignty, or words such as 'integration' and 'co-operation'. These words all mean taking away powers from national institutions. They give the impression of an

---

[36] First published on 28 June 2013 at http://www.win-white.org

absolute attitude to sovereignty. In other words, they are used in such a way as to imply that a reserve of sovereignty remains with the Member State-donor, which graciously grants lumps of sovereignty to the foreign or alien body but can withdraw co-operation – and thus reclaim all its sovereignty – at any time. That notion has some validity, of course. It is true that, formally and practically, the relevant powers do remain with the national institutions and Member States can withdraw co-operation, and sometimes do. This absolute conceptualisation of sovereignty has been adopted implicitly by both supporters and opponents of the E.U., however it is represents a highly-misleading picture. A true understanding of the E.U. and its legal relationship to its Member States can only be gained if we see sovereignty as a fundamentally pragmatic concept, conceived-of relativistically.

We have already touched on the E.U.'s modus, which is a gradual accumulation of powers and supervisory competence to the European institutions. This represents a creeping movement towards the E.U. having legal integrity, a form of nationhood, in its own right. This, the E.U.'s true project, could not be successful without a pragmatic understanding of sovereignty among Europe's various stato-nationalist leaders. The single currency project is the most overt and blatant example of this creeping statehood and 'pragmatic sovereignty' in action. More auspiciously, the E.U. has been successful in evolving distinctive competences in foreign policy, commercial policy, customs matters and fisheries, all of which transcend national boundaries to some degree of other: in the case of fisheries, radically so. This is the reality behind the idealistic pleadings of 'sovereignty', in both directions, from the E.U.'s technocrats, political personalities, supporters, enemies and opponents. Looked at historically, the E.U.'s modus is not innovative. In fact, it is entirely consistent with philosophic concepts of international law and stato-nationhood going back to the Peace of Westphalia of 1648. The reality is that the E.U. is consistent in development with established traditions of European legal, political and constitutional thought. This raises a number of questions and points that, at first sight, may seem perplexing in the mind of the ethno-motivated stato-nationalist dissident, and which have formed the backcloth of much political debate in Britain over the last few decades. Why would these ancient, ethnic nation-states permit an evolutionary process to enter into train that would involve the practical bleeding of sovereignty from their own institutions? How could such a project be carried out so harmoniously and contentedly, without significant resistance from stato-national political or economic elites and without rioting in the streets?

That the E.U. has been a harmonious alignment is because its various stato-national leaders – in both politics and business – have willed it, as this was their project. They would not have willed it to fail or fall apart. That the E.U. has, generally, achieved its intermediate objectives and remains on course for "ever closer union" among its Member States is a testament to its consistent success in attracting public assent or support throughout the various Member States. It is the people-at-large who wanted, or at least were willing to accept, integration (and thus, the ceding of sovereignty). This may be because they were misinformed – were "lied-to" – or it could be that they lacked other political choices, but they wanted or accepted these changes nonetheless. The point illustrates a reality that few stato-nationalists wish to recognise or acknowledge. Their usual response is to complain about the E.U.'s true agenda as if it is some conspiratorial secret, but it isn't a secret. The true agenda has been out in the open from the beginning. Even so, the stato-nationalist diagnosis and the prognosis are correct and the complaint has an accurate basis; it is, in fact, the treatment prescribed that is harmful, if not dangerous, to our racial prospects. If sovereignty is pragmatic and relativist, and if the world is evolving in a way that reflects this, then the correct response is not to fight the rest of the world because of the way it is or the forces of history because of what they have led to and will likely lead to. That is a war that would surely prove futile. Flogging the poor old tired horse may be emotionally-satisfying, but it is hardly useful. What we need is a new horse.

Debates about the 'evils' of the E.U. in Britain are, then, a distraction. The fault – in so far as there is fault – for 'problems' with 'Europe' is with the institutions of Britain itself, specifically the UK Parliament. These are not European problems, caused by some distant, out-of-touch cartoon bureaucrats in Brussels or wherever, so much as British problems caused by people in London. This is true even on the terms of the 'anti-E.U.' politicians and agitators themselves. If we accept UKIP propaganda, then it is in the UK Parliament, for the time being, that reserve sovereignty is still vested. It is there that the necessary resolution would see us removed from the E.U., de facto and de jure, should that be considered desirable. When this point is made, the 'Eurosceptics' and anti-E.U. politicians reply that the 'problem' (whatever they define that to be) is not some foreign committee, but in fact that the political class in this country is out-of-touch with the population. There is, indeed, a political class in Britain, and they are out-of-touch, but even a remote elite must broadly reflect its population representatively. If there were a genuine desire to withdraw from the E.U. among the population, then by now we would have at least entered into serious negotiations to withdraw. The reason we have not done so is that there is no such desire. Not a serious desire at any rate, not in the country, not in Parliament and not in UKIP itself. Those who believe otherwise are deluding themselves on two fronts: first, they are deluded that the E.U. actually matters in racial terms, when in fact it is a side-issue and, at best, a distraction; and second, quite apart from the relative significance of the E.U., what is not grasped is that we have the type of society that disregards national and racial identity because the majority of people have either affirmed or acquiesced in the changes that brought about its existence, and UKIP – a globalist, right-wing, materialist faction of the Tory party – is a product of this general attitudinal climate. Do not mistake my logic for an affirmation of this country's democratic credentials. I do not believe in democracy in the first place, nor do I accept this country is a democracy in anything but the most limited sense. However, even the most beligerent dictator cannot survive without either the tacit acceptance or acquiescence of his people – consent, in other words – and if we are sufficiently clear-headed to acknowledge this, then these difficult issues become easier to grapple with.

We are the foreigners in Britain: those of us who are racially-conscious that is. Those among us who wish to preserve Britain politically must ask themselves what it is they are seeking to preserve. A mixed-racial, alien-infested hellhole perhaps? Or maybe the most unequal British society since the Edwardian era? Or perhaps what matters is preserving mass drug dependency, pornography and alcoholism? The reality is that Britain is not Britain. It is somewhere else, a sick, depraved, dysgenic society that cannot be saved, and those who, on any terms, call for its preservation are (consciously or otherwise) joining a different chorus, the fractured, dissonant clatter of our enemies who welcome all-sorts to their shebang. That is not to say that an idealised racial 'Europe' is the answer. We cannot instantly re-create the society that we want, and any concrete attempts to do so via remote country retreats and other sundry discursions will lead to nothing. What we must recognise is that though geo-demographics are crucial politically, what we are engaged in is not so much a territorial battle as a war for the human mind and spirit. Our destination must be 'Nowhere' in the truest sense. We are fighting for a future we will not see, but our contribution is critical – and the European identity of that future is inescapable.

'Europe' is a problematic word for Nationalists due to the association it now has with the discredited, pseudo-Communist excesses of the E.U. Yet a vision of the unity of Europe is entirely compatible, if not a predicate, for white racial survival. In that sense, as I see it, the difference between a British stato-nationalist and a White Nationalist is fundamental, and I do not accept that the two positions are complementary. There is a conflict between the pull of the invented nation and the reality of race, and increasingly as the British Mixed Race State shows itself to be treasonous as to race, that conflict manifests itself in so many ways so as to almost render the two positions opposite. Despite this, for practical purposes, a state of complementarity has continued within Nationalism for many years, so that British nationalists have worked alongside White Nationalists, and some have even adopted the claim of holding both positions at once. This unhappy marriage cannot continue. Those of us who are White Nationalists do not reject our British identity. Far from it, but nor is this merely a cold debate about political structures. It is true that we do not attach any significant weight to the current political construct that is the British State: what I call, the British Mixed Race State, a phraseology I use to emphasise the fact that the British State is mixed-racialist in its nature and purpose, and is thus anti-white. However, the difference goes deeper and can best to summarised by differentiating the terms 'patriot' and 'Nationalist'. A patriot in the stato-nationalist sense is akin (to paraphrase Popper) with the 'uncritical rationalist'. He accepts, worships in fact, the manifestations of absolute sovereignty. A Nationalist, on the other hand, is Popper's 'critical rationalist'. He confronts the brutal truth and dismisses idealistic notions of absolute sovereignty as an empirical nonsense. He accepts that sovereignty in the stato-national sense is pragmatic and relativist. He holds that the only sovereignty that matters is racial sovereignty. Accordingly, he treats the deceptive manifestations of absolute sovereignty with cold expediency. When the nation-state no longer serves its purpose, the Nationalist gathers together his worn tools and builds up a new Nation. That is what we Nationalists must now do.

Some would say that the issue between British stato-nationalists and White Nationalists is insubstantial and semantic, in that it's all nothing more than how one defines a 'Nationalist'. I disagree. It is not merely that I am free, if I wish, to define 'Nation' in racial terms. It is that the term 'Nation' has no meaning unless it is defined racially. The idea of mixed-racial nations, Singaporean administrative units for the management of human populations, is as sinister and nonsensical as it sounds, but I must acknowledge the reality that the choice of the alternative has been taken from me. The British population voted for this Westphalian perversion, this Rainbow international legal order that hides behind idealistic myths of absolute sovereignty. They want this. That we few, the Nationalists, want a quite different world in which human beings have strong indigenous identities, and that we see such a world as a precondition to human dignity and freedom, is a point completely lost on our uneducated fellows. To them, we are: "Nazi!", "Racist!", "Misogynist!", or whatever is the in-term. There comes a point when one must acknowledge that the horse is well-enough flogged, and it so happens that this horse is comatose. The historians of the future will be startled to find that the cause of the horse's condition was not some tragic accident or sinister plot sprung by malicious crypto-Jews acting in league with David Icke and a council of lizards. The explanation is more prosaic, and less comical. The horse lost its spirit. It laid down to die. This truth must now be confronted, coldly and soberly.

If our nation cannot be Britain, then we must lift our sights higher. Our Nation will be Europe, i.e. a White Nation that is a white European community of whatever geographic location, and that is cohesive in the racial sense. The petty ethnic and linguistic divides within the White National Community that once swayed masses now amount to little, for the majority who were charged with the eternal task of assuring our genetic destiny have set their course, a road to a cosmopolitan Nothing in which ethnoism is a deracinated construct. This cosmpolitian world will be as cold as the pavement outside. It will be a world in which everyone is equal, and therefore everyone is nothing; a world in which everyone is, truly, a citizen of the world, and therefore a citizen of nowhere: alas, not the Nowhere that William Morris had in mind, but instead a Nothing kind of Nowhere in which each person will live a life of softened servitude. I refuse to join that journey into spiritual obsolescence, and as it is Europe that is the ancestral homeland of our race – the greatest people to walk the face of the Earth, the White Race – then those of us who remain of the pre-Modern mind, of the visceral racial consciousness, must set a quite different course, towards a world of meaning, towards a New Europe.

The modus of the New Europeans will not be some crude Schumanisme, an extension of the existing civic Europe. Ours will be a New Order, a New Tribe, but we need a means to get there. What I propose is that Nationalists now turn the greater part of their efforts towards community-building strategies that are explicitly race-conscious. In North America, wonderful efforts are underway to create Pioneer Little Europe communities. In Europe, we must iterate this brilliant movement, but we must do so in a way that is more appropriate to our distinct civic, social and political environment. I therefore propose a new concept, Racial Intentional Community, which honours our debt to PLE and to a large extent simply replicates it, but which also reflects the more communitarian, social and fascistic philosophical basis that we, the Nationalists of Europe, wish to see in our societies, on our Continent, including here in Britain. Let us confront the choice that faces each of us.

Arguments among friends are often the most brutal, as a reading of the history of various white civil wars will show. There are times when friends must, bitterly and tearfully, part for the good of the whole. We have arrived at such a moment. The white race is stood on the precipice of destiny. One day it will be our very survival that is called to the dock of Fate. In that trial of fire and steel, Mother Nature will look on with withering contempt at those who do not accept the imperatives of genetic and racial perpetuation, and She is remorseless. There is no room for the liberal mentality of seeing both sides of it, of having it forwards, sidewards and backwards. There is survival and there is extinction, and now each of us must choose. What we are witnessing is the beginning of the making of that choice. A critical but necessary schism is appearing in our milieu. It will be a slow but sure separation of the true, racially-conscious Nationalists from the reflexively racist ultra-Tories and national chauvinists clinging to the comforting wreckage of the British Mixed-Race State. The latter are now a dead-weight due to their inability to evolve politically. A significant minority of them were never sincere racialists in the first place, rather they masqueraded as Nationalists, often due to a psychological need to wear the black hat. These obstinate 'Britishers', whether purblind, reactionary or just plain stupid, will now take their rightful place among the 'racially liberated' masses, happy to be appeased by whichever right-wing puppet the Establishment throws up from time-to-time. By contrast, those for whom the bottom line is, and always will be, race – the Nationalists – must forge a new future as New Europeans. For these few, the nation-state is a transient construct, a means to an end that can be adopted and discarded coldly according to the expediencies of racial survival. We, that small minority, who are conscious of our racial destiny, must come to the painful mental acceptance that the most cherished patient has finally croaked, and while it certainly deserves – and will one day receive – a dignified burial, wrapped in its own Union Flag, we are set on Fate: Britain as a political entity must now be left to die, lest it brings the entire white race down with it. A New Europe must arise!

## 6.2.

*This is the second in a series of articles I wrote in the summer of 2013 for the White Independent Nation website. Again, I stand by today what I wrote then, only I would probably be more explicit now about the role of Jewish influence in the media, whereas in the above article it is only hinted at very subtly.*

### Bias Towards Whom?[37]

We often hear or read about complaints concerning the alleged bias of one mainstream media organisation or another. The BBC, for instance, is regularly accused of having a kind of 'left-wing' bias. Sometimes this allegation is broadened to all media in Britain, so that it is said most press and broadcast media have a general liberal or Left bias.

The reverse allegation is, of course, often heard from the Left, in that they claim the mainstream media is bias towards the political Right or is against the Left in various ways. Admittedly, most of us will readily accept that bias is a natural state of mind that is difficult to conceal when commenting on news or current events. We all approach comment from a perspective that is our own and a strong level of objectivity is difficult to achieve in those circumstances. The root of the complaint, then, is in the belief that those who journalise or report on what is happening in the world are expected to resist ordinary, base temptations of partiality. Perhaps unrealistically, bias is thought to be the preserve of commentary, while news should be gathered by a kind of Quixotic cadre of objective public servants who, idealistically, report what they see and nothing else.

Of course, the real world doesn't work like this. We only need look at history. Bias in media has existed since the dawn of the first printing press. In the early days, the capital needed for establishing a serious and viable press was such that the technology was concentrated in relatively few hands. Naturally, great reliance was placed on the financial sponsor, with the result that only a narrow range of opinions were published and circulated from the first printing presses. This informal censorship, if one might call it that, later took on legislative form in the infamous licensing laws imposed by Parliament during the 17th. century. These laws restricted what types of opinions might be published and circulated. As you might expect, views that were hostile to the political elite of the day could be suppressed, and were often prevented from being published at all. It was only with the rise of the modern journalist trade during the late 17th. and early 18th. century that the liberty to speak freely in Britain took on meaning in the public space, as publications such as Tatler and the early Spectator emerged.

The modern equivalent of the parliamentary licensors and the wealthy print owners are the BBC executives and their counterparts in the private sector. The BBC executives often have close involvement in a variety of political and cultural activities outside their immediate responsibilities at the Corporation. The private sector media owners are invariably hugely influential figures in business and across society, especially in politics. Together they form a media and political class: class being the apt term, since they act cohesively, and consciously, in their collective interest.

---

[37] First published on 14th. August 2013 at http://www.win-white.org

These people will generally tolerate only a narrow bandwidth of 'acceptable opinion', and it is within this Potemkin Village that the public is presented with its political choices, through newspapers, various online channels, the radio and the TV. These 'choices' are in fact largely a series of 'false opposites', the falsity being that on closer examination, it becomes apparent that almost-all of the political parties are presenting the proverbial 'business as usual' agenda, while minority views that might challenge the status quo are not permitted to find expression.

The emergence of the web as an alternative media is slowly threatening this domination by wealthy interests of news and opinion. The web is a means by which information can be disseminated democratically and on a mass basis relatively cheaply, but even with the rise of internet news and commentary, the economic structure of media still harks back to the wealthy print owners and their parliamentary licensors. The reason for the continuing struggle for 'information democracy' is the economic power of the media barons, who still have available to them 'soft' means of censorship and control. Their methods, tried and tested, include, inter alia, powerful advertising and marketing techniques; the use of propaganda to dissuade serious consideration of alternative viewpoints; the promotion of concision in broadcasting; the control of what is 'acceptable language'; and the simple denial of airspace (or print space). The rudiments of this information control apparatus give a whole new dimension to the term 'bias'. Its Middle French origin word, biais, meant a slant, slope or oblique. We see here also a possible origin for the term 'spin': i.e. the giving to favourable slant on events and news stories. In keeping with that etymology, and in spite of the web's democratic potential, what is broadcast, published and consumed by the public day after day is still a slanted reality, a simulacrum in which a distorted, even alien, picture of the world is presented, yet a picture that at the same time uncannily reflects the priorities of our everyday oppressors: be they employers, official types or a hostile government. But what is all this in aid of? What is being protected?

We must remember that self-perpetuation is in the nature of a hierarchy. This gives rise to a variety of materialist expediencies, which we see manifested in everyday news about politics, and in the mundanities of our own lives. What the politicians and information managers wish to protect most of all is their own sinecures. It is the case that a wave of Nationalist support in Britain would imperil the livelihoods and material interests of a large part of the ruling elite. And we know that the same could be said about a rise in support for the extreme Left, which is anti-capitalist, yet we note with frustration and dismay the appeasement and co-option of the social liberal perspective by the Establishment, including mainstream media. The explanation for this must be deeper than mere cultural bias. There have to be materialist considerations at play. We can also observe that it is Nationalism – and the broader far-Right – that suffers most of the British State's overt oppression, and while the far-Left does also at times receive its share of official attention, it is the far-Right and Nationalists that are openly reviled and despised by the British State, and also, significantly, among the mainstream media.

Does this overt biasing both against Nationalists and toward social liberal attitudes suggest a deeper, systemic partiality among media institutions? Or are the allegations of left-wing bias, levelled especially against the BBC, just another clever distraction that, when repeated by Nationalists, serve to take attention away from the country's real problems? The monsterisation of the so-called 'Left' is an easy and clever way for the elites to distract attention. The Tories in particular enjoy the fact that those of a populist bent rail against the so-called 'Marxist' or 'left-wing' BBC while overlooking the destructive, anti-social and anti-national policies of the government itself, not to mention its 'Loyal Opposition'. That most of the people who use the term 'Marxist' in this context have little or no idea what it means is hardly relevant. The point is that there is a need for a diversion, a scapegoat, and it must be plausible. And it is plausible that the BBC is infested with what is called Cultural Marxism. What exactly is meant by the phrase 'Cultural Marxism' depends on who is speaking or writing, but in non-academic hands the vague gist is that it is an extreme, socially-liberal type of leftism involving a wish for a more egalitarian, racially-mixed and internationalist society. Does the BBC support this sort of thing? Officially, the BBC is impartial. Unofficially, however, its various journalists, broadcasters and reporters do seem to promote a certain partial outlook, and while it is difficult to define precisely what that outlook is, we can say with relative ease what it isn't. It is not socially-, morally- and culturally-conservative, nationalistic, or family-centred. In fact, it is uncomfortable with these things. But is it left-wing? The question, and indeed the accusation, are circular in that the Left are people and groups with a variety of different ideological positions. However, it is clear that when the issue of media biasing is addressed by Nationalists and the far-Right, then the Left is being defined as those who believe in, or prioritise, social, economic and racial equality. Few could or would disagree with that as a fairly inclusive description, if not a definition. We can include within it almost-all political groups that identify with the egalitarian Left culturally, if not ideologically, and propound equality as a good in itself. To what extent does the BBC align itself with this 'ideology of equality'?

The evidence is mixed, but a clear picture does emerge. The BBC often broadcasts programmes that are deeply pro-business in character. We only have to look at 'reality' series such as The Apprentice, Dragon's Den, etc. as a case in point, as they celebrate business and the vague idea that one must be competitive and cut-throat in order to 'get ahead'. Then there is the BBC's news and current affairs output, with items and stories that often have a pro-business focus. On the other hand, we can detect with the BBC an editorial slant that is equalitarian, in that stories and news items are selected that highlight certain issues. We see this in the BBC's coverage of business issues. There is often a focus on the supposed pay gap between male and female workers, and the issue will be presented in a way that is favourable to those who believe that female workers suffer a raw deal. Coverage of the immigration controversy will be presented from an angle that highlights the business and economic benefits that migrants supposedly bring to the UK. Some programmes show a more overt editorial biasing. An edition of Countryfile in December 2012 highlighted the supposed 'problem' of a lack of ethnic minority people living in or visiting the countryside. That and other particularly egregious examples do suggest an equalitarian bias that is anti-national and anti-white in character, but to label this as 'left-wing' does not necessarily tell us a great deal. It is not that the BBC and its cousins in the media are institutionally 'left-wing'. Nor are they institutionally 'right-wing', necessarily just because they produce pro-business programmes. That is not to let the Left (in both the Labour and Tory parties, and their cultural friends, etc.) off the hook concerning their failed policies in this country, rather it is to seek a closer understanding of precisely what is being propagandised and promoted through our media and why. Do these people really keep yapping about 'equality' because they're all left-wing or involved in some sinister neo-Marxist plot? Or is the real reason more prosaic? We really need to ask the age-old question: Who benefits? A different, and arguably more accurate, way to summarise the situation is that the media, including the BBC, tend to be 'metropolitan' in attitude.

By 'metropolitan' I refer to the adoption of certain mores, norms and attitudes that are modish and reflect the lifestyle of those who might benefit from or look more favourably on a more liberal outlook in society. In British society today, we can see that a new 'metropolitan class' is emerging that could be likened to the patrician class of the late Roman Republic, occupying the strata of elite political, cultural and administrative posts in society and evolving into an ersatz Nomenklatura, with its own class signifiers. One such signifier is a distinct anti-plebeian attitude and an overt disdain for working people and their provincial mores and needs. A stark example of the phenomenon is found in discussion about immigration. A common provincial complaint is how problems with open-door immigration are not discussed in public, yet in truth, the subject is dealt with at length in public discourse. The difficulty is not in its absence from public discussion, but in the perspective from which it is dealt with, which invariably emphasises the priorities of both big business and metropolitan types, two groups that loudly welcome the 'benefits' of open immigration policies in the form of low-cost, pliable labour and cheap restaurants, etc. Likewise, in some ways it benefits the business class to promote the idea that all women are potential victims of 'sexism' or that 'racism' is widespread, as this encourages division and individuation in the workplace, as opposed to solidarity. If working people unite, they are strong – especially if they unite within effective unions. If, on the other hand, working people are encouraged to divide and becomes suspicious of each other, maybe also compete with each other for illusory 'middle class' careers, there is less a sense of solidarity, and the bosses are stronger. To an extent, these priorities manifest in open snobbery towards the 'ignorant provincials' who dare to challenge the established order of things. Insults such as 'racist', 'bigot', 'Nazi', 'red', 'commie' and so on are a reflection of a class bias, with one class using verbal intimidation to block reasoned debate about its assumed privileges and the damaging and anti-social effect they have on the country-at-large. Simple class snobbery also plays its role. You might say that the provincials are the 'workers', while the metropolitans are the 'bosses' and the workers really should know their place and keep quiet. This type of attitudinal cringe is of course nothing new in Britain, but it is important to understand that class prejudice is not merely a cultural phenomenon, it is also economic in character – in other words, it serves a purpose, with a long antecedence into the traditional feudal economic structure of British, particularly English, society.

What we will also consider here is the interaction of basic socio-geography. Britain – particularly England – is London-centric, and this is reflected in the priorities of the media. In a more pluralistic society with diffuse and autonomous power structures, there might be more room for the provincial attitude to take root. Nevertheless, and despite superficial appearances offered by devolution to the sub-national level, Britain remains a heavily centralised society with its power structures concentrated in London. A 'British media' does not, as such, exist. What we have in fact is a London media that broadcasts to the entire country, adopting a metropolitan social, cultural and political orientation. In London, and among Londoners, the 'anti-plebeian' and 'metropolitan' values are pervasive because of what London is. It's a metropolis. Its people tend to see things in metropolitan terms. That's only natural. In fact, no matter how conservative you are, or think you are, if you lived in London you would over time begin to allow accommodations to the social environment around you. If you were sufficiently robust mentally, you could resist it to a degree, but not totally. Most media people either live or work in London, or both, and where they do neither, they still work for a media organisation that is London-centric in the sense of either being located in London or being under London-centric cultural influences, or both. Most successful media people also spend the formative years of their careers in the London media environment. However, the metropolitan mindset is only a tendency – so, there are exceptions, and there are 'metro' people who will flit in-and-out of the tendency and exhibit a more provincial or conservative mindset from time-to-time, depending on the issue. But to display a provincial, anti-metropolitan viewpoint consistently would require the journalist or broadcaster to rebel against his own paymasters. That is something that most journalists – and certainly nearly-all young journalists – will not do. The media are cliquely and McCarthyite in their treatment of their own, and will shun and exile professionally any journalist who does not articulate and repeat the Zeitgeist, and so understandably many journalists will not reveal their true thoughts or betray inner doubts.

Those of us outside London, especially those like myself who live in areas that are still traditionally quite conservative, working class and white-dominated, look at the goings-on in the 'mainstream media' with bafflement. The gossip and parliamentary tittle-tattle; the petty arguments over who said what on Twitter; the strange and fanatical crusade to purge racism among white people; the obsession with house prices and abstract growth figures; and so on. To the provincial mindset, none of this is particularly relevant or equates to the common experience, still less makes sense. Nevertheless, the circus rumbles on, on all channels, purveying the metropolitan, anti-plebeian perspective. Recently, on Channel Four (another, supposedly, 'left-wing' channel), we were treated to the dubious delights of a fresh series of Undercover Boss, a risible programme that infantilises and humiliates ordinary workers. The perspective of the programme-makers is deeply patrician. They believe implicitly that ordinary people are helpless and should not take responsibility for the material conditions in their working environment. Instead, they should look to their munificent 'boss' who, like a knight in shining armour, will come to the rescue to make their working conditions 'fair' and give a few quid to charity in the process. The picture is of ordinary people not in control of their own lives while carrying out difficult and arduous work that the 'boss' can't do, yet the boss earns several times their salary. It's fitting for a society in which selfishness and greed have been elevated to a virtue that is then crystallised in patronising workplace munificence; a society in which the ordinary worker is denied union membership and basic dignity; a society in which what matters is getting one up on the other fellow. Most of the participants in the series are low-paid and unskilled and not in any position to answer back to an impertinent boss who understands his own company so poorly that he needs a camera to follow him round while he discovers just how bad a manager he is and how good his workers are. I think it is safe to say that Undercover Boss is not a left-wing programme, though it may unintentionally fill the more astute Channel Four viewer with some very left-wing ideas as he or she angrily throws a shoe at the TV set and contemplates what they would do if they got their hands on the stupid boss being featured that week.

Our metropolitan media are happy for us to believe that they are simply a bunch of 'left-wing' revolutionaries, but the truth is not quite like this. What they – and their friends in politics – really are is the propaganda arm of an anti-social predator class in society. These modern 'licensors' are the mouthpieces of society's capitalists, and just as in the 17th. century the parliamentary licensors did the bidding of their wealthy constituents, today the political and media class work against the people in pursuit of a self-enriching agenda. The BBC, in common with all broadcasters, is certainly biased. This bias may, from time-to-time, appear in 'left-wing' or 'right-wing' form, but its true nature is more complicated. You may be sure that the real bias is toward those who wish to maintain their profits at the expense of the people and will do everything possible to stop a Popular Nationalist movement arising. This is because in a Nationalist society the community will place the health, welfare and dignity of its folk above all else, and give its children a future – and the modern licensors will not be welcome. As we work towards that society, we may require from time-to-time policies or initiatives that resemble the Left or the Right, but are in fact Nationalist. That is our only bias: we are merely working for the interests of our own people.

**6.3.**

*Below is an article published last year on the White Independent Nation website.*

### Who's The Bigot?[38]

I grew-up in a predominantly white, working class area of northern England, in which support for the Labour Party was taken as a given, and in which I myself supported and voted for Labour. I was even a Labour Party activist during my teenage years.

The votes were weighed, rather than counted, and it is my understanding that they still are. However, back then it was not an area in which today's 'Left' would have felt at home or remotely welcome. The people, and most of their Labour politicians, held to traditional views about society and the family. They supported the collective rights of their class and folk and were outraged at the attack on trade unions by both Labour and Conservative governments. They were nationalists in the generic sense of being for their own people, but they were not specially patriotic. They tended to look favourably on European integration, seeing themselves (as many northern English do) vaguely as northern regionalists and separate from the more market-oriented southern English. They had no time for the emerging social liberalism in society and disliked anti-family policies, and innovations such as gay rights. They tended to loathe mass immigration. At that time, it was common to hear in political meetings ordinary working men speak in highly-prejudicial terms about a range of modish issues. There was, then, a class-based cleave in the Labour Party, between the traditionally conservative branches found in the working class areas and the more social-liberal perspective found in the middle-class, metropolitan branches.

If I make my birthplace sound ugly to more decadent or sensitive souls, it is not out of disloyalty, but I do have some reason. I was born in Pontefract, the town immortalised by J. S. Fletcher in his classic satiric novel, The Town of Crooked Ways. It is also the town that gave us the corrupt architectural designer, John Poulson. From my own researches, I know that Pontefract had a rough, perhaps even corrupt, political environment over the years, but particularly during the 1960s and 1970s. For a good guide to what politics in the north of England during that era was like, watch the excellent 1990s TV series, Our Friends In The North, which depicts similarly-corrupt local politics in the north-east of England. Pontefract also has a unique claim as the place to hold the first secret ballot in the Northern Hemisphere, which took place on 15 August 1872. However, the place typifies the north of England towns, with its blind tribal loyalty to the local municipal Labour Party; in its combination of quaint medieval buildings alongside brutalist 1960s architecture; and especially in the ordinary views and attitudes of its people, which cannot be dissimilar to the views of ordinary people everywhere in our country. It is an attitude of mind that the modish would describe dismissively as 'bigotry'. For an example of this patronisation, recall if you will that during the 2010 popularity contest, the then-Prime Minister called an ordinary retiree in Rochdale, Gillian Duffy, a 'bigoted woman'. This was once she was out of earshot. It is clear that he felt her (fairly mild) views on immigration did not deserve serious consideration, but the phrase 'bigoted woman' was a perjorative employed to dismiss not just Ms. Duffy's

---

[38] First published on 20th. August 2013 at http://www.win-white.org

views, but Ms. Duffy as a person. Mr. Brown was making an assessment about Ms. Duffy herself and her moral qualities; he was not merely dismissing her views.

Bigotry can indeed be an ugly impulse, but its presence does not necessarily make for an unpleasant society. In fact, quite the opposite. A nation of bigots can be strong for its bigotry. The views I have described above, and those of Ms. Duffy, remain common among most ordinary people – i.e. the type of people who have to work for a living, or who have retired from real jobs – except that now this bigotry has to remain silent and hidden. This unspoken shared consciousness among working people is not just a narrow provincial mindset and cannot be dismissed as such. It is, rather, a kind of folk wisdom, a common body of knowledge and experience as to what makes for good families and stable communities. The usual response to its opponents in national culture, politics and in the workplace is a la Gordon Brown – "She's just a sort of bigoted woman that said she used to be Labour...". Ms. Duffy, who used to be Labour, discovered the value of her genuine and honest views to the patrician Gordon Brown. However, Ms. Duffy and her community were, perhaps, fortunate. The more usual response to such outrageous outbursts from "bigoted women who used to be Labour" is to recruit an army of middle-class social-worky liberals (think Stella Creasy crossed with Harriet Harman) to descend on whichever working class community is deemed 'too Saxon' (i.e. too white), to do their 'civilising' work reductio ad Hitlerum, 'educating' the 'ignorant' natives. The media will, helpfully, chime in with alarmist, but essentially truthful, perspectives on the economic degradation of the area, often forgetting the context that the loyalty shown by these "bigoted" working people "who used to vote Labour" was rewarded with asset-stripping and industrial defoliation.

What is missed by these 'intelligent' 'educators' amidst their enthusiasm for cultural rapine is the background traditions of the people they patronise and look down on. The patrician mind is mistaken. The ordinary people are not ignorant. They just know what is best for them, yet they are trapped in a 'Normanised' political system run by a Bohemian metropolitan class who want to dictate what is best for them, and what is considered best – 'fair', 'just', 'moral' – normally coincides with what might result in the most economic opportunity for the people who actually own the country. Deindustrialisation – i.e. the destruction of manufacturing jobs, and with it trade union influence – is supported by both the political Right and their friends in the metropolitan Left. White working class men can then be coerced into service sector jobs, casualised labour or self-employment of some kind, or just left to live on benefits (the people the Daily Mail calls 'scroungers'). None of this 'economic activity' has any serious trade union representation, or is politically- or industrially-represented at all. But it's good for business. Mass immigration means cheap labour and generally lower labour costs as migrants are pliable, which is good for business. Racial integration (race-mixing) means gradual social acceptance of the immigrant aliens, which solidifies the new social order and makes it harder to argue coherently against ever-more immigration. And so on. These things, and more besides, are regarded as 'progress', but we should bear in mind that not all progress is advancement. 'Progress' seems to demand that an entire section of the population loses its political and industrial voice – and conveniently, this just happens to be the section of the population that holds to its own folk wisdom, in conflict with the 'humane', 'fair', and 'moral' values of the rulers. Which again, is good for business. We can see that the unspoken auchtonomy that once-governed and accounted for things was not the preserve of narrow provincial mindsets, or ignorant country bumpkins, but actually served an economic purpose. Against that background, bigotry looks like the privilege of the intelligent.

But let's consider what bigotry really is. It might be defined as prejudice based on some ascribed trait such as sex, race or nationality. In itself, bigotry is neither a good nor a bad thing. After all, we measure, variously, the 'goodness' or 'badness' of things by evaluating their outcomes, not by their innate nature. Killing another human being can be a good or a bad thing, depending on the consequences of the act. We use man-made laws to roughly apply a system of ethics, so that our actions can be policed according to their consequences and certain actions that are 'bad' can be discouraged. It is not, therefore, illegal to be racist, as racism is, in itself, inconsequential. However certain acts that involve racism are considered contrary to law. This modern transitory, from neutrality as to the thing-in-itself to moral and legal mobilisation against the act, brings to mind the Stoic introspection of Marcus Aurelius in Meditation X (Book Eight) [to quote]:

*"This, what is it in itself, and by itself, according to its proper constitution? What is the substance of it? What is the matter, or proper use? What is the form, or efficient cause? What is it for in this world, and how long will it abide? Thus must thou examine all things that present themselves unto thee."*

To paraphrase Marcus Aurelius into our own, quite different, context, it could be said that the human mind is 'the unknowable', the neumenon of the Greek philosophers, or indeed the ding an sich of Kantian philosophy. Whether it is sexual fantasy or some sort of bigotry or love or hatred, we cannot really know ourselves fully, let alone know what is in the minds of others. We must therefore borrow the solution outlined above in Meditation X and consider the act – that is, the consequences of the thought – in light of what we surmise in the world around us, and then judge accordingly. In a traditional community, this Stoic transitory mindset is not very difficult to adopt and follow as a kind of social 'golden rule'. Ordinary folk, I would suggest, are essentially 'little Stoics', pragmatically judging others on their conduct, while accepting everyone on a prior assumption of good faith. The notion that someone should be judged for being 'racist' or 'sexist' is an alien concept to the Stoic mind, for two reasons. First, it makes little practical sense in a community to judge people on what they may or may not think; and second, it is difficult to ascribe a 'sexist' or 'racist' quality to an act, for these are purely abstract ascriptions. We know, roughly-speaking, when an act is 'good' or bad'. Our 'moral common-sense' provides a yardstick for measuring the 'goodness' or 'badness' of the act, and we normally needn't trouble ourselves with further complicated discursions on the matter so far as day-to-day conduct is concerned. What is more difficult is applying notions that are purely abstract. Thus, you rarely hear from ordinary people accusations that such-and-such a person is a 'racist cyclist'. Yes, I can hear you laughing as you read that. Indeed, the notion is ridiculous, yet a comparable accusation is frequently accepted in the media without serious question.

If I told you that tomorrow's newspapers would be printing a story about a professional sports cyclist having made some racist remark or other, then you might indeed believe me when I say that the hypothesis of the 'racist cyclist' is not as silly as it might first seem. Mention 'racist' or 'sexist' and the accusation is widely-accepted on the basis of fairly flimsy and summary evidence about what the target had said, even in private. We may imagine that our 'racist cyclist' would then be shunned by his commercial sponsors, some of his friends, and all 'respectable' people, in much the same way that in the traditional community a person who committed some egregious or scandalous criminal act might be shunned. Yet, in the traditional community, it is Stoicism that is the impulse at work, a judgement based on actions and consequences; whereas, in the media, there is an orchestrated anti-Stoicism in operation: a harken, if you like, to the opposite Greek tradition of Aristotle, with its pseudo-faith in the idealistic and incorporeal. Our hypothetical 'racist cyclist' is, on the terms of this society, to be subjected to an organised campaign of libel and slander without any solid basis. His appeals to reason and common-sense cannot be considered cogent, for the Stoic understanding of social relations is gone. Efforts are made to force him to apologise for his 'bigotry' and beg for forgiveness.

Why? Because the Stoicism of our ancestors cannot work in a mixed-racial society. When we look around us, we see that there are no longer communities, and even the existence of families is in doubt. There are only individuals, of different racial and cultural heritage, striving for their own ambition and satisfaction. The former, traditional informalities of manners, dress, speech, behaviour and body language, and so on, that permitted discretion, understanding and judgement within a 'common culture' – in which people understood one another implicitly – have now gone, perhaps forever. We are now an individuated mass, and notions of community must now give way to legalistic prescription, which – necessarily – intrudes into areas that were formerly properly considered private. Instead of judgement of others based on conduct alone, which is the traditional, Stoic, basis of English criminal law, there is now an imperative to police our thoughts, in so far as this is practically possible, and there are special words that are used to describe the thoughts that are considered improper. On the face of it, the law continues to respect the Stoic transitory, but in practice there is a creeping tendency, both in the letter of the law and its application to day-to-day life, towards suppressing views and opinions that are impolitic, so that whereas Marcus Aurelius – the rather arrogant, imperious Roman Emperor – might have humbly conceded that he could not understand the thing in itself except via the fruit of its expression, our own rulers seek a relentless Inquisition of the 'thing' and will, if they think it necessary, stamp on it in lieu of any understanding.

This presents those of us who are the 'Gillian Duffys' of the world with a dilemma, for our own bigotry – if it may be called that – is natural, though not unthinking. The application of our bigotry could be seen as a necessary defence mechanism. Our racial views, expressed here on the W.I.N. website, are a typical example. I would say ours is a 'positive' type of bigotry, neither morally good nor bad, but simply a necessitous and inevitable result of a survival instinct. Our visceral attitudes towards other races are to do with that natural instinct, which is spoken and written here and elsewhere as an insatiable desire to preserve our race and way of life. By contrast, the more 'negative' charge of bigotry, presumably levelled by the racial liberals against W.I.N. and similar initiatives, and familiar to most who rely on mainstream media, is really an attempt to dehumanise us and deter our instinctive survival responses. It is here that the positive-negative cleave in bigotry becomes important in our efforts at persuasion. Those who submit to the brainwashing and implicitly accept the 'negative' charge of bigotry develop a neurosis, believing that they are in some way dirty and unclean for having what are in truth perfectly natural thoughts. Only interested in marrying a white woman? "That's racism!" Want to only socialise with white people? "Well really, how racist!"

Indeed it is (negative) bigotry to have these impulses – to that extent, our opponents and critics are actually right – but that in itself doesn't really tell us much, other than that such thoughts can seem a little ugly in that no-one really wants to judge anyone based purely on appearance, even if there is a solid, racial, basis to the discrimination. We must consider what has brought these impulses about. If it were not for the enforced mixed-racialism and its multi-culturalism, there would be none of this 'negative' kind of bigotry, as constructed by media. There would be no reason for it, because different peoples would not be forced together. Instead, people would accept 'positive' bigotry – i.e. Nationalism – as the norm, and most people would simply marry others of the same race because that is the natural thing to do. Likewise, those of a more adventurous bent or who might wish to learn about other races and cultures close-up would be able to travel or enter education to do so, and would be free to follow their own desires, interests and passions in whatever way they liked. In this sense, it can be seen that Nationalism is not necessarily an authoritarian philosophy, it is merely a perspective that prioritises the interests of a discrete racial community, which – after all – is the most natural impulse, and has operated throughout recorded human history. A Nationalist world would not require closed borders or police states – that is a misconception. Instead, people would have a shared mentality that there are collective rights and responsibilities to sustain a community, and that human diversity must, and can be, respected. That would be a world free of 'negative' bigotry and its people would be happier, more diverse and more willing to understand one another as we share our human journey. But that dream cannot become reality if people are forced to mix together and so adopt 'negative' bigotry as a defence against their unwelcome neighbours.

Our opponents point to the need for greater commonality among human beings, as a route to what they would call 'peace' and 'fairness'. This is a laudable goal, but it will not be achieved by forcing people to live together cheek-by-jowl. We all want to live in a world that is peaceful and without needless ('negative') bigotry, but that is only possible if different peoples adopt the 'positive' bigotry that is their birth right and respect national and cultural boundaries. Peace, after all, requires understanding, and understanding is only possible when differing peoples first respect one another. That requires boundaries, both visible and invisible. For our ancestors, this was little more than a common sense insight. If people today would finally begin to revive this 'common sense', then the ugliness might stop.

**6.4.**

*This was another article published in the autumn of 2013 on the website of White Independent Nation. Although the events it refers to are no longer current, and if I were to write this again I would phrase some of it differently, I do think the general message of the article is nevertheless still ripe. We must not allow ourselves to get sucked in by these populist movements again. We must retain our focus. The article ends with an appeal to the generic PLE concept, though I would favour the specific model offered by White Independent Nation. I would, however, now suggest that whites should broaden out their strategy to building a new alternative sub-culture: what I call the White Alternative.*

## Uncle 'Tommy' and his Anti-English League[39]

The latest espial machinations of the British treason state are proving a little obvious, even for the more obtuse or thick-headed. Even those treasured British qualities of subtlety and understatement have been cast aside for what might be indelicately called DDR tactics, in a desperate scramble to neuter a golem that has, frankly, spiralled out of control. Thus, that well-known and successful [MI5/Special Branch*] asset, Stephen Yaxely-Lennon, aka. 'Tommy Robinson', has now – finally – bowed to the inevitable and assumed his rightful place in that unfortunate Pantheon of high profile race traitors – in the process, confirming all that was suspected about him by anyone with multiple functioning brain cells.

Tommy's confessional press conference, now well and truly down the memory hole, was positively Orwellian. Perhaps it was just my imagination, but it appeared to me that our ersatz 'Winston Smith' was sweating and shaking throughout proceedings. 'Tommy' seemed agitated and worried, and at times distracted, almost as if he had just undergone some kind of lengthy inquisition and torture at the hands of sinister, black-clad interrogators. But whatever had just happened in Room 101, what transpired at the hastily-arranged press conference was, in its own little way, quite extraordinary, and outrageous too. In the manner of an errant member of the Politburo who had just been caught selling tractors on the sly, 'Winston'/'Tommy' informed us frankly of his 'thoughtcrimes' against the 'Party' and how he would repent for these gross felonies by (inter alia) helping the 'Thought Police' rat out 'racists' in the organisation he had led.

Now, it's easy to sneer, but this article will only do so a little bit – for entertainment purposes. 'Tommy' deserves it a little because of that disgusting pledge he made to betray his own followers. No doubt he has had his role to play for the State security services, and will continue to, just like (most probably) our 'Nigel' in UKIP, but one also suspects in Tommy's case the devices of knaves inflicted on an earnest, well-meaning dupe rather than anything more sinister. There are, after all, degrees of treachery and not all traitors derive glee or satisfaction from their own duplicity, however egregious. It's true that 'Tommy' did his best, and received all kinds of threats against both himself and his family for his trouble. Which of us would care to step into his shoes? It would be indulgent and hypocritical to overlook this. Having such a high profile, and furthermore, facing the prospect of yet another criminal trial this month on the usual trumped-up charges, with the looming possibility of a

---

[39] First published on 13th. November 2013 at http://www.win-white.org

custodial sentence, it is inevitable that he would feel the strain and might be persuaded to accept a 'respectable way out'. Who can blame him for this? I can't. That is not to excuse his oblique treachery, nor the very obvious collusion in which he has partaken for his own benefit, but in his defence it is worth pausing to reflect that his motives might have been more personal than is widely appreciated.

So 'Tommy' joins his anti-English friends in a well-paid state sinecure, probably as a sort of 'expert' on 'anti-racism', or some such. He is no more nor less qualified than others found supping from that Faustian chalice. Despite this, I must confess to having a soft spot for dear 'Tommy', with his tanning shop (slightly amusing in the circumstances, but on a more serious note: also admirable in that he ran his own business); his strained vowels, which are unmistakably from the English Home Counties; his avuncular mannerisms; and his Everyman tendency to say "I'm just a bloke from Luton town, innit", whenever he is asked to consider some imponderable. No doubt that was the idea: I was supposed to relate to 'Uncle Tommy'. Alas, I and many others were not taken in, and there are a number of reasons why the true nature of the EDL was obvious from the start. Nevertheless, it's important to assess the EDL phenomenon on its own merits and consider, objectively, what are the real lessons to be drawn.

The first problem with the EDL was its unfocused and confused message. It was never precisely clear what this amorphous organisation actually stood for, other than being vaguely against some of the more overtly nastier and militant elements of Islam. The controlled media often asked 'Tommy' whether the EDL was against Islamic infiltration of the West generally or just extremist Islam? Agonised studio discursions followed in which countless hairs were split and many hands were wrung. Islam is not the same as 'Islamism', we were informed. Most Muslims respect 'British values', we were assured. 'Tommy' was told it's naughty to confuse 'radical' or 'extremist' Muslims with 'moderates' and he shouldn't do it again, or presumably he'd be off to bed without any supper – or maybe off to prison. Lots of people clapped, whooped and cheered, but most of us watching at home were baffled, and none the wiser. In reality, all this was bumbling semantics, the purpose of which was to distract the more gullible and credulous from recognising the plain truth. 'Islamism' shares the same goal and objects as Islam, and the apparently 'moderate' mass of Muslims are nothing more than a Trojan Horse for 'extremists'. What the 'extremists' desire is the same as what the 'moderates' desire – that is, total demographic displacement of Europeans in favour of Muslims. The difference is that the 'extremists' are honest about this, whereas the 'moderates' are dishonest about it and try to keep it to themselves. The problem the Muslims have is that it's all rather obvious, and so a means is needed to distract people – hence 'public debates' between 'reasonable' Muslims and false opponents or state-run dupes, like Uncle Tommy.

Rather than sticking to a simple and truthful message, the EDL acquiesced in the media's dissembling agenda which elides the, essentially, semantic distinctions between 'extremist' and 'moderate', 'literalist' and 'reformist'. In so far as Islam matters, the real issue was and remains the demographic threat that Muslim populations represent for European civilisation, and the way in which Islam acts as an ideological front for racial interests that are opposed to ours. This did not seem to matter to the EDL, as it allowed Muslims to attend its marches; it grovelled before

Muslims in fake debates on the telescreen; and, it openly courted support from influential individuals and organisations within the Muslim community, who were sympathetic to the goal of combating what the media like to call 'extremism'.

The EDL was also wrong-footed by the pro-Israel/Zionist tendency. It is this lobby that are the true cheerleaders for the encroachment of Islam and general mixed-racialism in European societies. That is not to say there is no place for an anti-Islamic or anti-Jihadist organisation that focuses purely on the Islamic threat, but it is to say that such activities should be a way of introducing the masses to the real existential threat to whites – Israeli nationalism and Zionism – which use Islam as a means to undermine the racial integrity of European societies. Yet this point was completely missed or overlooked. Instead, the EDL did the precise opposite: going out of its way to court Zionist and Jewish support. EDL followers were to be found flying and displaying the Israeli national flag on official marches, completely unchallenged. The message seemed to be much the same as that touted by many 'respectable conservatives' – yawn – in both Europe and North America: i.e. that the Jews and Europeans are somehow natural allies against Muslims, rather than bitter enemies.

One could, perhaps, understand all this if the EDL were operating tactically and merely paying lip-service to Islamic and Zionist interests for pragmatic reasons. Given the political climate, this might even be seen as inevitable for such a high-profile group, but 'Tommy' went far beyond mere formalities. He accepted funding from Jewish backers; permitted a Jewish division of the EDL to be established (as well as a Hindu division); and, gradually – and absurdly – turned himself into a kind of unofficial conciliator with the Muslim community, publicly-declaring the EDL to be anti-racist and anti-fascist. The man was a muddle-head and a dupe, but when assessed coolly, his active connivance with the interests and personalities of those he putatively opposed can be seen as a harbinger. Uncle Tommy was running nothing more than an Anti-English League, the effect of which was to legitimise the arguments that the EDL should have been vigorously opposing.

I have not yet mentioned, but now will, the EDL's comical embrace of the various fetishist messages of the liberal metropolitan Left. Supposedly, the EDL had a pro-homosexual division, among other ad hoc absurdities. To the greater part of the population, it may seem curious that I should be troubled by this. Isn't this the 21st. century after all? Shouldn't we all be tolerant and understanding now? The problem is not with tolerance, which is a positive feature in society – provided it is tolerance of things done privately and which only inflict the most marginal personal and social harm. The difficulty here is with the new modish anti-tolerance that corrodes the original virtue. The very defence of civilisation requires that our values should not only be conserved and maintained, but preserved and passed down to future generations. That, in essence, is what reasoned traditionalism is: a belief in the permanence of a civilizational code that each generation seizes, then fashions and refines to the distinct needs of its own time, but leaves coherent and undisturbed for the next generation. Homosexuality is a threat to all this. It is a threat to our survival, especially in present circumstances, in that Europeans are facing an unprecedented demographic assault. Thus, to defend the propagation of homosexuality reflects only surface coherence about 'tolerance'. Looked at properly, the Anti-English League was working for our extinction, happily adding dry mote and wood to the pyre while busily fussing about Muslims.

Why do the EDL, and Western cultural dissidents in general, feel the need to backslide like this? The reasons are legion, but the key points can be summarised as follows. First, it is evident that there is no longer any significant support in the West for racial politics, whether conservative or radical. There is, among the Everyman, a seed of reactionary and reflexive race awareness that might well have been germinated before now and could have flowered under different circumstances, but its potential has been irradiated by a toxic political class. Even the most mild, reasoned opposition to immigration is characterised as 'racism'. It certainly is racism – the accusation is true – but the disinhibiting power of the accusation is such that most are dissuaded from acting on their natural, latent tendencies. Other social and cultural issues that are tangentially racial are treated in the same way. For example, justified scepticism concerning equality for homosexuals, along with traditional support for the promotion of age-old conjugal relations is viewed as 'gay-bashing'. This pressure from above, percolated through powerful media, has contributed to a climate in which a 'street movement' such as the EDL, regardless of the original sincerity or not of its founders, becomes a watered-down reactionary force, constantly having to make concessions to 'popular' modish sentiment. In fact, such sentiment is not really 'popular' at all, as the EDL's successful record in organising demonstrates, but the EDL was never a conscious movement with a clear and focused message, and so the very real concerns of its marchers have been lost and, to outsider, look like clatter and din.

Thus the EDL neither contributes to, nor stems from, consciousness at the street and workplace level. Oddly, a 'street movement' that was apparently (and in some ways, actually) raised from ordinary people served to embody neither class consciousness nor race consciousness and, in time, just degenerated into a convoluted form of escapism – a kind of 'lifestyle politics' mixed-up in brawling, drinking and shouting. Those marchers who stood behind the EDL banner may as well have gone on holiday to Majorca and done their shouting and inane sloganeering there. They were as aimless as their parents, who, in their own formative years – the Sixties – marched for similarly escapist slogans of peace and free love.

That's not to say it was a complete waste of time. Just as the Sixties provided an influential counterweight to a reactionary Establishment, the very physical reality of the EDL and its presence on the streets, has provided a visible symbol of resistance, but just as the Sixties generation later became practising neo-thatcherites, the EDL organisation has, in the fullness of time, become a creature of the people it was, in principle, meant to oppose; and, its own marchers will, in time, meld into the mixed-racial masses. The same thing, in different ways, has happened, and is happening, to other racially-attuned opposition movements. Take the BNP, which was extensively-liberalised, especially under Griffin. To an extent, the reforms of the Griffin era were actually quite sensible when viewed in the context of a party with serious electoral aspirations, but the BNP of today is no longer a Nationalist party. Whatever pretence it might make at being otherwise, the BNP is now part of the mixed-racial Establishment and serves its agenda, albeit as a rebel rather than a favoured son. The National Front, likewise, promotes an agenda that is right-wing rather than Nationalist and that serves to legitimise the very structures that have brought about a mixed-racial society in the first place. That is not to mount a slur on all the people involved – especially in the National Front, which consists of sincere people. What applies to Uncle Tommy applies also to others: not all betrayals are carried out consciously, or even willingly. Many so-called 'traitors' act out of genuine motives and are just misguided, but the point is that those who campaign for 'democracy' eventually become institutionalised and committed as democrats, a position that directly conflicts with the revolutionary nature of Nationalism.

Nationalism is fascist, not democratic. To be a Nationalist is to recognise the natural order of things and that the best must be at the forefront of society. Democracy, by contrast, is about recognising the lowest common denominator and allowing the weakest to dictate to the rest of us. This is what our society calls 'moral' and this is how our society really is. This implicitly requires a rejection of Nature and a celebration of mediocrity. The Uncle Tommys and the 'democratic' leaders of the BNP, etc., are quite at home in this democracy. They enjoy its perks and have borrowed the language of the modish Left, deploying it with glee and bleating like sheep about their 'rights' and the need for 'integration' of all and sundry.

Why does this happen? While it is not solely a British phenomenon, it is true that in Britain any genuine political racialism and fascism has long been drowned-out by the 'voices of moderation'. That is not to say we never hear fascist or racialist arguments – in fact, there are plenty – but they normally take on the form of pale imitators of the real thing: mostly, right-wing demagogues and ultra-Tory civic nationalists posing as 'men of the people'. In this respect, the anti-racists and anti-fascists are actually correct. Whether or not Nigel Farage, for instance, is a real and actual racialist is a little beside the point, since his arguments do point logically in that direction anyway. Alas, no amount of UKIP posturing, in or out of office, will ever lead us to a Nationalist position. To point in that direction is not the same as to lead us there, since the means being employed are democratic and thus redundant. More 'moderate' politicians, in both the Labour and Tory Party, will also deploy 'national' arguments and narratives when it suits them – an obvious example that springs to mind is the 2010 Labour slogan, 'British Jobs For British Workers', which was apparently originally used by the National Front some thirty years before. At a deeper level, most politics are still practised within a 'national' frame of reference. Yet these narratives are entirely false and counterfeit, as there is no longer any national (i.e. racial) consciousness behind them. Appeals to nationhood are not for the advancement of a progressive society in which identity is recognised and celebrated, but only for the encouragement of blind obedience to some profitable scheme or other. Mr. Farage, for instance, is a creature of capital. He will be told quietly to have a care, though, lest he go too far with his arguments and damage Britain's relationship with one of the world's largest trading blocs. In short, Nationalism in Britain, such as it is, remains a force for ruling class interests, not working class interests. To an extent, this is a problem around the world – Nationalism being a worldwide impulse – but it is also fair to say that the type of frustrating Potemkin Village politics we have in Britain is a peculiar Anglophone problem, and in our case, reflects a structural problem in the British political ferment.

Unlike on the Continent, there is no autonomous, trade unionist or syndicalist basis for broader pro-European nationalism in the United Kingdom. There is no Nationalist current on the Left, for instance. We seem to be entirely a Movement of the political

Right. I wonder if this is either desirable or healthy? I, for one, certainly do not feel 'right-wing', and though I fully-appreciate the malleability of such terms, in most respects I have common cause with the Left and even with Marxists. To me, Nationalism is an indigenous impulse and belongs to the working people. The real dividing line ideologically is on the matter of Race. Yet it is on that sole issue that so much now hangs. It seems to be a Marxoid ploy to eradicate human identity, but this invidious scheme has little or nothing to do with real Marxism or indeed the genuine, indigenous working class movements that have characterised Britain – the Diggers, the Roundheads, the Chartists, the suffragettes, the Social Democratic Federation, and so on. I, too, belong to that seditious working class tradition known as 'socialism', yet I see nothing of that reflected in Nationalism today. Consequently, there is nothing of our ideas in the workplace among workers themselves, and so we cannot relate to the struggles of ordinary people. Instead, we have Union Flags and bulldogs and Daily Mail (i.e. Jewish and Zionist) opinions. The 'Movement', such as we are, is essentially elitist and lacks organic dynamism. Our strength in numbers on the web is clear and is much commented-on, with veiled hints of repression here and there, but just as with the EDL, our flaw is that we have been captured by the opposition and are being turned and used for the opposition's purposes.

Beneath the surface, we have yet to realise our real mission, which is not about plastic flags and 'Pomp and Circumstance', but about the real Britain and the real Europe of working people who share a common heritage and civilisation. This requires that we link our racial protest to the material protests of ordinary people. I believe the only way to do this is through the strategy of building race conscious communities, from which a new Popular Nationalism can be raised-up that is preoccupied not with idealistic patriotism, cartoon 'Nazis' and other flights of fancy, but with the more mundane material needs of white people, including their survival.

The EDL, for years the only street protest movement going, has provided a depressing mirror on our current state, but we must learn from its ultimate failure. It was unanchored in any conscious community or workplace agitation. Thus it emerged in a bubble, fuelled by understandable media sensationalism about Muslims burning poppies rather than genuine grievances relating to people's lives. It seemed to be a street movement, yet many of its marchers were from the 'affluent' end of the working class: middle-managers, technicians and professionals, a demographic we sorely need, but also a group that tends make up the hobbyists and holds to reactionary views. Consequently, the protests always had a hint of hyper-reality about them, with the 'plastic' civic nationalist emblems and the over-the-top rhetoric. They were easily contained because the EDL were nothing more than an elaborate and perspicacious stunt – a very successful prank, and very English in that respect – and thus eminently containable. In the end, it provided little more than an outlet for a type of reflexive or casual racism, which is widespread but easily tackled by the Establishment, capitalists and the Left through formal repressive measures and media suffocation strategies.

For his part, Uncle 'Tommy' may have started-out on his political journey as a dupe, and he may now be a traitor, but to his credit, he has wised-up massively. He now seems to realise the limitations of unanchored street protesting (and also its dangers to his own life, limb and finances, hence his 'conversion'). Pursuing a 'democratic' strategy and begging the British treason state to make changes that it doesn't want to make and which no longer have wide public support is akin to howling at the Moon. It's not that the maintenance of a street movement would be misguided or is inappropriate. Rather, it's that such tactics represent 'putting the cart before the horse'. Unless undergirded by a strong community of ideologically- committed and race-conscious people, it's little more than feathers blowing in the wind, and ripe for manipulation by state controllers.

For Uncle Tommy then, all that's left is a 'satisfying' (and no doubt well-remunerated) 'career' as some kind of 'race relations' waffler. Think of it as akin to being 'kicked upstairs'. Tommy has outlasted his usefulness to the Politburo now, and the choice is that he can either stick to his 'principles' (trumped-up charges, then prison, etc.) or just take the money and be pensioned-off. He predictably chose the latter, and to be fair, that's what ordinary men like him are expected to do. His only hardship is that he must grin and bear it while being associated with the disingenuous utterings of his new colleagues, but that's no more than what is expected of any employee with a modern employer in our wonderful, enriched society. The answer for those who care for the preservation of European civilisation is a massive and concerted effort to build race-conscious communities, with the more traditional avenues of electoral politics and street activity having complementarity rather than centrality. The PLE concept is the model and we are now already seeing derivations of it from skilled and talented emulators across the White National Community. It is my respectful contention that if we are to preserve anything of our Race, these efforts must be the focus of our collective physical, intellectual and psychical energies.

# 7. How The Law Protects The Invader

# How The Law Protects The Invader[40]

*DISCLAIMER: This is a draft, as-yet unreferenced article that I prepared last year for submission to the White Independent Nation (WIN) website. The subject is the way that the law is used to further a racial survival strategy for the Jews. My reason for writing it in the first place was that I think there is a need for a close, revisionist examination of deeper Jewish influence in our society and the way that ancient Jewish culture and ritual metastasised into our institutional life. At almost 13,000 words, the article is very lengthy, an important warning for anyone who might be thinking of reading it. The article does require considerable revision and improvement, and does not necessarily represent my complete views on any topic. For example, there is a discussion below on Cultural Marxism which I think needs improvement, including more on the involvement of Jews (of all political and social stripes). I would also change a lot of the terminology used. The article was included on the WIN site in edited form (thanks to Nick Grifford of WIN for reading and editing the piece) and I re-post it here to give the patient reader a more thorough understanding of my philosophical position. It's an admittedly eclectic mix of contradictory perspectives: Nietzscheanism and 'White [Esoteric] Marxism', Traditionalism and Anti-Traditionalism. Given the chance and opportunity in the future, I will be re-visiting some of the themes in this lengthy article in a more digestible form: particularly the problem of how conservatives and the Right have, as I see it, misinterpreted Cultural Marxism.*

## Introduction

This essay looks at our society, our purported future and the deliberate engineering of who we are as 'social animals' through the lens of the Law, with a particular focus on attempts to innovate the Law away from collectivist indigenous traditions towards individuated rights that are more suitable for a deracinated, transactional social environment. The case is made for an alternative vision, that of a New European who will be forged in a 'Racial Intentional Community' and herald a return to the more authentic European ethos of fraternité, communauté, nationalité, identité – and mission, grounded in the natural laws that bind all of Man and which express our imperative for racial and genetic perpetuation. This new, life-affirming coda will be articulated ultimately in our own Rechtsstaat Homo Superior.

We will begin with a discussion of an important and, at the time, much-remarked on speech of February 2008, by the then-Archbishop of Canterbury, Dr. Rowan Williams, who indicated that he would not object to the intrusion of Sharia law into the United Kingdom. I have selected Dr. Williams purposefully, for at the time he made this speech he was head of the Church of England, that is to say, the most senior clerical personality in the Anglican Communion, and thus his thoughts and ideas might be considered emblematic in some ways of the spiritual health of Western society. What he (and his successor) says and does not say is a rough, but accurate, barometer of the moralistic ideals in the society. It is suggested here that the meaning derivable from Dr. Williams', and other obscure technically-laden speeches by key decision-makers, goes far beyond what is consciously intended and betrays the true intent of the ruling elites towards the indigenous Europeans. We

---

[40] First published on 30th. January 2014 at http://www.win-white.org

will go on to discuss how this can be the case, with reference to the Law itself as both the source and consequence of memetic influences in society.

## Archaeology of the Now

If you want to find out the truth about our society, then the quickest and most effective route is to read the more obscure written contributions of those with power or influence. The business pages of the Establishment newspapers, for instance, are a reliable mine of revelatory information for amateur archaeologists of veracity. In amongst the dry analysis will be found the true thoughts of those who run the country. With brutal honesty, and without the rhetorical contortions found in commentary on political and cultural matters, business journalists and columnists reveal whose interests they serve. They do so unconsciously, and unapologetically, but plainly enough for anyone with eyes to see. And for those with ears to hear, just occasionally, but perhaps more frequently in recent years than in the past, a prominent public figure will let slip in some speech or other the true agenda of the multi-racialists. One of the most revealing speeches of the last decade can be attributed to an unexpected source, Dr. Rowan Williams, who in February 2008, when Archbishop of Canterbury, shared his thoughts on Sharia law in a considered, erudite address at the Royal Courts of Justice.

## The Parable of the Archbishop

The speech itself was the epitome of liberal-minded intellectual genuflection. In dense, tortured soliloquy, informed by the masochistic character of his Faith, the Archbishop attempted to justify the unjustifiable: that is to say, justify the co-existence of European civilisation with Islam through a visage of legal development in Britain, specifically the construct of "supplementary jurisdictions" that would exist to "compete" with the established legal order in society. When this risible address met with the public outrage and evisceration it deserved, Dr. Williams moved from justifying the unjustifiable to defending the indefensible. I call in aid here the quote from a Radio Four interview given by Dr. Williams at the height of the controversy caused by the speech:

**Dr. Williams:** *An approach to law which simply says there's one law for everybody and that is all there is to be said, and anything else that commands your loyalty or your allegiance is completely irrelevant in the processes of the courts, I think that is a bit of a danger.*

**Interviewer:** *And that is why Sharia should have its place?*

**Dr. Williams:** *That is why there is a place for finding what would be a constructive accommodation with some aspects of Muslim law.*

The "constructive accommodation" that Dr. Williams tacitly seeks is that the indigenous white Europeans should hand their society over to non-whites, including Islam, and that white people should live under the racially-chauvinist rule of Islam and other alien creeds. That is not what Dr. Williams said (at least, not in so many words), and that may even not be the proximate meaning of what he says, or even his intention (who knows?), but that is the true message and purpose of Dr. Williams' speech, whatever his conscious thoughts, and most specially this arrant peroration:

*"...if we are to think intelligently about the relations between Islam and British law, we need a fair amount of 'deconstruction' of crude oppositions and mythologies, whether of the nature of sharia or the nature of the Enlightenment."*

The 'deconstruction' sought is that of the Western rationalist mind, lest it be resistant to the Islamic mentality and that of other alien racial colonisers. As usual, and as expected, this truth was lost among the distracting clatter and din of the state-controlled opposition, i.e. the solicitous choir of social and moral conservatives, British stato-'nationalists' and anti-Islamists, who in unison condemned Dr. Williams for his call that Sharia law be brought to the UK, on the shallow grounds that Sharia brings with it various 'extreme', 'barbaric' or 'inhuman' punishments. This canard, recycled and regurgitated on demand across the news cycle whenever a vaguely-relevant incident arises, serves the interests of the Islamists, for it masks the true, conscious agenda of their religion. Presumably, if the good bishop had called upon the authorities to grant parallel legal consideration for an essentially harmless, but racially alien, creed, then there would be no objection? Some would have maintained their objection, it is true, but they would have been flummoxed unless they could finally summon the courage to voice the one true, valid objection to Islamic incursion in Europe: that it is a racial meme destined ineluctably to subvert and destroy white civilisation itself, and that racial and social liberalism are the inhibitors designed to prevent the host from reacting in the appropriate way to ensure its own survival. That is why the true significance of Dr. Williams' comments was racial, a point underscored by Dr. Williams' other radio comment that the adoption of certain aspects of Sharia law "seems unavoidable". Why might it be 'unavoidable'? On the face of it, this is a strange choice of words: until, that is, the racial realities are appreciated.

The obscurantist storm of criticism that gave a misleading impression of Dr. Williams' views is a symptom of a congenital inability among people across the political spectrum – Right and Left, and far-Right as well, to face inconvenient truths. As usual, it is our racial enemies who are left to state or infer the truth for us, provided one is accustomed to reading between the lines. For instance, this from Baroness Warsi:

*"The Archbishop's comments are unhelpful and may add to the confusion that already exists in our communities.*

*"All British citizens must be subject to British laws developed through Parliament and the courts. He said people should be able to opt in or out of the system. I have very great concern about that."*

We can conclude that Dr. Williams' comments were "unhelpful" because the good bishop had, in his earnest erudition, revealed more than he had intended, and this alarmed Baroness Warsi and other non-whites who fear – with good reason – the arousal of white racial consciousness.

None of this is to say that Dr. Williams consciously or intentionally wishes for the end of white European civilisation (though he might). His problem is that he is blinded by a psychological complex afflicting much of the Western intellectual classes. To Dr. Williams – the very archetype of philobarbarist condescension – Muslims are jolly nice people with some rather strange customs: a kind of anthropological oddity rescuable by amalgamation into superior Western culture. In the process, he tacitly acknowledges Western moral superiority – an inconsistency on his part – but rather like a cell welcoming a viral organelle, he sees no barrier to the intrusion of an alien belief system into England, that would carry with it the coda for the destruction of the host's cultural DNA, and ultimately its actual DNA, in modest incremental steps initially, but no less sure for it. The racial implications, inescapable though they are, are lost on him. Admittedly, and to his significant credit, Dr. Williams demonstrates much the superior understanding of Law and its role in society compared to his dim critics, but that does not alter his purblind nature. That his comments also had the merit of honesty is also beyond question, though whether he himself was (or is) conscious of this attribute in his own remarks is anyone's guess.

Dr. Williams at least did us a spiritual service, by obliging with his own living, breathing example of the perils of the forked tongue disguised in fancy talk. Perhaps at this point a biblical quotation would be apt. Psalm 12:2 states pessimistically:

*"They speak vanity every one with his neighbour: with flattering lips and with a double heart do they speak."*

However, not to fear, as Psalm 12:6 assures us:

*"The words of the Lord are pure words: as silver tried in a furnace of earth, purified seven times."*

No doubt Dr. Williams would arrogantly call on such words: a justification for his own perverted 'truths' in the permanency of his 'God'. As an atheist steeped in the Anglican tradition, I prefer to treat those words as a reminder of human treachery and the constancy of truth.

### What the Law 'is': the civilisational poverty of pseudo-positivism

Dr. Williams' speech reflected his visage of British society: a multi-racial and muti-cultural space in which the Law might adapt and evolve to address the challenge of different sorts of people living together. This brings into focus certain fundamental questions. The unspoken, commonsensical, assumption that the Law exists to regulate the affairs of a given territory, and relations between the people in it, usually satisfies when ordinary political issues are discussed. When faced with an unsatisfactory turn of events that can be blamed on some governmental authority or legislative decision, the man on the street will, understandably, tend to blame the putative legislators or decision-makers in terms that assume there is a problem to be fixed or a remediable decision to be made, rather like fixing a car. In short, we tend to assume that the Law is technocratic in character, a function of evidence-laden policy-making, and when something 'bad' happens, we surely only need better decision-making. When confronted with facts that suggest a deviation from this logic, we either instinctively suppress such thoughts, or we lash out irrationally (though sometimes also accurately) and denounce all-and-sundry as "corrupt", "dishonest", "self-serving", or whatever. The former tendency reflects a mental timidity, which we all exhibit from time-to-time, and which is part of our evolutionary inheritance. Human beings are social animals and there is a very powerful instinct in each of us against 'rocking the boat' and becoming a 'troublemaker'. We really want to conform, but more importantly, there are also strong interests in society that need our conformity. It's why those who do 'rock the boat', whether Left or Right politically, are subjected to organised campaigns of name-calling: "racist", "Nazi", "weirdo", "misogynist", "commie", "anarchist", etc. The latter tendency reflects an inability to address matters in our lives soberly and rationally. This, in turn, is borne out of powerlessness. We live under a social system – democratic capitalism – that, contrary to its own propaganda, discourages any attempt toward self-government and self-reliance.

These behaviours have their genesis in a philosophical school of thought that has broad currency not just in academe, but as a casual reflex in ordinary society: legal positivism, which is to say, the view that the Law is entirely man-made and not necessarily reflective of any underlying objective moral or ethical principle. If the legal positivist viewpoint is tacitly accepted, then certain conclusions naturally follow from it. For instance, the notion that the Law might be a means for one group in society to oppress another is discomforting to the positivist mindset, though not inconsistent with it. Positivists do not always reject the idea of ideological influence in Law, but they do not like to acknowledge it either. This is because, in the positivist frame of reference, the Law itself is meant to emerge from practices in society, not out of any grand ideological schema. It should be no surprise, then, that legal positivism is particularly attractive to the traditionally liberal mindset. By 'traditionally liberal', I refer not to liberalism's more recent social and racial bastardisation, but rather to the emptier. I am not sure we should imply that modern liberals are somehow brimming with cogent ideas and feasible solutions, Victorian notion of liberalism, in the sense of society as the crucible of progress and enlightenment. People who accept such traditionalist notions tend to be somewhat vacant, often socially-privileged, and their interest in politics tends to be practical more than intellectual. In Britain, they populate mainly the Conservative Party, including its leadership, and to a lesser extent the mainstream of the Labour Party. They are predominantly interested in gossip and what happens at Westminster. They tend to go along with prevailing social and political currents, and on some issues this can be in either direction – so they will either support multi-culturalism because that's what 'respectable' people do, or evince scepticism about it because lots of people appear to be opposed to it. They tend to see social issues in transactional and materialist terms – for instance, if 'against' immigration, it will be for primarily economic reasons, and if 'for' immigration, again that will be for economic reasons. They tend to weigh-up most social policy matters according to an economic or financial algebra, and see themselves as living in the 'real world' as they prioritise budgetary acumen over other considerations. They tend to hold a romanticised view of British legal development – emphasising the English juridical and political contribution to liberty, Magna Carta, etc., but have little detailed knowledge or understanding of these historical achievements and, if and when expedient, will support policies that subvert the principles that under-girded them and of which they are truly ignorant. Their overarching view is one of a society moving relentlessly towards some vague abstract notion of progress. This 'progress' is empty and the policies it justifies are not always progressive. In fact, they can be quite regressive and cruel. In the liberal mind, a vicious and savage war might be justified by the need for 'democracy', or 'progress' and 'enlightenment'.

This liberal, pseudo-positivist mindset could easily be mistaken for philosophical pragmatism, and is often labelled non-technically as pragmatism, or even 'common sense', but in truth, the liberal position is itself ideological, and as with any ideology, it has permeated through society in the form of various pseudo-positivistic common-sense notions that govern the thoughts of most ordinary people about politics and a range of other social matters. Often the nature and manner of our interaction with Law reflects this type of mindset. We recognise easily the legislative and political aspects of Law, the matters of policy in the hands of our benighted law-makers, though we often perceive the issues in purely technocratic terms. Our own involvement with the legal system – with professional lawyers, perhaps with the courts and maybe the police – is ideologically-sterile, and it would hardly ever occur to us that the Law itself, and its machinery, including the police, judges, lawyers and courts, might also be political in nature. It is tempting to see Dr. Williams' speech, and others like it, through that lazy mindset, and indeed, that is the way it was seen by very many at the time the speech was made. The notion was of a naïve liberal intellectual venturing to share his metropolitan opinions about 'what should be done' on an issue to do with multi-racialism that was – and is – ripe for discussion.

This, I would suggest, is a mistaken view. The language and direction of Dr. Williams' speech was purposeful, even if he may not have been conscious of the consequences of the ideas and assumptions he is repeating. What is missing from the pseudo-positivist perspective at its barest is an acknowledgement of this, the essential ideological and purposive nature of Law itself and discussions of Law. Any concept of Law must accept the civilisational values that underpin it, and which provide the context for any sane process of law-making. Consciously or otherwise, Dr. Williams, and others like him, are promoting values that are at odds with the juridical settlement that undergirds our civilisation. Yet we should also take note that Dr. Williams himself is far from positivistic, and so a positivistic political or critical response both to him and his ideological and cultural allies will be inadequate. It is necessary to fight culture with culture. While it is acceptable that the legal positivist should leave open questions about the practice and interpretation of Law, it cannot be accepted that legal positivism is to be excused as a mere philosophy of Law or credo for jurists and scholars. In its pseud, more reflexive form, it is also a mindset. If we fail to recognise this, and if we fail to reject the morally-impoverished pseudo-positivist perspective and re-assert our civilisational values with a muscular response to this multi-cultural desertification, then we are in effect admitting defeat on the ideological field of battle.

## Law as ideology

A more sophisticated – some would say, 'realist' – view than legal positivism recognises that ideology (belief systems) and Law are inseparable. Of course, we must here recognise what ideology is and its limited relevance to understanding. Ideology is neither a cause nor an explanation. It can be seen merely as the motivating system of ideas for any particular group. For all that, it is still very important, but it is a mistake to ascribe to the ideological construct itself any determinative or causative influence. A historical example that will illustrate the point is the Black Act. This was a criminal statute enacted by Parliament in 1723 to deal with groups of forest poachers, mostly in Hampshire, who would blacken their faces when undertaking poaching raids: hence the term for them, 'Blacks'. It is probable that a degree of social and political resentment prefigured in the poachers' actions, but in any event, the Black Act is an example of law designed to support the economic interests of a ruling elite. The Act prescribed the death penalty for more than fifty criminal offences, a savage 'legal' means to enforce what were basically merely property rights, so the Law here was used as a means to uphold private property ideology, but the ideology itself does not tell us exactly why the Law was enacted. What might assist us is an examination of who benefited from its passage. In this case, the landowners derived immediate benefit from the Black Act due to its formal deterrence effect, however this too does not take us to the root of the matter.

The Law itself is an intrinsic part of a belief system. It is the same belief system that compels you to wake-up at a particular time in the morning and go to work. It is the belief system that compels you to do (within reason) what your boss tells you to do. It is likely you are under a contractual obligation to arrive at work by a certain time, not leave before a certain time, and follow reasonable instructions from your superiors. These contractual, legally-enforceable obligations are manifestations of employment ideology. You, as the non-owner (the employee) must do as the owner (employer) says in return for a payment (your wage or salary). The ideological justifications for this – various types of propaganda that you have been brainwashed with since school and that encourage your compliance at work – ensure that you most likely do not think too much about the economic sense of your situation, other than very narrow questions such as whether the wage or salary is sufficient for your needs. This narrowing of the thought process, or concision, is a symptom of a heavily-ideological environment. The ideology does not exist for its own sake or just for fun. It exists to protect the economic interest of the owner, the employer, and is necessary in order to distract your attention and ensure that you do not think too much about the justice of your position as a non-owner in economic activity, i.e. as an employee.

Much of our Law is explicitly in place to advance the interests of an owning class in society, and to support ideological justifications for their advantageous position. The Black Act was supported ideologically by notions of the sanctity of private property, i.e. poaching is 'stealing', etc.. Whatever their moral basis, these ideological precepts serve a materialist purpose in encouraging compliance with laws that may work against the economic interest of the greater part of the population[emphasis added - Ed]. It can easily be seen, however, that the agents of society's ideological base – be they employers or Archbishops – do not necessarily work consciously to uphold a governing ideology in the interests of a ruling group. It would probably not have occurred to Dr. Williams, for instance, that by adopting the precepts of conventional wisdom on multi-racialism in Western societies, he is aiding in the weakening and division of the ordinary working populations of those societies, something that is manifestly in the interests of the ruling capitalist elite. To the unconscious Dr. Williams, the issues are purely legal and cultural, and to his zero-conscious audience, the issues are purely technocratic and concern whether amorphous "extremists" and "barbarians" should be permitted into British society. The notion of history as a process of underlying, unseen, causes and consequences, is lost on them.

One of the intellectual failings evident in our society is this inability or unwillingness to perceive the influence of the economic base and the social relations of capital on what goes on, and an unwillingness to identify the ideological – indeed, intellectual – justifications for it as no more than justifications. It is the case that most public discussion is ideologically-arid. We see professional intellectuals – academics and journalists – of both the Left and Right political persuasion, deploy arguments of an essentially liberal/positivistic or philosophically pragmatic nature to explain history, politics or current events in a way that is sterile of any motivating insight, except the practicalities of whatever is the present issue. Thus, most of the public remain ignorant of their true place in society, and more important, their real power. The real power to overthrow the present hierarchical social system is in the gift of its subjects, for the working population forms an overwhelming numerical majority. Capitalism could be overthrown tomorrow if the people would will it.

## Real Power Is With The People

We must ask ourselves why people are not, on the whole, conscious of their true economic position in society and the power they have collectively? The immediate answer is that the capitalist system has various means to shape the thoughts of ordinary people through daily propaganda, and means of state can be used to subdue and discredit dissenters and divert subversive activity into dead-ends. The real war is a war of the mind: it is an intellectual battle of which street agitation, guer[r]illaism and war are an extension.

To borrow Marxist terminology, most people suffer to some degree from 'false consciousness', which in simplistic terms describes a compliant state of mind in which a person is not conscious of his true economic position and the class nature of society, i.e. the division between a ruling class and a working class. It follows somewhat that the system that we know as 'Democracy' (though not necessary democracy, as such) is essentially a confidence trick. Most ordinary people might think this is rather to state the obvious, yet it would not occur to them that there is both a reason and a cause for this, and that the 'reason' and 'cause' are eminently rational. What underpins the deception that is Democracy is our social relationship to society's economic base. A practical state of political equality might exist from time-to-time, but it cannot cure economic inequality unless democratic principles are applied to the economy as well. Regardless, most people are content to wallow in a state of entheogenesis, wishing for some real democracy to come their way out of nowhere – a consequence of the liberal/positivistic mind. Populist political parties such as, say, UKIP, that are thrown-up by the Establishment from time-to-time to distract the masses, play-up to these misconceptions. UKIP will wax lyrical about the "out-of-touch political classes", "corrupt politicians", "Cultural Marxists", "left-wingers" or whatever it is, and occasionally some of this might be accurate, rather like a drunk darts player who accidentally hits the bullseye, but none of it gets to the root of the matter. It's just a clever way to occupy the public and thus maintain the system essentially as it is.

However, there is a more fundamental problem with democracy in society more broadly. Democracy as presented in the West is an abstract, an ideation of Enlightenment thought, and in itself a rather empty notion. A moment's thought should emphasise the practical difficulty that if everyone has a say, then no-one has a say. As a system, in the mass sense, it appeals very much to the lowest common denominator. The Athenians had a much better grasp of democracy as a real, living practical principle, and, notably, their scope for civic participation was limited to those who would serve the state body in the martial sense, which is how the notion of 'citizenship' originated. Many of the Loyalists of the American Revolution were motivated by a dislike of the prospect of 'mob rule', which they believed would be the natural outcome of republican government at that time. In much the same way, the minarchists of the early 19th. century American West sought to replace capitalist democracy, an oxymoron and which they saw as a damaging, disenfranchising system, with a type of self-government based on private property principles. Fascism, as both an ideology and a governmental philosophy, can be seen as an refined iteration of the Enlightenment notions of democracy. The fascists in the 20th. century sought to militate against the damaging social and national effects of mass democracy by creating a society in which important interests would be mobilised to co-operate in government for the interests of the people. To a fascist mind, a 'democratic' society that permits the perversion of the ethno-national interest is not worthy of the name. If you live in a society infested with pornography, drug addiction and other vices and debasements, in which you are surrounded by people who do not share your race or culture, or even language, then the fact that you might have a vote every four years starts to look rather beside the point, and any fancy talk about 'democracy' and 'equality' and 'human rights' begins to look worthless.

The point is that what is idealised as Democracy in our society has not been idealised by all societies, and there are rational and intelligent people who reject notions of citizenship and enfranchisement for all. Fortunes are spent on keeping the ordinary public from thinking too much about these matters. The mental world of the average 'citizen' can be likened to a zero-conscious state in which the mind is hypnotised by a rapid kaleidoscope of soundbites, sentimental pop music and imagery designed to induce compliance. This is done to maintain certain illusions: most specially, a broad, lazy assumption that society works in the interests of all. Any thoughtful person must recognise that it cannot, and any society that purports to do so must tell lies to its people, the biggest lie of all being 'democracy'. Democracy is a means of control for a dysgenic society that seeks to treat its people as mindless consumers, shorn of meaning and identity. The response of Nationalists to this during the 20th. century has, understandably, largely been of a revanchist nature, concentrating on the need to maintain the nation-state as a source of sovereignty and spiritual meaning, but as the nation-states of Europe reveal themselves to be racially- and nationally-treasonous and stato-nationalism becomes less politically-relevant, there is a need for a New Nationalism that rejects the reactive prescriptions of the Right. We will explore what that will be here, but first let us consider the reaction to the Marxist critique among the political Right and Western cultural conservatives more broadly: the thesis of 'Cultural Marxism' – in the view of this author, a jaundiced, semi-accurate critique of Marxism.

## 'Cultural Marxism': object of frenzy

It is common for cultural commissars and commentators to sneeringly disparage the ordinary public for its tendency to engage in spirals of emotional frenzy, but what is not recognised is the extent to which daily public concerns reflect the preoccupations of intellectuals. We have discussed the liberal, pseudo-positivist mentality and how the intellectual mind can be preoccupied by second-order ideas that merely reflect the practical concerns of society. Now we will consider how the intellectual class and their pseudo-intellectual imitators will engage in their own frenzies and amplify mistaken and distorted interpretations of ideas.

It has grown fashionable among commentators on the political Right and in Nationalism to speak of 'Cultural Marxism' (and less commonly, but arguably more accurately, 'neo-Bolshevism'). The term as a label has become an auto-response to a perception that there is a damaging moral and cultural liberalism in society. In a more specific sense, 'Cultural Marxism' is a reference to an academic school of neo-Marxists of 1920s Europe, the Frankfurt School, who developed a critique of what they saw as the morally-repressive society around them. The connection of the Frankfurt School to actual Marxist thinking was weak, at best, but these thinkers concluded that there was a need to subvert society with critical, counter-cultural values that reflected neo-Marxist ideas in the social and cultural sense. The term Cultural Marxist itself is of questionable validity, but it is used here for convenience.

There is no evidence that the Frankfurt School actually favoured multi-racial, multi-culturalism in the West. The main focus of the School was on attitudes to sex and power structures in existing Western society (though later critical theorists who claimed a broad intellectual inheritance from the Frankfurt School did examine Western ideas about race subversively). If we seek an ideological motivation for multi-racialism, we are more likely to find it in the propaganda of capitalism, for divisive multi-racial societies fulfil the needs of market economies much more efficiently than racially-cohesive societies in which the working class is socially- and politically-cohesive. Nevertheless, the notion that multi-racialism is attributable to the Frankfurt School or some other sinister left-wing academic movement has common currency on the political Right. It does contain some truth, but it is – at best – only a partial explanation. Its adoption as an almost-complete and automatic response to liberal ideas generally, not just multi-racial culture, is akin to vapid conspiracism. What it illustrates is the danger of ideological thinking that is not anchored in rational explanations. Critical thinkers, i.e. those who examine ideological motivations in society, are just as susceptible to modish thinking and irrational frenzies as the general population. The 'Cultural Marxist' frenzy permeates into society, so that the pseudo-intellectual begins to talk in terms that tacitly disparage rational (i.e. economic) explanations, thus a further psychological or mental barrier is erected to prevent ordinary people perceiving and recognising the influence of the economic base on society.

To put this in real terms: on Tuesday, the ordinary man will say that "socialists" are "scum", because he heard it from some erudite shock-jock raving about 'Cultural Marxists' and the Frankfurt School. Then on Wednesday the following week, the same ordinary man will announce that "Nazis" are "scum", because he heard it from a news presenter. These are not accidental or isolated examples of borrowed sloppy thinking, rather they are a consequence of the misdirection of intellectual work. The object of frenzy needn't be "socialists" or "Nazis", it could be something else. The point is that the ordinary man understands neither socialism nor National Socialism, still less Nazism, but ignorance is bliss and a desire for an explanation is compelling, in the face of which an easy explanation cannot be resisted, and so he will happily repeat what the "informed" people on the news have told him, who in turn accept their direction from the cultural architects in politics and academe. These intellectuals, just like any number of ordinary work-a-day folk, need a bauble to distract them, but it needs to be something of intellectual character that will engage sufficient interest. It needs to have a sense of verisimilitude about it. When the distraction ploy works, it can almost be likened to a synecdoche of the truth. Those with an interest in perpetuating these distraction do not sit and plan matters and are not even necessarily conscious about politics or cultural matters. In fact, the forces in society that self-perpetuate and hide the true nature of social relations issue these divertissements organically and unconsciously.

## Consciousness is the real battlefield

It is my contention that the issue of political economy in society has been decided theoretically in favour of the co-operativism (or what could be very broadly called 'socialism'). The Earth enjoys abundant resources, largely due to the economic success of capitalism, but capitalism cannot accommodate the insatiable drive for human freedom, and so a co-operative society is now needed. That is not to say such a society is inevitable. Capitalism will not collapse. It will be brought to an end by the conscious will of a majority of people. The issue is how to get there, and what exact form this co-operative society should take.

The problem with Marxism is that it confines itself to the materialist questions. Again, in rather simplistic terms, this is what can be called 'economic determinism' (a clumsy, but necessary shorthand phrase in summative discussions like this)– i.e., a belief that the social relations of capital determine what happens in society. This is the orthodox or classical Marxist view, and indeed represents the key to understanding a critical perspective on capitalist society, but while it unquestionably has considerable validity and utility in explaining society, it does not and cannot explain everything. The great failure of the Marxists has not been due to some technical error. Their analysis of capitalism, especially Marx's original critique, is essentially correct in its technical aspects. The problem has been a failure of consciousness – in plain and brutal terms, an inability to convince sufficient numbers of people of their case to mount the necessary democratic assault on capitalist institutions. I believe the major reason for this is the tin ear of Marx to issues of the Self, which palpably reverberates among neo-Marxists.

Marx himself did not even have a conception of human beings, as such, a concept he dismissed as wholly ahistorical and idealistic. He saw men and women not as wholly autonomous beings defined by their rights arising out of our inherent natures, but as specie beings defined by our ability to satisfy our needs and make use of our abilities. The difficulty with this is the focus on external causes and the reliance on historical conditions that denies to Man an essential nature. In the early 20th. century, an attempt was made among some neo-Marxist scholars to synthesise Marxist thinking with Freudian analysis, to unite the macro (i.e. the external and historical analysis of Marx) with the micro (i.e. the internal and psychoanalytical insights of Freud). This interesting synthesis meets its most potent expression in some of the ideas of Cultural Marxism, and ultimately has met with some influence in the growing rejection by the mainstream centre-Left in politics of racial and national boundaries, but ultimately neo-Marxists have failed to mobile themselves as a genuine revolutionary social force. Instead, even their most revolutionary social and cultural ideas have become absorbed within the cultural bloodstream of capitalism, which has adapted to them.

More significantly perhaps, it is also evident that the culturally and racially-liberal thinking that has emerged out of what, broadly-speaking, might be called (admittedly, not entirely accurately) the 'Cultural Marxist' attack on society is alienating to the vast majority of people. The difficulty for neo-Marxists is that, while their structural and economic arguments are impeccable, they are seeking and demanding the fall of racial and national boundaries, and thus inadvertently seeking to deny an essentialist component of human identity and human biodiversity, a facet of ourselves that is inextricably tied to our consciousness, our sense of ourselves. Or, to put it plainly – family, kith and kin will tend to trump common economic interest. The arguments that can be (clumsily) summarised as 'economic determinism' are not enough for a full understanding, and to pretend that they are dangerous in that it leads us down the road to compulsion and authoritarianism, whether in an overtly democratic guise, or in a Stalinist . We can, conceivably, create the libertarian society that orthodox Marxists want, but there would be grave problems if that is the only aim, as kin relations cannot be terraformed. What can be created and maintained are the structures in society that encourage kin relations, and that is what Nationalism essentially is.

What has often been seen as the ghoul of William Morris that hangs around at the edge of Nationalism might better be seen as a ghost, a spirit with the unfinished business of syncrecity. The other tradition can be embraced. The Right thesis of Cultural Marxism represents, I believe, a misplaced reaction against this and needs to be seen for what it is, a dead-end, and discarded. The true ideological battlefield is not over politico-economic structures – something that is already theoretically decided – or ad hoc questions about societal behaviour, which can be decided by people , but over the consciousness of Man. It is not a battle between Marxism and Nationalism, as such. The warring parties are more amorphous than those pedestrian 19th. century definitions suggest, and not easily definable. It is really an argument over the Enlightenment legacy, between those who wish to advance the rational socio-political settlement toward a hollowing-out of our racial and spiritual nature and those who embrace Man as Man and wish to re-emphasise and retain our National Community in whatever politico-economic terrain might exist in the future.

## Law as racial expression

What of race and identity? This brings us to back four-square to a discussion of Law, for it is the Law – and rules – of a culture that hold a national community together as a reflection of its values. We might say it is a Law of Nature, consistent throughout recorded history, that we as human beings, in common with the rest of the animal kingdom, live and act for the purpose of reproduction of our genes. The basis of our survival is our fecundity, and thus sex and the behavioural relations around sex is of vital importance to human society. It follows, in my view, that a sane human society has as its priority the racial and genetic perpetuation of its own kind, and those who ignore this natural law die out. Any system of Law in society should be elaborated only from these axiomatic principles.

To speak of a Law of Nature is not in any way to reject existing legal orders. While there is a tradition among lawyers and jurists to refer to 'reason' rather than 'nature' in the context of Law, it might be observed that most positive law – organised systems of law – are an extension of a kind of natural law grounded in virtue, English common law most specially so. However, when I use the term Law in relation to a National Community, I am advancing a different, more immanent, concept of Law as a memetic coda, a racial or tribal expression, a means of communicating and enforcing in society the racial and genetic interests of one group against another. I believe that is the truth of what Law is, and I think the former Archbishop, Dr. Williams, provided us with a glimpse of this truth in his considered speech on Sharia law. A couple of further, specific, historical examples are offered here as a means of further elucidation.

The Mosaic Laws are a set of religious laws, rules and customs in various normative modes that remain of fundamental moral and ceremonial importance to Jews today, and which also influence heavily civil and criminal law in the West. Much of that Western influence came merely in the form of concerted scholarly efforts at intertextuality during the Medieval period, and most of the Mosaic Laws might now be considered archaic on a literal reading and tend to be supported only among Orthodox Jews. Furthermore, to an extent any influence that might have been exerted by the moral and ethical content of the Mosaic Laws is now being overshadowed in the West by the more secular and multi-racial influences of the contemporary universalist legal and moral order. Nevertheless, the Mosaic Laws retain a social and cultural significance, both to Jews themselves, and also to mainstream society beyond, in the sense of what observers like to call the 'Judeo-Christian tradition', in which we can surmise a heavy influence of Jewish legal and ethical principles in English case law. For those who identify as Jews, the Mosaic Laws part of a coherent ethnic identity that is passed down the generations. Furthermore, English law does permit (or, to be more precise, does not preclude or outlaw) limited jurisdiction of Jewish law between Jews, particularly in marriage disputes and commercial litigation, with adjudication in rabbinical courts, known as Beth Din, however Beth Din remain under the supremacy and coercion of English law.

The Anglo-Saxon laws and customs that existed in England until the Norman Conquest were a continuation of the traditions and customs of their Germanic progenitors. Before the Byzantium incursion in the Early Middle Ages, the Anglo-Saxons of Britain had little influence from the institutionalised civilisations of southern Europe and relied on the oral transmission of laws and customs such as folk-right, which amounted to an expression of the judicial consciousness of the ethnic sub-group. We know from what records that were compiled (after some of the Anglo-Saxon legal traditions became written) that there was a significant ethnic transference from other North Sea cultures – the Saxons, Frisians and Scandinavians in particular – with reference not just to law-making and enforcement, but also broader social customs, administrative organisation and political ideas, as well as a faithful maintenance of judicial principles within each discrete sub-group, as a distinct ethnic expression of that sub-group.

**Law as a meme of cultural and racial expansion**

Notwithstanding the historical evidence, perhaps a reason the notion of Law as a racial expression is not discussed is that it would seem anti-intellectual to relegate Law to the status of some kind of a primaeval or cultural force, as opposed to having a purely rational basis, but if we examine the validity of the assertion in light of accepted legal developments in our own, supposedly 'rational', society, we can surmise that Law is not just essential to the cohesiveness of a racial group, but also a means of cultural expansiveness. For instance, the first Anglo-Saxon written legal code, King Æthelberht's law code, set out fines for molesting the property of the Christian Church. This was enacted shortly after the arrival of an evangelical mission to Britain by Augustine. The Norman conquerors imposed a superstructure of law and justice that, in time, altered the nature of English society, and which survives to this day. Whereas in the Anglo-Saxon era, the legal culture was steeped in collectivist tribal traditions, with rights and privileges interpretable in relation to blood and social ties, the Norman influences in contrast brought individualistic notions into English law, with regard to property-ownership, rights, and so on. It is was also after the Norman Conquest that a new alien racial group was brought into English society, the Jews. William the Conqueror brought Jews to England from Rouen, in Normandy, to take advantage of their commercial skills, believing that they would assist in bringing greater prosperity to the country. The individualistic legal traditions and feudal and hierarchical emphasis of Norman society supplanted into England suited these commercially-astute racial interlopers who lacked any roots in the society and had less of an interest or stake in the permanency of culture and kin relations. The Jews in turn began to exert significant influence on the English legal tradition, particularly common law. Much of this influence reflected the philosophic influence of the Torah-Talmud, including the post-Talmudic common law tradition of responsa, which had a direct influence on the evolution of English common law. Also, the jury trial method, and much of our other due process, arose from Talmudic guidelines. Over the centuries, the Jews became significant pillars of the business community, with a vital influence on the direction of the country and were able to establish themselves as an autonomous niche set apart from the rest of society and outside the English feudal system, protected as servi camera (servants of the King), as they were recognised to be of crucial importance to the country's treasury.

The tumultuous history of the Jews in England will not be laboured here, but suffice it to say that over time, and between edicts and expulsions and other turmoil and resentment from the native English, the Jews have managed to establish themselves as a prosperous, distinctly racial community in England, and other Western societies as well, that inevitably puts them in antagonism with the indigenous populations. Due to their prominent commercial role in society, Jews also played a causative and contributory role in the great European Civil Wars of 1914 to 1945 (the First and Second World Wars). In hindsight, these Wars can be seen analogously in much the same way that classical scholars view, say, Caesar's Civil War as signalling the fall of the Roman Republic and heralding an imperial era, the Roman Empire. A Rubicon was crossed that saw the defeat of White Racial Nationalism – ersatz Roman 'republican' government – at the hands of the brutal proxy forces of International Jewry, the ersatz imperialists. The subsequent Nuremberg Hearings (known as the Nuremberg Trial(s)), in which various personalities of National Socialism were subjected to kangaroo trials for crimes both real and imagined, signalled a new juridical and moral settlement in which the cultural notion, until then only pregnant and incipient, that the white man is evil, could at last be codified and allowed to permeate the bloodstream of European societies, which in turn lost their 'republican' civic integrity as Third World invaders swamped their lands. For the Jews, the black and Muslim invaders of more recent times represent an important opportunity to divide the population and weaken the grip of the indigenous white British on their own society. Dr. Williams' speech on Sharia law has to be seen in this context.

## How the Law protects the invader

t is the author's contention that the [Sephardic and Ashkenazic - Ed] Jews are a discrete racial group within Western societies pursuing a long-term racial survival strategy based on financial and cultural parasitism. It is critical in maintaining their successful long-term status that the Jewish identity in mainstream society is deliberately kept somewhat nebulous as to the white racial majority. Hence most Jews resemble white people physiognomically, with the result that only a tiny group of racially-conscious whites will perceive the truth, that Jews are racially different and antagonistic to the interests of whites. It will be noted in contrast that more recent racial invaders to Europe are marked in appearance and easily separable and usable as racial scapegoats. This includes Blacks, Muslims – and Orthodox Jews. The Jew's strategy is staganographic, hiding among the white population while using Orthodox Jews, Muslims and blacks as cover, with the unconscious help of useful idiots, including liberal whites, conservatives and various types of stato-nationalists. This Jewish racial survival strategy leads to division in society, which is worsened by mass revolutionary immigration. As the atomisation accelerates, encouraged by other anti-social economic policies, those with a pre-disposition toward dissident thinking will gravitate towards one or several state-controlled opposition parties. UKIP is the current state-controlled safety valve for pseudo-nationalist opposition, distracting and diverting valuable time and energy from building a real Nationalist opposition and counter-culture.

A long-term legal strategy is also needed by the Jews, and in this regard we can liken the Law to a process of engineering. Under heavy philosophic influence from Jewish religious coda, the Torah and the Talmud, the Law has been shaped according to Judaic racial interests, to facilitate commerce and investment, and to create a Judaic legal culture based on individualism rather than collectivism, which is the essential basis of Judeo-capitalism. As a result, white people have over the course of time faced legal and ethical possibilities that are, essentially, alien to them, something that is congruent with the notion of Law as a means of racial expression. As the Jew has shown his hand more overtly in the 20th. century, the tables have been soundly turned, and the Law itself is now, more fully and overtly than ever, a means for our most prominent racial competitor to oppress and bully us into silence, compliance and submission. The membranous defences have broken-down under the diabolical assault of a killer virus. Apparently benign concepts such as 'liberal democracy', 'equality', 'human rights', 'feminism' are in fact the means to destroy the White Race. Politicians and others who indulge in such terms are repeating the coda of our racial-genetic enemies. This includes those who claim to defend white people. For instance, the BNP – the British stato-nationalists – themselves have co-opted into this language and started to believe in the democratic system and place it ideology and interests above any type of 'nationalism' it might have stood for, using the language of the system: democracy, equality, human rights, etc. That is how any ideological system arrogates and co-opts its opponents and enemies. It is a supreme, and cruel, irony that this 'democracy' rewards the BNP with a civil action, by the Equalities and Human Rights Commission, that forces this putatively "nationalist" political party to change its constitution to admit non-whites into membership, under threat of imprisonment. In contesting this legal claim, the BNP used the same 'enlightened' language of 'democracy', 'equality', 'human rights', and so on that was used by their opponents. The outcome was predictable, in that all these terms are codewords for an anti-white agenda.

The appeal of these 'enlightened' ideas of 'democracy', 'equality' and 'human rights' is their apparent 'moralism'. It would not be difficult for me, if I were so minded, to convince even the most obdurate person of the value of human rights as an abstract, and furthermore, it would not be much of a challenge for me to convince the average person that a strong belief in human rights, again in the abstract, is 'right'. This position is apparently moralistic, but morals can only find imperfect expression in Law. Mother Nature is thoroughly amoral and unconcerned with the individuation of luck and chance or the assertion of pretend 'rights', and so any attempt to advance 'human rights', 'democracy' and 'equality' must always fail if pursued at face value. In reality, of course, the concepts are not advanced sincerely, but as part of a genetic campaign against the pre-eminent racial group, an anti-white agenda. The Jews, and the Muslims, of course know how the natural laws operate, and they already have a strong, membranous coda which inculcates each and every single member of their tribes in the predicates of racial survival and perpetuation. In reality, the strange liberal praxis of 'democracy', 'equality' and 'human rights' is a coda to be learnt by whites only, for its purpose is thoroughly dysgenic – for the white race.

In legal practice, arguably the most significant discipline is the seemingly hum-drum field of employment law, because this – above all others – affects social relations in day-to-day business and in the workplace. It is here that the alien virus has been most penetrative and successful against its host body, Western societies, particularly in the EU Member States. In the UK, Kafkaesque laws and regulations have been enacted that institutionalise division and conflict in the workplace and allow for entirely subjective tests of harassment and discrimination, with the result that ordinary employers live in constant fear of a financially-devastating legal claim. These perverse laws are supported by the weird sub-culture of Employment Tribunals, which adjudicate on disputes in an inquisitorial fashion. One of the major misconceptions in the UK is that its employment laws and Employment Tribunals are institutionally biased against employers. In fact, these laws and regulations generally serve an agenda that helps employers by emphasising individual rights over collective rights and thus keeping workplaces divided. The crux is the advancement of identity politics, in the workplace and elsewhere, which focuses on the differences amongst employees and so discourages the emergence of a sense of collective rights and privileges. This in turn improves the economic power of employers. Employees are generally no longer conscious of their collective interests or their real power as a numerically-superior body. Any racial group in society, such as the Jews, that harboured an interest in undermining white domination might wish to encourage these warped and masochistic perceptions among ordinary white working people, helped along by mass revolutionary levels of immigration of Third World people of disparate racial and cultural origins. After all, a national work force of atomised individuals with individual 'human rights' and with starkly different racial and cultural backgrounds is unlikely to form any sense of cohesive identity, and unlikely to challenge the social and economic order or damaging anti-social policies, such as those implemented in the UK by successive neo-liberal governments. [emphasis added - Ed].

An essential requisite of this legal order is a racial-cultural attack on the dominant, national majority, group. An important component of employment law, for instance, is discrimination law, an entirely specialist sub-discipline that emerged in the UK from the late 1970s onwards. There was significant theoretical influence in this legal development from U.S. Supreme Court authorities and appellate decisions and statutory law in the United States as well as the Continental Roman law concepts of the then-E.E.C. Discrimination law, conceptually and practically, is an archetypal liberal meme, designed to subvert and undermine the social and economic dominance of white men in society in two ways. First, via an overt attack on white male control of the workplace, through the means of legal claims and the threat of legal claims. Second, through the inculcation of neurosis and conflict in the workplace by means of an individuated concept of rights. If white men, whether in a managerial capacity or on the shop-floor, are made to see themselves socially and economically as individuals, rather than as a cohesive bloc, then it becomes harder for them to act as a group and to retain group loyalties. This in turn means that, gradually, over the course of years, the informal bonds that tie people together in society begin to break. Whereas white people in Europe historically evolved socially out of community cultures, the modern White Man is expected to be some kind of a bold Randian individualist, a condition that cannot be sustained given our fundamentally social nature, thus the neurosis of the white male proliferates and manifests in yobbery, crime, drug and alcohol abuse and other dysfunctions. Yet in a different legal field in which we note a racial attack on the national majority racial group, international law, notions of Man as an interdependent animal are maintained, even celebrated. A panoply of treaties, international committees and aid organisations are in place to give legal and practical protection and assistance to indigenous peoples, whose collective rights are readily-acknowledged and afforded legal recognition by modern industrial nation-states. Only, here the accepted legal definition of 'indigenous' in the international law sense specifically excludes white peoples by reference to groups in society that are numerically non-dominant.

Changes such as these that are dysgenic in society require a spiritual weakening in the dominant group whose genes are under attack. The White European Civil Wars of 1914 to 1945 certainly weakened the genetic strength of the white populations by removing entire strata of fit, healthy, young men who would otherwise have provided the strong core of our society's progeny. Not to disregard or disrespect the brave contribution of men and women who did fight and survived, nor to doubt the worth and intelligence of those few – on both the Left and Right politically – who saw the true nature of those terrible events and for that reason refused to participate, but what is left of the White Race in Europe are largely those who are descended from the lucky, cowardly, puny and weak, many of whom (though by no means all) found some way to avoid or minimise dangerous service. That said, if the matter is looked-at on a genomic level, the poor quality of our base human material can be considered irrelevant. Those of us who live in this sick, depraved society are, at times, weak, dishonourable, dishonest, criminal, yobbish, promiscuous and licentious, but even the worst of us white men have good genes. We each carry the spark that created most recognisable culture on planet Earth: most worthwhile art, science, mathematics, philosophy, literature and civic and juridical understanding is within us. As individuals, we may not reckon much in the ruminations of the unfathomable, but as carriers of these valuable genes, our worth is inestimable. What we have to confront is that our racial competitors have worked, and are continuing to work, diligently to deny us this essential self-knowledge, to deny us our heritage and thus deny us a future. They cannot be blamed for this. They must play their own genetic game and follow their nature, but they would mould a different kind of white Man: a mindless, zero-conscious 'democratic' consumer, and until now they have succeeded handsomely. This is a war of consciousness, and the task before us is in conditioning the Self.

## The rise of Judeo-Capitalist Man

We have discussed the dangers of the liberal, pseudo-positivist mind, which is fermented in the Western intellectual classes and ubiquitously reflexed in our society. It is not an accidental mindset, but the deliberative basis of the Judeo-Capitalist White Man, a New Man engineered with devilish torments, including financial and sexual liberalism, shorn of heritage and any sense of history, living in a transactional climate in which what matters is an ideated existentialism that prioritises the cares and practicalities of the present, not the past or the future. All of this is designed to weaken the racial and genetic basis of Western society. It is ignorance of history that is most crucially important in shaping the mind of this diabolical Epimetheus. If you do not know or understand the past, then you have no future, nor care for one.

In politics, the Judeo-Capitalist White Man plays a two-handed game with regard to most issues. Take, just as one example, the question of European political integration. On the one hand, the European institutions are said to be an authoritarian construct, related in some way to 'communism' (applying the term in a clumsy and illiterate fashion). "Communism", then, is meant to be a "bad" thing, though few people who use the word 'communism' – including most of our professional intellectuals – actually have any idea what it is or entails, or why it has anything to do with people in Brussels and Strasbourg. Thus 'Europe' itself becomes a dirty word in a discursive climate in which the only legitimate narrative is one that divides whites, and even maligns other white stato-nationalities. Others, in contrast, feel the need to support some kind of European integration on one of several, mostly economic, grounds. The confusion and double-talk on both sides of the debate is a symptom of the liberal mind that refuses to see matters in racial terms, but instead prioritises, one way or the other, material questions.

Take another, related, example: the question of human rights. The debate among the pseudo-positivists and sundry other useful idiots tends to centre around whether this or that judicial ruling has gone too far. Such debates are essentially redundant, since you cannot operate legal and juridical principles of a universal nature without an acceptance that the rules must be interpreted in such a way that they apply in all relevant cases. This rudimentary legal positivism is fairly self-evident to any thinking person, but still some people believe that exceptions should be made so this or that individual either is granted or denied 'human rights', or some other legal privilege, normally according to the relative sympathy or popularity of the individual involved.

The extreme, and thoroughly confused, form of the Useful Idiot tendency argues that we should withdraw altogether from entreated courts that declare human rights because they are "foreign" or "go too far" or represent "political correctness gone mad". [emphasis added - Ed].

What no-one seems ask is why we should have or need a human rights culture at all. Partly this is because to discuss this question would require a proper understanding of history, a subject that has been eviscerated at most scholastic levels. In a community that is cohesive and worthy of the name, it is unlikely that notions of human rights would even have need to be conceptualised. We discussed earlier how, with Byzantium incursion in the Early Middle Ages, then the Norman Conquest and the Jewish influence of the Talmud and other Judaic philosophy on the engineering of Anglo-Norman legal structures, including English common law, rights in England's legal and commercial culture became individuated and shifted away from notions of collective and ethnic unity. An idea of human rights was not, and could not be, conceived by the Anglo-Saxon culture alone. That is not to say there were no 'rights' that could be attached to individuals. In fact, there were individual rights (for instance, there was a considerable body of legal rights for women), but there was never any need for a coherent body of 'human rights' that could be interpreted, defended and upheld in its own right. The progenitors of the 'human rights' idea were found in Rome not Germania, and only emerged in earnest as part of the English legal tradition after the Norman Conquest.

When discussing the relative dangers and benefits of a 'human rights' culture, the debate among pseudo-positivist minds tends to divide into two separate camps. There is usually an artificial common ground along the lines of: most right-thinking people would accept that in a civilised society, there must be a recognition of rights. It is normally observed among pseudo-positivists that any tendency to dismiss human rights arguments conceptually or practically, especially if the challenge or objection is knee-jerk or reactionary in nature, is not a serious or substantial argument given that, it is said, the philosophical and juridical tradition of human rights is ages-old, with its roots in Medieval law and custom, and Roman law before it. In the first camp, the 'right-wing' pseudo-positivists, i.e. the Tory protagonists, will try to advance the notion that the judiciary are promoting an attitude to human rights that decouples Law from the interests of the society it is meant to serve. In the other camp, the 'left-wing' pseudo-positivists, i.e., the more noticeably liberal types, tend in response to this to be reduced to a more purely or classically positivistic argument in their defence of the human rights concept, along the lines of 'rules are rules'. Both camps are giving inadequate, unsophisticated responses to what is, fundamentally, a question of what sort of society we wish to live in. The reality is that human rights innovations are part of an ancient challenge to indigenous, communitarian legal traditions, and are pursued for racial and ideological purposes, even if the relevant judicial actors are not themselves conscious of this. The memetic coda, that might be summatively expressed in the mantra, liberté, égalité, fraternité, or similar, invites an individuation of rights that leads to dysgenic social and racial trends and general cultural degeneracy, so that we soon have féminité and even altérité. The Judeo-Capitalist White Man that has been moulded and engineered out of all this is a thorough-going materialist. He is of the present and of the eros, having abandoned his storge and thus his long-term vitality. He has no sense of the past, still less of his heritage, and places no value in his identity or in its preservation.

## Prometheanism and the New European

The challenge facing us, then, is not so much political as a sociological and psychological struggle, though at times the endeavour may find political expression. The legacy nation-states of the tired Westphalian system to which Nationalists have given their implicit political loyalty are now showing themselves to be racially treasonous, particularly since after the White European Civil Wars of the early 20th. century. Thus, one of the hardest steps for Nationalists will be to mentally transition from an intellectual condition of raison d'État toward a raison d'être, from asking 'What is good for the nation-state?' to 'What is good for our race?'. To borrow a form from Popper, we must be 'critical nationalists' (c.f. 'critical rationalists'). We must become more fully soldiers in an intellectual war. This will in turn require a kind of sociological and psychological engineering: the Law will become a necessary tool in the social and cultural terraforming of our society, but we must recognise that any such campaign, no matter how patient or sophisticated, must ultimately fail if the essential requisites of physical and demographic advantage are not also addressed. This is in the hands of Nationalists themselves, but part of the answer also is adopting the correct legal and organisational strategies. Any gains made territorially, culturally and demographically can only be preserved and assured with intentional communities that recapture territory for whites and build strong legal and ideological defensive membranes against attack.

These new intentional communities, which I call 'Racial Intentional Community', will initially exist in many separate geographic locations simultaneously. They will be held together, both internally and federatively, by the political, legal and managerial acuity of their planners and by the ideological commitment of participants, but simple racial consciousness will not be enough. For the new nomos that will lift the Racial Intentional Community into a White Independent Nation, we must be our own Prometheus and with our humble clay and worn-out potter's tools mould the New European who will be infused with the values of the natio. The Epimetheus, meanwhile, who lacked foresight of his common human destiny, will – must – be left to wilt and die, his genetic inheritance defiled and his future forgotten, but if we, the would-be Prometheus, are not to follow our wretched, diabolical cousins into spiritual obsolescence and, ultimately, genetic oblivion, then the Racial Intentional Community must be the first step on the road to the new Nation. We must reflect for a moment on how the natio concept was first regarded and understood by Roman thinkers, particularly Cicero. Only a community, civitas, can be guarded and insured against slavery, for it is in the community – in communitarian bonding – that a common identity, our best insurance, is forged. Only then can a true nation will arise, but only out the most honest recognition of our nature and the eternal laws.

## Man is a social AND biological animal

Man is not merely a social animal, but a thorough-going socio-biological animal. Notions of liberty, equality and fraternity can be worthy goals in abstract, but only if caveated by the reality of identity, which is the building block for psychological health and integrity in that it is our sense of ourselves. If pursued outwith the context of identity, individuated goals are liable to slide into official compulsion, and ultimately, the actual totalitarianism of 'Democracy'. To put it plainly: you cannot equalise diversity or liberate human beings from their differences, and any attempt to do so will crush any semblance of fraternity among Man. That human beings the world over cannot yet perceive their common economic (class) enemy may be ascribable to this compulsive and suicidal mission of forcing different peoples to live together cheek-by-jowl, so denying and crushing their essential identities. Man is a viscerally racial animal, ergo social and biological.

Those who wish for us to co-opt the anti-white internationalist coda and seek the comfort of protest within it will ultimately meet with disappointment, for talk of 'human rights', 'equality' and 'democracy' in relation to a rights for indigenous whites can be no more than a further mechanism for distraction. What is needed is nothing less than a new social and legal order, a White Independent Nation whose philosophic banner shall be not liberté, égalité, fraternité but fraternité, communauté, nationalité, identité – and mission. Our mission shall be no less than the imperative of natural law, that binds all Nature, and upon which Mother Nature looks with weary reassurance.

**Towards a 'Rechtsstaat Homo Superior'**

If we recognise the role and value of Law in assuring the necessary, requisite, communitarian bond described above and inhibiting the infiltration of alien and counter-cultural racial influences, then in building our White Independent Nation we must settle on a corpus that will represent our survivalist coda, i.e. 'what is good for our race is good for us'. In short, a Rechtsstaat Homo Superior, a body of laws and morals of a New Tribe, the New Europeans, but in the spirit of the Urvolkes from whom we claim our legitimacy. As the New Europeans will be without an expressive political state or volk, the Rechtsstaat Homo Superior will be a corpus of a Nation, not of a state, and will evolve 'in exile', in the shadow of the supremacy and coercion of the increasingly alien values of the universalist Law in multi-cultural, multi-racial, societies. Unlike with the development of Mosaic Law and practical Judaic jurisprudence, the Rechtsstaat Homo Superior will be at odds with the societies that surround it, rather than seeking to adapt, accommodate and invade them. Racial Intentional Community must, I believe, be a society organised on co-operative and community principles, restoring European laws and folkways to the White National Community and re-visiting appropriate aspects of the more communitarian legal culture of the Anglo-Saxons and comparable indigenous European cultures. A crucial formative aspect is that European whites cast-aside ethnic differences and unite in shared living space, hence Racial Intentional Community.

Strategically, Racial Intentional Community can be likened to an intermezzo, linking the conscious participants to the immaculate final act: the White Independent Nation that will one day arise. During this transitional phase, racially-conscious, intentionalist whites will, unavoidably, be confederated to some extent or other with the treasonous, anti-white nation-states and so will have to comply, for better or ill, with those laws that exist, however inimical they may be (or find some accepted means of avoidance, which itself imputes compliance). However, the Community concept will provide some means of dealing with this and will form the basis of a liveable Nationalist alternative in which materialist endeavours are minimised and skills and talents are exchanged freely in the interests of all. That is not to say that

Racial Intentional Community will be detached from society or autonomous of society in any way, and that is certainly not what is meant or intended. Racial Intentional Community is, rather, a iteration of the Pioneer Little Europe concept, adjusted for European civic and social conditions. Like PLE, it will be street-based, and can be used as a tactical method for checking non-white urban incursion as much as for suburban or semi-rural living.

That said, Racial Intentional Community differs from the PLE model in that I believe any dissident community-building activity in Europe will, if successful, need to take account of the centralised political structures, heavy state intervention and institutionalised anti-white values which are prevalent here, even in nominally federal states like Germany. In that civic and political environment, the first priority will be to ensure that there are strong, membranous legal structures which provide for a defence against legal attack. This will in turn inculcate and encourage a communitarian ethos. Ultimately, the New Europeans will forge their own White Independent Nation, and codify their own Rechtsstaat Homo Superior, but for now there has to be a recognition of a humbler objective, which is that systems, plans and structures must be in place that protect a white intentional situation and assure its preservation and long-term existence. To simply establish a white intentional presence in a community without discrete formal structures, as PLE appears to envisage, will not work well in Europe. A more considered approach is needed.

**Parable Revisited**

I began this essay with a story about the drippy bishop, Dr. Rowan Williams. I did so purposefully. Dr. Williams is a spiritual man and a spiritual figure in society, and we are here embarked on a spiritual battle, a war over the soul and consciousness of Man. It is therefore both apt and fitting that the words of this forked-tongued fool, lettered as he is in theology, should form the proscenium of our debate. What is missed by the mainstream commentators of Left and Right is that Dr. Williams' apparent backsliding is part of a systematic campaign of dysgenics, the biggest in human history: the eradication of the White Race, via cultural – and moral – assault and miscegenation. Dr. Williams' speech was an attempt to provide a spiritual and religious gloss on what in reality is a materialist argument. His role as a commissar is to help provide the intellectual apologia, the ideological justification, for ethnic cleansing. His implicit message, that as we are all human we should tolerate living together, notwithstanding our differences, and we should be accommodating to those whose cultures jar with ours, is spiritually bankrupt and anti-human – and besides, cannot work in practice.

While the non-whites, especially Jews, are certainly our opponents, it is white people like Dr. Williams who represent our most worthy and dangerous adversaries. In the vision of the future conjured by the likes of Dr. Williams, the White Children will bow timidly to 'intellectuals' such as him, and will be enslaved to the sneering, simpering, masochistic idiot class he represents, with their prestigious degrees and empty, cattle-prod language of liberté, égalité, fraternité, 'democracy', 'human rights' and 'equality': the demented prattle of the Western intellectual and the pseudo-positivist.

However, we are in the era of Reckoning. That future cannot happen. We, the carriers of the flame, may be sickened, infected and dishonoured, but the genes still exist within us and so the beauty of White Women will endure and our children's children will one day tell the 'Parable of the Archbishop' to their own children: the story of the foolish but important man who spoke with a forked tongue, as he placed slimy ingratiation to a coloniser above the principled defence of his own people. The lesson they will tell, and retell, will be our coda, a new ethos built not on the empty promises of liberal idealism, but on the iron predicates of racial survival. No longer will the Law be a means for subversion or a tool for corrupt and empty-headed men to betray their own kind. The Law will become, again, part of the membranous defence of our folk.

**END**